The AI Revolution

A Vision for a Responsible and Inclusive Future

Volodymyr Rybaiev

Table of Contents

Table of Contents 1
Introduction to Artificial Intelligence and Machine Learning 5
    Chapter 1: The Dawn of AI: From Ancient Dreams to Modern Realities 5
        The First Sparks of Artificial Intelligence in Ancient Myths and Legends 5
        How Alan Turing's Enigma Machine Paved the Way for Modern AI 9
        The Birth of Machine Learning: From Perceptrons to Neural Networks 13
    Chapter 2: Under the Hood: How AI and Machine Learning Work 18
        A Laymangs Guide to Algorithms and Data 18
        The Magic of Neural Networks: How They Learn and Adapt . 23
        Deep Dives into Supervised, Unsupervised, and Reinforcement Learning 28
    Chapter 3: The AI Toolkit: Essential Techniques and Technologies 33
        Natural Language Processing: Teaching Machines to Understand Us 33
        Computer Vision: Giving Machines the Gift of Sight 39
        Robotics: The Rise of the Machines in Our Daily Lives 43
Real-World Applications and Case Studies 49
    Chapter 4: AI in Everyday Life: From Smartphones to Smart Homes 49

Table of Contents

How AI Powers Your Favorite Apps and Gadgets 49

The Future of Smart Homes: AI-Driven Convenience and Security 55

Case Study: Amazon Alexa and the Voice-Activated Revolution 61

Chapter 5: AI in Healthcare: Saving Lives with Smart Technology 66

How AI is Transforming Medical Diagnostics and Treatment 66

The Role of Machine Learning in Personalized Medicine 72

Case Study: IBM Watson and the Fight Against Cancer 78

Chapter 6: AI in Finance: Revolutionizing the Way We Handle Money 85

The Impact of AI on Banking and Investment 85

Fraud Detection and Cybersecurity: AI as a Guardian 91

Case Study: PayPal's AI-Driven Fraud Prevention System 97

The Impact of AI on Various Industries 104

Chapter 7: AI in Manufacturing: The Factory of the Future... 104

Automation and the Rise of Smart Factories 104

Predictive Maintenance: Keeping Machines Running Smoothly 110

Case Study: Tesla's AI-Driven Manufacturing Innovations . 116

Chapter 8: AI in Retail: Personalizing the Shopping Experience 123

How AI is Changing the Way We Shop 123

Personalized Recommendations and Targeted Marketing. 128

Case Study: Netflix's Recommendation Engine 135

Chapter 9: AI in Transportation: The Road to Autonomous Vehicles 142

    The Evolution of Self-Driving Cars 142

    AI in Logistics and Supply Chain Management 149

    Case Study: Waymo and the Future of Autonomous Driving 155

Ethical Considerations and Challenges 162

    Chapter 10: The Ethics of AI: Navigating the Moral Maze 162

        Bias in AI: The Dangers of Unintended Discrimination 162

        Privacy Concerns: Balancing Innovation and Personal Data 167

        The Debate Over AI Regulation and Governance 173

    Chapter 11: The Dark Side of AI: Cybersecurity and Misuse .. 178

        The Threat of AI-Powered Cyber Attacks............................. 178

        Deepfakes and the Erosion of Trust in Digital Media 183

        Case Study: The Cambridge Analytica Scandal 187

    Chapter 12: AI and the Future of Work: Opportunities and Challenges 192

        The Impact of Automation on Jobs and the Economy......... 192

        Upskilling and Reskilling: Preparing for the AI-Driven Workforce... 199

        Case Study: The Gig Economy and the Role of AI 206

        Practical Tips for Implementing AI in Businesses................ 212

Practical Tips for Implementing AI in Businesses 222

    Chapter 13: Getting Started with AI: A Roadmap for Businesses 222

        Identifying AI Opportunities in Your Business 222

Building an AI-Ready Team and Infrastructure 230

Case Study: How Small Businesses Are Leveraging AI 239

Chapter 14: Data Strategy: The Fuel for AI Success 246

Collecting, Storing, and Managing Data Effectively 246

Data Privacy and Security Best Practices 252

Case Study: Data-Driven Success Stories 259

Chapter 15: Implementing AI: From Pilot Projects to Full-Scale Deployment 265

Designing and Executing AI Pilot Projects 265

Scaling AI Solutions Across the Enterprise 272

Case Study: AI Implementation in Fortune 500 Companies 280

Chapter 16: Measuring Success: Metrics and KPIs for AI Projects 286

Defining Success Metrics for AI Initiatives 286

Continuous Improvement and Optimization 294

Case Study: Measuring the Impact of AI in Customer Service 301

Conclusion: The AI Revolution: Where We Go from Here .. 308

Conclusion: The AI Revolution: Where We Go from Here 314

Chapter 17: The Future of AI: Predictions and Possibilities ... 314

Emerging Trends and Technologies in AI 314

The Role of AI in Solving Global Challenges 321

A Vision for a Responsible and Inclusive AI Future 328

INTRODUCTION TO ARTIFICIAL INTELLIGENCE AND MACHINE LEARNING

Chapter 1: The Dawn of AI: From Ancient Dreams to Modern Realities

The First Sparks of Artificial Intelligence in Ancient Myths and Legends

Introduction: A Tale as Old as Time

Folks, gather 'round and let me spin you a yarn about a time long before computers and smartphones, a time when the first sparks of artificial intelligence flickered in the minds of our ancestors. You see, the idea of creating intelligent beings isngt some newfangled notion; it's been with us since the dawn of civilization. So, let's take a journey back in time, back to the days of gods and heroes, and see where the seeds of AI were first planted.

Ancient Greece: The Birthplace of AI Dreams

Now, if you're looking for the roots of AI, you gotta start with the Greeks. They had a knack for dreaming up all sorts of fantastical creatures and machines. Take Hephaestus, the god of blacksmiths and craftsmen. This fella was the original inventor, the Edison of the ancient world. He crafted mechanical servants called automatons to help him out in his forge. These werengt just your average robots; they were made of gold and could move and think on their own. Imagine that! A bunch of shiny, golden helpers buzzing around, doing all the heavy lifting.

But Hephaestus didngt stop there. He also created a couple of golden dogs to guard the entrance to his workshop. These critters were smart as a whip and could sniff out intruders better than any bloodhound. And if that aingt enough, he even made himself a set of golden tripods that could wheel themselves around and serve food at his parties. Talk about a handy gadget!

The Myth of Talos: The First Robot?

But perhaps the most famous of Hephaestus's creations was Talos, a giant bronze man who guarded the island of Crete. This here was no ordinary statue. Talos was said to be alive, with veins of molten metal running through his body. He could patrol the island, keeping an eye out for invaders, and even hurl boulders at 'em if they got too close. Some say Talos was the first true robot, a mechanical man with a mind of his own.

Now, you might be thinking, "That's all well and good, but what does this have to do with AI?" Well, hold your horses, 'cause I'm getting to that. You see, these ancient myths show us that humans have always been fascinated by the idea of creating intelligent beings. We've always wanted to build something that could think and act on its own, something that could help us out and make our lives easier. And that, my friends, is the essence of artificial intelligence.

The Middle Ages: Alchemy and Automatons

Fast forward a few centuries, and you'll find that the dream of AI didngt die with the Greeks. In the Middle Ages, alchemists and inventors were still trying to create intelligent machines. Take Roger Bacon, for instance. This English friar was way ahead of his time. He wrote about all sorts of marvelous inventions, including a talking brass head that could answer any question you asked it. Now, whether or not he actually built such a thing is up for debate, but the idea itself is pure AI.

And then there was Leonardo da Vinci, the original Renaissance man. He sketched out designs for all sorts of mechanical marvels, including a robot knight that could sit up, move its arms, and even open its visor. Now, Leonardo's robot wasngt exactly intelligent, but it was a step in the right direction. It showed that humans were still thinking about how to create machines that could mimic the actions of living beings.

The Enlightenment: The Age of Automatons

But it wasngt until the Enlightenment that the idea of AI really started to take off. This was the age of reason, the age of science and invention. And it was also the age of automatons. These mechanical marvels were all the rage among the rich and famous. They could play music, write poems, even draw pictures. And while they werengt exactly intelligent, they were a darn sight closer to AI than anything that had come before.

Take the Turk, for instance. This here was a chess-playing automaton that toured the courts of Europe, beating some of the best players of the day. Now, it turns out the Turk was a bit of a trick. There was a human chess master hiding inside, pulling the strings. But the idea of a chess-playing machine captured the imagination of the public and set the stage for the development of true AI.

The Modern Era: From Myth to Reality

And that, my friends, brings us to the modern era. The age of computers, of algorithms, of neural networks and machine learning. The age where the dreams of the ancients are finally coming true. We've come a long way since the days of Hephaestus and his golden servants, but the spirit of AI remains the same. It's the spirit of invention, of curiosity, of pushing the boundaries of what's possible.

So, the next time you fire up your smartphone or ask Alexa to play your favorite tune, remember that you're standing on the shoulders of giants. You're part of a tradition that stretches back thousands of years, a tradition of dreaming big and thinking bold. And who knows? Maybe one day, we'll create something that even Hephaestus would be proud of.

Chapter 1: The Dawn of AI: From Ancient Dreams to Modern Realities

How Alan Turing's Enigma Machine Paved the Way for Modern AI

Introduction: The Man Who Changed the World

Ladies and gentlemen, let me spin you a yarn about a man who changed the world. A man whose genius laid the groundwork for the digital age we live in today. A man whose name is synonymous with the birth of modern computing and artificial intelligence. I'm talking about Alan Turing, the British mathematician and computer scientist who cracked the Enigma code and paved the way for the future.

The Enigma Machine: A Code That Couldngt Be Broken

Now, to understand how Turing's work paved the way for modern AI, we gotta go back to the dark days of World War II. The Germans had this darned clever machine called the Enigma. It was a cipher device that could encrypt messages in such a way that they were nearly impossible to decipher. The Enigma machine was a marvel of engineering, with a complex system of rotors and plugs that could create billions of different combinations. It was the ultimate code, and the Germans thought it was unbreakable.

But here's where our hero, Alan Turing, comes in. Turing was a brilliant mathematician with a knack for solving puzzles. He was recruited by the British government to work at Bletchley Park, a top-secret facility dedicated to breaking the Enigma code. Turing and his team faced a monumental task. They had to decipher messages that were encrypted with a machine that could change its settings every single day. It was like trying to solve a puzzle that kept changing its pieces.

The Bombe: Turing's Secret Weapon

But Turing wasngt the kind of fella to back down from a challenge. He set to work, analyzing the Enigma machine and looking for patterns in the encrypted messages. He realized that the key to breaking the code lay in finding a way to automate the process of decryption. So, he invented a machine called the Bombe.

The Bombe was a marvel of its own. It was a massive, electromechanical device that could simulate the workings of the Enigma machine and test thousands of possible settings in a matter of hours. It was like having a team of super-fast codebreakers working around the clock. The Bombe was so effective that it significantly reduced the time it took to decipher Enigma messages, giving the Allies a crucial advantage in the war.

The Birth of Modern Computing

But the Bombe wasngt just a codebreaking machine. It was also a precursor to the modern computer. You see, Turing's work on the Bombe laid the foundation for the development of programmable machines. He realized that if you could build a machine to solve one complex problem, you could build a machine to solve any complex problem. This idea would eventually lead to the creation of the first general-purpose computers.

And that, my friends, is where the story of modern AI begins. Because without computers, there would be no artificial intelligence. Computers are the backbone of AI, the engines that power the algorithms and neural networks that make AI possible. And it all started with Alan Turing and his Bombe.

The Turing Machine: A Blueprint for AI

But Turing's contributions to AI didngt stop with the Bombe. In 1936, long before he started working on the Enigma code, Turing published a groundbreaking paper called "On Computable

Numbers, with an Application to the Entscheidungsproblem." Now, that's a mouthful, but what it boils down to is this: Turing proposed the idea of a universal machine that could simulate any process of logical reasoning.

This hypothetical machine, which came to be known as the Turing Machine, was a blueprint for the modern computer. It was a machine that could read and write symbols on an infinite tape, following a set of predefined rules. The Turing Machine was a theoretical construct, but it laid the groundwork for the development of real-world computers.

The Turing Test: The Ultimate AI Challenge

And then there was the Turing Test. In 1950, Turing proposed a test to determine whether a machine could exhibit intelligent behavior indistinguishable from that of a human. The test involved a human evaluator who would communicate with both a human and a machine, without knowing which was which. If the evaluator couldngt tell the difference, the machine would be considered to have passed the test.

The Turing Test became a benchmark for AI research, a goal that scientists and engineers have been striking for ever since. It's a testament to Turing's vision of a future where machines could think and reason like humans. And while we're not quite there yet, we're getting closer every day.

The Legacy of Alan Turing

Alan Turing's work on the Enigma machine and his contributions to the field of computing laid the foundation for the development of modern AI. His ideas about universal machines and intelligent behavior have shaped the way we think about artificial intelligence and the potential of machines to mimic human thought.

But Turing's legacy goes beyond his scientific achievements. He was a pioneer, a visionary, and a man who dared to dream of a future where machines could think. His work has inspired generations of scientists and engineers, and his name is synonymous with the birth of the digital age.

So, the next time you fire up your laptop or ask Siri for directions, remember the man who made it all possible. Remember Alan Turing, the genius who cracked the Enigma code and paved the way for the future of artificial intelligence.

The Birth of Machine Learning: From Perceptrons to Neural Networks

Introduction: A Journey Through Time

Folks, gather 'round and let me spin you a yarn about the birth of machine learning. It's a tale of pioneers and visionaries, of breakthroughs and setbacks, and of the incredible journey from simple perceptrons to the complex neural networks that power today's AI. So, buckle up and get ready for a wild ride through the history of machine learning.

The Dawn of Machine Learning: The Perceptron

Now, to understand where machine learning came from, we gotta go back to the 1950s. This was a time of great excitement and innovation in the field of artificial intelligence. Scientists and engineers were just starting to explore the possibilities of teaching machines to think and learn.

Enter Frank Rosenblatt, a psychologist and computer scientist who had a brilliant idea. He proposed a simple model for a machine that could learn from experience. He called it the perceptron. The perceptron was a single-layer neural network, designed to mimic the way the human brain processes information. It was a groundbreaking concept, the first step on the road to modern machine learning.

The perceptron worked like this: it took in a set of inputs, applied a set of weights to those inputs, and then used a simple mathematical function to produce an output. If the output was correct, the perceptron would reinforce the weights that led to that decision. If the output was wrong, the perceptron would adjust the weights to improve its performance. It was a simple but powerful idea, and it captured the imagination of the scientific community.

The Perceptron in Action: Teaching Machines to See

Rosenblatt's perceptron was a hit. It was hailed as a major breakthrough in the field of AI, and it sparked a wave of excitement and optimism. Scientists and engineers started experimenting with perceptrons, trying to teach them to recognize patterns and make decisions.

One of the most famous experiments involved teaching a perceptron to recognize handwritten digits. The perceptron was fed a series of images of handwritten numbers, and it was trained to identify each digit correctly. It was a remarkable achievement, a demonstration of the power of machine learning to solve real-world problems.

But the perceptron had its limitations. It could only handle simple, linearly separable problems. In other words, it could only make decisions based on straight lines. If the problem was more complex, if it involved curves or multiple dimensions, the perceptron was stumped.

The Dark Ages: The Fall of the Perceptron

And that, my friends, is where the trouble began. In 1969, a mathematician named Marvin Minsky published a paper that dealt a devastating blow to the perceptron. Minsky pointed out the limitations of the perceptron, arguing that it was fundamentally flawed and incapable of solving complex problems.

Minsky's paper had a chilling effect on the field of machine learning. Funding dried up, research slowed down, and the perceptron was all but abandoned. It was a dark time for AI, a period of stagnation and disillusionment. But, as they say, every cloud has a silver lining.

The Renaissance: The Rise of Neural Networks

Fast forward to the 1980s, and the field of machine learning was starting to come back to life. A new generation of scientists and engineers was taking a fresh look at the problems of AI, and they were coming up with new solutions.

One of the key breakthroughs came from a group of researchers led by Geoffrey Hinton, a British cognitive psychologist and computer scientist. Hinton and his colleagues realized that the perceptrongs limitations could be overcome by adding more layers to the neural network. They proposed a new model called the multilayer perceptron, which was capable of solving more complex problems.

The multilayer perceptron was a game-changer. It opened the door to a whole new world of possibilities in machine learning. Suddenly, scientists and engineers were able to tackle problems that were previously thought to be unsolvable. They could teach machines to recognize faces, understand speech, and even play games like chess and Go.

The Power of Backpropagation

But the multilayer perceptron was just the beginning. The real breakthrough came with the development of a technique called backpropagation. Backpropagation is a method for training neural networks that allows them to learn from their mistakes and improve their performance over time.

Here's how it works: when a neural network makes a prediction, it compares the predicted output to the actual output. If there's a difference, the network calculates the error and uses it to adjust the weights of the connections between the neurons. This process is repeated over and over again, with the network gradually improving its performance until it reaches a satisfactory level of accuracy.

Backpropagation was a revolution in the field of machine learning. It allowed scientists and engineers to train neural networks to solve complex problems with unprecedented accuracy. It was the key that unlocked the power of deep learning, the technique that underpins many of today's most advanced AI systems.

The Modern Era: The Age of Deep Learning

And that, my friends, brings us to the modern era. The age of deep learning, where neural networks with dozens or even hundreds of layers are capable of achieving remarkable feats of intelligence. From self-driving cars to virtual assistants, from medical diagnostics to financial analysis, deep learning is transforming the world in ways that were once thought impossible.

But the journey from perceptrons to neural networks wasngt easy. It was a path filled with challenges and setbacks, with moments of brilliance and moments of despair. It was a journey that required the collective efforts of thousands of scientists and engineers, each building on the work of those who came before them.

And it's a journey that's far from over. As we look to the future, we can only imagine what new breakthroughs and discoveries lie ahead. The field of machine learning is still in its infancy, and the possibilities are endless.

The Future of Machine Learning

So, what does the future hold for machine learning? Well, that's a question that's as exciting as it is unpredictable. But one thing is for sure: the journey from perceptrons to neural networks has taught us that the power of AI lies in its ability to learn and adapt.

As we continue to push the boundaries of what's possible, we can expect to see machine learning play an increasingly important role in our lives. From healthcare to education, from entertainment to transportation, the potential applications of AI are limitless.

And as we look to the future, we can take inspiration from the pioneers who came before us. From Frank Rosenblatt and his perceptron to Geoffrey Hinton and his multilayer neural networks, the story of machine learning is a story of innovation, of perseverance, and of the power of human ingenuity.

So, let's raise a glass to the pioneers of machine learning, to the visionaries who dared to dream of a future where machines could think and learn. And let's look forward to the exciting journey that lies ahead, as we continue to explore the boundless possibilities of artificial intelligence.

Chapter 2: Under the Hood: How AI and Machine Learning Work

A Laymangs Guide to Algorithms and Data

Introduction: Welcome to the World of Algorithms and Data

Folks, gather 'round and let me spin you a yarn about the magical world of algorithms and data. Now, I know what you're thinking: "Algorithms? Data? Sounds like a bunch of techno-babble to me." But fear not, my friends, for I'm here to make it all as clear as a summer's day. So, grab your favorite chair, pour yourself a glass of lemonade, and let's dive right in.

What in Tarnation is an Algorithm?

Now, let's start with the basics. What exactly is an algorithm? Well, think of it like a recipe. Just like a recipe tells you how to bake a pie, an algorithm tells a computer how to solve a problem. It's a set of step-by-step instructions that a computer follows to get from point A to point B.

Imagine you're trying to find the shortest route from your house to the grocery store. You could just wander around aimlessly, hoping to stumble upon the right path. But that'd be a mighty inefficient way to go about it, wouldngt it? Instead, you'd probably use a map or a GPS to guide you. And that, my friends, is what an algorithm does. It's the GPS of the computer world, guiding it through complex problems to find the best solution.

The Power of Algorithms: From Search Engines to Self-Driving Cars

Algorithms are everywhere, folks. They're the backbone of the digital age, the engines that power the technology we use every day. Take Google, for instance. When you type a question into that little search bar, an algorithm kicks into gear, scouring the internet for the most relevant answers. It's like having a librarian who knows every book in the world, ready to help you find exactly what you're looking for.

And then there are self-driving cars. These marvels of modern engineering rely on a whole suite of algorithms to navigate the roads safely. They use algorithms to detect obstacles, to plan routes, and to make split-second decisions. It's like having a chauffeur who never gets tired, never gets distracted, and always knows the best way to go.

Data: The Fuel That Powers Algorithms

But algorithms aingt nothing without data. Data is the lifeblood of the digital age, the fuel that powers the engines of AI. Think of it like this: if an algorithm is a recipe, data is the ingredients. Without the right ingredients, even the best recipe in the world aingt worth a hill of beans.

So, what exactly is data? Well, it's information, pure and simple. It's the numbers, the words, the images, and the videos that we generate every day. It's the tweets we post, the emails we send, the photos we share. It's the data that tells us how many people live in a city, how many cars are on the road, and how many stars are in the sky.

The Data Explosion: More Information Than Ever Before

We're living in a world of data, folks. Every day, we generate more information than ever before. According to some estimates, we produce about 2.5 quintillion bytes of data every single day. That's a number so big, it's hard to even wrap your head around it. It's like trying to count the grains of sand on a beach.

But all that data is a goldmine of information. It's the key to unlocking insights and solving problems that were once thought impossible. Take healthcare, for instance. By analyzing vast amounts of medical data, scientists can identify patterns and trends that could lead to new treatments and cures. It's like having a crystal ball that can peer into the future and show us the way forward.

The Art of Data Collection: Gathering the Ingredients

But where does all this data come from? Well, it comes from all sorts of places. It comes from sensors and cameras, from smartphones and laptops, from satellites and drones. It comes from the internet, from social media, from e-commerce sites. It comes from everywhere and anywhere, all the time.

And collecting all that data is a science in itself. It's about knowing where to look, what to look for, and how to look for it. It's about using the right tools and techniques to gather the information you need, when you need it. It's like being a detective, piecing together clues to solve a mystery.

The Magic of Data Analysis: Turning Information into Insights

But collecting data is just the beginning. The real magic happens when you start to analyze it. That's when you turn raw information into valuable insights. That's when you start to see the patterns and trends that were hidden beneath the surface.

Take Amazon, for instance. They use data analysis to recommend products to their customers. By analyzing your browsing history, your purchase history, and your search history, they can predict what you might be interested in buying. It's like having a personal shopper who knows you better than you know yourself.

The Tools of the Trade: Algorithms for Data Analysis

Chapter 2: Under the Hood: How AI and Machine Learning Work

But how do you analyze all that data? Well, that's where algorithms come in again. There are all sorts of algorithms designed specifically for data analysis. There are algorithms for sorting data, for filtering data, for clustering data, and for classifying data. There are algorithms for detecting anomalies, for predicting trends, and for optimizing processes.

And each of these algorithms has its own strengths and weaknesses. Some are better at handling large datasets, while others are better at handling complex relationships. Some are better at finding patterns, while others are better at making predictions. It's all about choosing the right tool for the job.

The Human Touch: The Role of Data Scientists

But algorithms and data aingt enough on their own. You also need the human touch. That's where data scientists come in. These folks are the magicians of the digital age, the wizards who can turn raw data into gold.

Data scientists are a special breed. They're part mathematician, part computer scientist, part detective, and part storyteller. They have the skills to collect data, to analyze data, and to interpret data. But more importantly, they have the ability to communicate their findings in a way that's clear and compelling.

Think of it like this: a data scientist is like a chef who can take a bunch of raw ingredients and turn them into a gourmet meal. They know how to combine the right ingredients in the right proportions to create something truly special. And they know how to present that meal in a way that's appetizing and appealing.

The Ethics of Data: Privacy, Security, and Responsibility

But with great power comes great responsibility. And when it comes to data, that responsibility is enormous. You see, data isngt just numbers and words. It's personal information, sensitive information, information that can be used for good or for ill.

That's why it's so important to handle data with care. It's why we need to think about privacy and security, about consent and transparency. It's why we need to be mindful of the ethical implications of our actions.

Take the Cambridge Analytica scandal, for instance. This was a case where data was used in a way that was unethical and irresponsible. Personal information was collected without consent, and it was used to manipulate and influence people. It was a violation of trust, a betrayal of the principles that should guide our use of data.

The Future of Algorithms and Data: A World of Possibilities

But despite the challenges, the future of algorithms and data is bright. It's a future filled with possibilities, with opportunities to solve problems and improve lives. It's a future where algorithms can help us cure diseases, where data can help us protect the environment, where AI can help us build a better world.

And it's a future that's already here. Every day, we're seeing new breakthroughs, new innovations, new ways of using algorithms and data to make the world a better place. It's exciting, it's inspiring, and it's just the beginning.

So, my friends, as we journey through this magical world of algorithms and data, let's remember the power and the potential that lies within. Let's remember the pioneers who came before us, the visionaries who dared to dream of a future where machines could think and learn. And let's look forward to the exciting journey that lies ahead, as we continue to explore the boundless possibilities of artificial intelligence.

Chapter 2: Under the Hood: How AI and Machine Learning Work

The Magic of Neural Networks: How They Learn and Adapt

Introduction: A Journey into the Mind of a Machine

Folks, gather 'round and let me spin you a yarn about the magic of neural networks. Now, I know what you're thinking: "Neural networks? Sounds like something out of a science fiction novel." But fear not, my friends, for I'm here to make it all as clear as a summer's day. So, grab your favorite chair, pour yourself a glass of lemonade, and let's dive right in.

What in Tarnation is a Neural Network?

Now, let's start with the basics. What exactly is a neural network? Well, think of it like a brain. Just like the human brain is made up of neurons that communicate with each other, a neural network is made up of artificial neurons that pass information back and forth. It's a complex web of connections, designed to mimic the way our own brains work.

But unlike the human brain, a neural network is made of code, not flesh and blood. It's a mathematical model, a set of algorithms that can learn and adapt. It's like having a digital brain that can think and reason, just like we do.

The Building Blocks: Neurons and Layers

To understand how neural networks work, we gotta start with the building blocks: neurons and layers. A neuron is the basic unit of a neural network. It takes in information, processes it, and then passes it on to the next neuron. Think of it like a little factory, taking in raw materials and turning them into finished products.

Now, these neurons are organized into layers. There are three main types of layers in a neural network: the input layer, the hidden layers, and the output layer. The input layer is where the data comes in. It's like the front door of the factory, where the raw materials are delivered. The hidden layers are where the magic happens. This is where the data is processed and transformed. And the output layer is where the final product comes out. It's like the loading dock, where the finished goods are shipped off.

The Power of Connections: Weights and Biases

But it's not just about the neurons and the layers. It's also about the connections between them. These connections are called weights, and they determine how much influence one neuron has on another. Think of it like a set of scales. If one weight is heavier than the others, it's gonna tip the scales in its favor.

And then there are biases. Biases are like the starting point of the scales. They determine the initial state of the neuron, before any data comes in. Together, weights and biases control the flow of information through the neural network, shaping the way it learns and adapts.

The Learning Process: Training a Neural Network

But how do neural networks learn? Well, that's where the training process comes in. Training a neural network is like teaching a child to read. You start with simple words and gradually move on to more complex sentences. The same goes for neural networks. You start with simple data and gradually feed it more complex information.

The key to training a neural network is a process called backpropagation. Backpropagation is like a feedback loop. It allows the neural network to learn from its mistakes and improve its performance over time. Here's how it works: when the neural network makes a prediction, it compares the predicted output to the actual output. If there's a difference, the network calculates the error and uses it to adjust the weights and biases of the connections between the neurons. This process is repeated over and over again, with the network gradually improving its performance until it reaches a satisfactory level of accuracy.

The Magic of Activation Functions

But there's more to neural networks than just weights and biases. There are also activation functions. Activation functions are like the on/off switches of the neural network. They determine whether a neuron should be activated or not, based on the input it receives.

Think of it like this: if the input to a neuron is strong enough, the activation function will turn it on. If the input is too weak, the activation function will turn it off. It's like having a light switch that only turns on when you press it hard enough.

There are all sorts of activation functions, each with its own strengths and weaknesses. Some are better at handling simple problems, while others are better at handling complex ones. Some are better at finding patterns, while others are better at making predictions. It's all about choosing the right tool for the job.

The Art of Deep Learning: Stacking Layers

But the real magic of neural networks comes from deep learning. Deep learning is like stacking layers on top of each other, creating a network that's deep and complex. The more layers you add, the more powerful the neural network becomes. It's like building a skyscraper, with each floor adding more space and more functionality.

Deep neural networks are capable of solving some of the most complex problems in the world. They can recognize faces, understand speech, and even play games like chess and Go. They're the backbone of modern AI, the engines that power the technology we use every day.

The Human Touch: The Role of Data Scientists

But neural networks aingt nothing without the human touch. That's where data scientists come in. These folks are the magicians of the digital age, the wizards who can turn raw data into gold. They have the skills to design, train, and optimize neural networks, turning them into powerful tools for solving real-world problems.

Data scientists are a special breed. They're part mathematician, part computer scientist, part detective, and part storyteller. They know how to collect data, how to analyze data, and how to interpret data. But more importantly, they know how to communicate their findings in a way that's clear and compelling.

Think of it like this: a data scientist is like a chef who can take a bunch of raw ingredients and turn them into a gourmet meal. They know how to combine the right ingredients in the right proportions to create something truly special. And they know how to present that meal in a way that's appetizing and appealing.

The Ethics of Neural Networks: Bias and Fairness

But with great power comes great responsibility. And when it comes to neural networks, that responsibility is enormous. You see, neural networks are only as good as the data they're trained on. If the data is biased, the neural network will be biased too. It's like the old saying: garbage in, garbage out.

That's why it's so important to handle data with care. It's why we need to think about bias and fairness, about transparency and accountability. It's why we need to be mindful of the ethical implications of our actions.

Take facial recognition, for instance. If the data used to train a facial recognition system is biased, the system will be biased too. It might be more likely to misidentify certain groups of people, leading to unfair treatment and discrimination. It's a serious problem, and it's one that we need to address head-on.

The Future of Neural Networks: A World of Possibilities

But despite the challenges, the future of neural networks is bright. It's a future filled with possibilities, with opportunities to solve problems and improve lives. It's a future where neural networks can help us cure diseases, where they can help us protect the environment, where they can help us build a better world.

And it's a future that's already here. Every day, we're seeing new breakthroughs, new innovations, new ways of using neural networks to make the world a better place. It's exciting, it's inspiring, and it's just the beginning.

So, my friends, as we journey through this magical world of neural networks, let's remember the power and the potential that lies within. Let's remember the pioneers who came before us, the visionaries who dared to dream of a future where machines could think and learn. And let's look forward to the exciting journey that lies ahead, as we continue to explore the boundless possibilities of artificial intelligence.

Chapter 2: Under the Hood: How AI and Machine Learning Work

Deep Dives into Supervised, Unsupervised, and Reinforcement Learning

Introduction: A Journey Through the Landscapes of Learning

Folks, gather 'round and let me spin you a yarn about the magical world of machine learning. Now, I know what you're thinking: "Machine learning? Sounds like something out of a science fiction novel." But fear not, my friends, for I'm here to make it all as clear as a summer's day. So, grab your favorite chair, pour yourself a glass of lemonade, and let's dive right in.

Supervised Learning: The Teacher's Pet

Let's start with the most straightforward type of machine learning: supervised learning. Think of it like a classroom where the teacher is always present, guiding the students every step of the way. In supervised learning, the algorithm is the student, and the data is the teacher.

How It Works

In supervised learning, the algorithm is trained on a dataset that includes both the inputs and the correct outputs. It's like giving a student a set of problems and the answers to those problems. The algorithm learns by comparing its predictions to the correct answers and adjusting its parameters to minimize the difference.

Example: Email Spam Filter

Imagine you're building an email spam filter. You start by collecting a bunch of emails, some of which are spam and some of which are not. You label each email as "spam" or "not spam." Then, you feed this labeled data into your supervised learning algorithm. The algorithm learns to recognize patterns in the spam emails and uses those patterns to classify new emails as either spam or not spam.

Applications

Supervised learning is used in all sorts of applications, from image recognition to speech recognition, from medical diagnostics to financial analysis. It's the workhorse of machine learning, the go-to method for solving a wide range of problems.

Challenges

But supervised learning aingt without its challenges. One of the biggest challenges is the need for large amounts of labeled data. Collecting and labeling data can be time-consuming and expensive. And if the data is biased or incomplete, the algorithm might not learn effectively.

Unsupervised Learning: The Independent Thinker

Now, let's move on to unsupervised learning. Think of it like a classroom where the teacher is absent, and the students have to figure things out on their own. In unsupervised learning, the algorithm is the student, and the data is the puzzle it has to solve.

How It Works

In unsupervised learning, the algorithm is trained on a dataset that includes only the inputs, with no labeled outputs. It's like giving a student a set of problems without the answers. The algorithm learns by finding patterns and structures in the data on its own.

Example: Customer Segmentation

Imagine you're working for a retail company, and you want to segment your customers into different groups based on their purchasing behavior. You collect data on each customer's purchases, but you dongt have any predefined groups. You feed this data into your unsupervised learning algorithm. The algorithm analyzes the data and identifies clusters of customers with similar purchasing behaviors.

Applications

Unsupervised learning is used in all sorts of applications, from market research to anomaly detection, from data compression to feature extraction. It's the explorer of machine learning, the method that helps us discover hidden patterns and insights in our data.

Challenges

But unsupervised learning also has its challenges. One of the biggest challenges is the lack of labeled data. Without labeled outputs, it can be difficult to evaluate the performance of the algorithm. And if the data is noisy or contains outliers, the algorithm might not find meaningful patterns.

Reinforcement Learning: The Adventurer

Finally, let's talk about reinforcement learning. Think of it like a classroom where the teacher is a coach, encouraging the students to explore and learn through trial and error. In reinforcement learning, the algorithm is the student, and the environment is the teacher.

How It Works

In reinforcement learning, the algorithm learns by interacting with an environment and receiving rewards or penalties based on its actions. It's like training a dog to do tricks. You reward the dog when it does something right and penalize it when it does something wrong. The algorithm learns to maximize its rewards over time by choosing the best actions.

Example: Self-Driving Car

Imagine you're building a self-driving car. You start by creating a simulated environment where the car can learn to drive. The car takes actions, like turning left or right, accelerating or braking. Based on these actions, the car receives rewards or penalties. For example, it might receive a reward for staying on the road and a penalty for crashing. Over time, the car learns to drive safely by maximizing its rewards.

Applications

Reinforcement learning is used in all sorts of applications, from game playing to robotics, from resource management to autonomous vehicles. It's the adventurer of machine learning, the method that helps us solve complex problems through exploration and discovery.

Challenges

But reinforcement learning also has its challenges. One of the biggest challenges is the need for a well-defined reward system. If the rewards are not designed properly, the algorithm might not learn effectively. And if the environment is too complex or unpredictable, the algorithm might struggle to find the best actions.

The Magic of Machine Learning: Bringing It All Together

So, there you have it, folks. A deep dive into the magical world of machine learning. From the teacher's pet of supervised learning to the independent thinker of unsupervised learning, from the adventurer of reinforcement learning to the boundless possibilities that lie ahead.

Machine learning is a powerful tool, a tool that can help us solve problems and improve lives. It's a tool that can help us cure diseases, protect the environment, and build a better world. And it's a tool that's already changing the way we live and work.

But machine learning aingt just about algorithms and data. It's also about people. It's about the scientists and engineers who are pushing the boundaries of what's possible. It's about the visionaries who are dreaming of a future where machines can think and learn. And it's about you, the reader, who is curious and eager to explore the wonders of this magical world.

So, let's raise a glass to the pioneers of machine learning, to the visionaries who dared to dream, and to the exciting journey that lies ahead. Let's celebrate the power and the potential of machine learning, and let's look forward to the boundless possibilities that await us.

Chapter 3: The AI Toolkit: Essential Techniques and Technologies

Natural Language Processing: Teaching Machines to Understand Us

Introduction: The Language of Machines and Men

Folks, gather 'round and let me spin you a yarn about the magical world of natural language processing (NLP). Now, I know what you're thinking: "Natural language processing? Sounds like something out of a science fiction novel." But fear not, my friends, for I'm here to make it all as clear as a summer's day. So, grab your favorite chair, pour yourself a glass of lemonade, and let's dive right in.

What in Tarnation is Natural Language Processing?

Natural language processing, or NLP for short, is the art and science of teaching machines to understand, interpret, and generate human language. Think of it like teaching a computer to speak and listen, just like we do. It's a field that combines linguistics, computer science, and artificial intelligence to bridge the gap between human communication and machine understanding.

The Building Blocks: Words, Sentences, and Meaning

To understand NLP, we gotta start with the building blocks: words, sentences, and meaning. Just like a house is made of bricks, language is made of words. And just like bricks are arranged into walls and rooms, words are arranged into sentences and paragraphs. But unlike bricks, words carry meaning, and that meaning is what makes language so powerful and so complex.

The Power of Words: Tokenization and Lemmatization

One of the first steps in NLP is breaking down language into its smallest parts: words. This process is called tokenization. Think of it like taking a sentence and cutting it up into little pieces, each piece representing a single word.

But words come in all shapes and sizes. They can be singular or plural, present or past tense, and so on. To make sense of all these variations, we use a process called lemmatization. Lemmatization is like finding the root of a word, the base form that all its variations come from. For example, the words "run," "ran," and "running" all come from the root word "run."

The Magic of Sentences: Parsing and Syntax

But words alone aingt enough. To understand language, we need to understand how words are put together into sentences. This is where parsing and syntax come in. Parsing is like breaking down a sentence into its grammatical parts: subjects, verbs, objects, and so on. Syntax is the set of rules that govern how these parts are arranged.

Think of it like this: parsing is like taking a sentence apart, like dismantling a machine to see how it works. Syntax is like the blueprint that tells you how to put the machine back together. Together, parsing and syntax help us understand the structure of language and the relationships between words.

The Meaning of Meaning: Semantics and Context

But structure aingt enough. To truly understand language, we need to understand meaning. This is where semantics and context come in. Semantics is the study of meaning, the way words and sentences convey information and ideas. Context is the situation or environment in which language is used, the background that gives words their meaning.

Think of it like this: semantics is like the paint on a canvas, the colors and shapes that create a picture. Context is like the frame around the canvas, the border that gives the picture its context and its meaning. Together, semantics and context help us understand the deeper layers of language, the nuances and subtleties that make communication so rich and so complex.

The Art of Understanding: Sentiment Analysis

One of the most powerful applications of NLP is sentiment analysis. Sentiment analysis is like reading between the lines, like understanding the emotions and attitudes behind the words. It's the art of determining whether a piece of text is positive, negative, or neutral.

Think of it like this: sentiment analysis is like having a friend who can tell how you're feeling just by listening to what you say. It's like having a sixth sense for emotions, a way of understanding the unspoken meaning behind the words.

Sentiment analysis is used in all sorts of applications, from customer feedback to social media analysis, from market research to political polling. It's a powerful tool for understanding public opinion and for making informed decisions.

The Magic of Generation: Text Generation and Machine Translation

But NLP aingt just about understanding language. It's also about generating language. This is where text generation and machine translation come in. Text generation is like writing a story, like creating new sentences and paragraphs from scratch. Machine translation is like speaking a foreign language, like converting text from one language to another.

Think of it like this: text generation is like having a ghostwriter who can create content for you, who can write articles, stories, and reports with the click of a button. Machine translation is like having a personal interpreter who can translate any language, who can bridge the gap between cultures and continents.

Text generation and machine translation are used in all sorts of applications, from content creation to language learning, from customer service to international business. They're powerful tools for communicating and for connecting people across the globe.

The Human Touch: The Role of Linguists and Data Scientists

But NLP aingt just about algorithms and data. It's also about people. It's about the linguists and data scientists who are pushing the boundaries of what's possible. It's about the visionaries who are dreaming of a future where machines can understand and generate language just like we do.

Linguists and data scientists are a special breed. They're part linguist, part computer scientist, part detective, and part storyteller. They know how to collect data, how to analyze data, and how to interpret data. But more importantly, they know how to communicate their findings in a way that's clear and compelling.

Think of it like this: a linguist is like a language expert who can decode the mysteries of communication. A data scientist is like a detective who can uncover the hidden patterns and insights in our data. Together, they're like a dynamic duo, working hand in hand to unlock the power of natural language processing.

The Ethics of NLP: Privacy, Bias, and Fairness

But with great power comes great responsibility. And when it comes to NLP, that responsibility is enormous. You see, language is personal. It's intimate. It's a reflection of who we are and what we believe. And when we teach machines to understand and generate language, we're giving them access to some of the most sensitive and private aspects of our lives.

That's why it's so important to handle language with care. It's why we need to think about privacy and security, about bias and fairness, about transparency and accountability. It's why we need to be mindful of the ethical implications of our actions.

Take the example of chatbots. Chatbots are automated systems that can engage in conversation with humans. They're used in all sorts of applications, from customer service to mental health support, from education to entertainment. But if a chatbot is biased or unfair, if it discriminates against certain groups of people or if it invades their privacy, it can cause real harm.

The Future of NLP: A World of Possibilities

But despite the challenges, the future of NLP is bright. It's a future filled with possibilities, with opportunities to solve problems and improve lives. It's a future where machines can understand and generate language just like we do, where they can communicate with us in ways that are natural and intuitive, where they can help us connect and collaborate across the globe.

And it's a future that's already here. Every day, we're seeing new breakthroughs, new innovations, new ways of using NLP to make the world a better place. It's exciting, it's inspiring, and it's just the beginning.

So, my friends, as we journey through this magical world of natural language processing, let's remember the power and the potential that lies within. Let's remember the pioneers who came before us, the visionaries who dared to dream of a future where machines could understand and generate language just like we do. And let's look forward to the exciting journey that lies ahead, as we continue to explore the boundless possibilities of artificial intelligence.

Computer Vision: Giving Machines the Gift of Sight

Introduction: The Eyes of the Future

Folks, gather 'round and let me spin you a yarn about the magical world of computer vision. Now, I know what you're thinking: "Computer vision? Sounds like something out of a science fiction novel." But fear not, my friends, for I'm here to make it all as clear as a summer's day. So, grab your favorite chair, pour yourself a glass of lemonade, and let's dive right in.

What in Tarnation is Computer Vision?

Computer vision, or CV for short, is the art and science of teaching machines to see and understand the world around them. Think of it like giving a computer a pair of eyes, like teaching it to recognize objects, interpret scenes, and make sense of visual information. It's a field that combines computer science, artificial intelligence, and engineering to bridge the gap between human vision and machine understanding.

The Building Blocks: Pixels, Images, and Vision

To understand computer vision, we gotta start with the building blocks: pixels, images, and vision. Just like a house is made of bricks, an image is made of pixels. And just like bricks are arranged into walls and rooms, pixels are arranged into shapes and colors. But unlike bricks, pixels carry information, and that information is what makes vision so powerful and so complex.

The Power of Pixels: Image Processing

One of the first steps in computer vision is processing images. This is where we take raw pixel data and turn it into something meaningful. Think of it like taking a photograph and enhancing it, like adjusting the brightness, the contrast, and the colors to make it look its best.

But image processing aingt just about making pictures look pretty. It's also about extracting information, about finding patterns and structures in the data. It's about turning raw pixels into useful insights.

The Magic of Recognition: Object Detection

But pixels alone aingt enough. To truly understand vision, we need to recognize objects. This is where object detection comes in. Object detection is like teaching a computer to spot things in an image, like identifyng a cat, a dog, or a car.

Think of it like this: object detection is like having a friend who can point out everything in a picture, who can say, "There's a cat, there's a dog, and there's a car." It's like having a sixth sense for objects, a way of seeing the world in all its complexity.

Object detection is used in all sorts of applications, from security cameras to autonomous vehicles, from medical imaging to robotics. It's a powerful tool for understanding the world around us and for making informed decisions.

The Art of Interpretation: Scene Understanding

But recognizing objects aingt enough. To truly understand vision, we need to interpret scenes. This is where scene understanding comes in. Scene understanding is like teaching a computer to make sense of a whole picture, to understand the relationships between objects and the context in which they appear.

Think of it like this: scene understanding is like having a friend who can describe a picture in detail, who can say, "There's a cat sitting on a chair, a dog lying on the floor, and a car parked

Chapter 3: The AI Toolkit: Essential Techniques and Technologies

outside." It's like having a storyteller who can bring a picture to life, who can paint a vivid image with words.

Scene understanding is used in all sorts of applications, from virtual reality to augmented reality, from video analysis to autonomous navigation. It's a powerful tool for creating immersive experiences and for understanding the world in all its richness and complexity.

The Human Touch: The Role of Engineers and Data Scientists

But computer vision aingt just about algorithms and data. It's also about people. It's about the engineers and data scientists who are pushing the boundaries of what's possible. It's about the visionaries who are dreaming of a future where machines can see and understand the world just like we do.

Engineers and data scientists are a special breed. They're part computer scientist, part engineer, part detective, and part storyteller. They know how to collect data, how to analyze data, and how to interpret data. But more importantly, they know how to communicate their findings in a way that's clear and compelling.

Think of it like this: an engineer is like a builder who can construct the tools and systems we need to make computer vision a reality. A data scientist is like a detective who can uncover the hidden patterns and insights in our data. Together, they're like a dynamic duo, working hand in hand to unlock the power of computer vision.

The Ethics of Computer Vision: Privacy, Bias, and Fairness

But with great power comes great responsibility. And when it comes to computer vision, that responsibility is enormous. You see, vision is personal. It's intimate. It's a reflection of who we are

Chapter 3: The AI Toolkit: Essential Techniques and Technologies

and what we see. And when we teach machines to see and understand the world, we're giving them access to some of the most sensitive and private aspects of our lives.

That's why it's so important to handle vision with care. It's why we need to think about privacy and security, about bias and fairness, about transparency and accountability. It's why we need to be mindful of the ethical implications of our actions.

Take the example of facial recognition. Facial recognition is a powerful tool for identifyng people, for securing buildings, and for preventing crime. But if a facial recognition system is biased or unfair, if it discriminates against certain groups of people or if it invades their privacy, it can cause real harm.

The Future of Computer Vision: A World of Possibilities

But despite the challenges, the future of computer vision is bright. It's a future filled with possibilities, with opportunities to solve problems and improve lives. It's a future where machines can see and understand the world just like we do, where they can help us navigate, explore, and discover.

And it's a future that's already here. Every day, we're seeing new breakthroughs, new innovations, new ways of using computer vision to make the world a better place. It's exciting, it's inspiring, and it's just the beginning.

So, my friends, as we journey through this magical world of computer vision, let's remember the power and the potential that lies within. Let's remember the pioneers who came before us, the visionaries who dared to dream of a future where machines could see and understand the world just like we do. And let's look forward to the exciting journey that lies ahead, as we continue to explore the boundless possibilities of artificial intelligence.

Robotics: The Rise of the Machines in Our Daily Lives

Introduction: The Machines Among Us

Folks, gather 'round and let me spin you a yarn about the magical world of robotics. Now, I know what you're thinking: "Robotics? Sounds like something out of a science fiction novel." But fear not, my friends, for I'm here to make it all as clear as a summer's day. So, grab your favorite chair, pour yourself a glass of lemonade, and let's dive right in.

What in Tarnation is Robotics?

Robotics, my friends, is the art and science of building and programming machines that can perform tasks autonomously. Think of it like giving a machine a brain and a body, like teaching it to move, to sense, and to think. It's a field that combines mechanics, electronics, computer science, and artificial intelligence to create machines that can interact with the world around them.

The Building Blocks: Mechanics, Electronics, and Software

To understand robotics, we gotta start with the building blocks: mechanics, electronics, and software. Just like a house is made of bricks, a robot is made of parts. And just like bricks are arranged into walls and rooms, parts are arranged into systems and subsystems. But unlike bricks, parts carry functions, and those functions are what make robots so powerful and so complex.

The Power of Mechanics: Movement and Manipulation

One of the first steps in robotics is understanding mechanics. This is where we take raw materials and turn them into moving parts. Think of it like building a car, like assembling the engine, the wheels, and the steering system to make it go.

But mechanics aingt just about making things move. It's also about manipulating the environment, about picking up objects, moving them around, and placing them precisely. It's about giving a robot the ability to interact with the world in a meaningful way.

The Magic of Electronics: Sensing and Control

But mechanics alone aingt enough. To truly understand robotics, we need to understand electronics. This is where we take electrical signals and turn them into actions. Think of it like building a remote control, like creating a system that can send and receive signals to make things happen.

But electronics aingt just about sending and receiving signals. It's also about sensing the environment, about detecting changes and responding to them. It's about giving a robot the ability to see, to hear, and to feel, just like we do.

The Art of Software: Intelligence and Autonomy

But electronics alone aingt enough. To truly understand robotics, we need to understand software. This is where we take algorithms and turn them into actions. Think of it like programming a computer, like writing code that can make a machine think and act.

But software aingt just about writing code. It's also about creating intelligence, about teaching a robot to learn, to adapt, and to make decisions. It's about giving a robot the ability to think and act autonomously, just like we do.

The Rise of the Machines: Industrial Robotics

Now, let's talk about the rise of the machines in our daily lives. One of the first places we saw robots was in the factories. Industrial robots are designed to perform repetitive tasks with precision and speed. They can weld, paint, assemble, and inspect, all without getting tired or making mistakes.

Think of it like this: industrial robots are like the workhorses of the modern factory. They can lift heavy objects, move them around, and place them precisely. They can perform tasks that are dangerous or difficult for humans, like working with hazardous materials or operating in extreme environments.

Industrial robots are used in all sorts of applications, from automotive manufacturing to electronics assembly, from food processing to pharmaceutical production. They're the backbone of modern industry, the engines that drive productivity and efficiency.

The Helpers Among Us: Service Robotics

But robots aingt just for factories. They're also for homes, for hospitals, for schools, and for offices. Service robots are designed to assist humans in their daily lives, to perform tasks that are helpful, convenient, or necessary.

Think of it like this: service robots are like the helpers among us. They can clean our homes, mow our lawns, and deliver our packages. They can assist the elderly, the disabled, and the sick, providing care and support when it's needed most. They can teach our children, entertain our families, and protect our properties.

Service robots are used in all sorts of applications, from healthcare to education, from entertainment to security. They're the helpers of the modern world, the assistants that make our lives easier, safer, and more enjoyable.

The Explorers Among Us: Mobile Robotics

But robots aingt just for staying in one place. They're also for exploring the world around us, for navigating through complex environments and discovering new horizons. Mobile robots are designed to move, to travel, and to explore.

Think of it like this: mobile robots are like the explorers among us. They can navigate through cities, through forests, and through oceans. They can explore the depths of the sea, the heights of the sky, and the surfaces of other planets. They can map the world, collect data, and perform tasks that are impossible for humans.

Mobile robots are used in all sorts of applications, from search and rescue to environmental monitoring, from space exploration to underwater research. They're the explorers of the modern world, the pioneers that push the boundaries of what's possible.

The Human Touch: The Role of Engineers and Scientists

But robotics aingt just about machines. It's also about people. It's about the engineers and scientists who are pushing the boundaries of what's possible. It's about the visionaries who are dreaming of a future where machines can think, act, and interact just like we do.

Engineers and scientists are a special breed. They're part mechanic, part electrician, part computer scientist, and part dreamer. They know how to design, build, and program robots. But more importantly, they know how to imagine, to innovate, and to create.

Think of it like this: an engineer is like a builder who can construct the machines we need to make robotics a reality. A scientist is like a dreamer who can envision the possibilities and the potentials of the future. Together, they're like a dynamic duo, working hand in hand to unlock the power of robotics.

The Ethics of Robotics: Safety, Privacy, and Responsibility

But with great power comes great responsibility. And when it comes to robotics, that responsibility is enormous. You see, robots are powerful tools, but they're also potentially dangerous. They can perform tasks that are helpful, but they can also cause harm if not used properly.

That's why it's so important to handle robots with care. It's why we need to think about safety, privacy, and responsibility. It's why we need to be mindful of the ethical implications of our actions.

Take the example of autonomous vehicles. Autonomous vehicles are designed to drive themselves, to navigate through traffic, and to make decisions without human intervention. But if an autonomous vehicle makes a mistake, if it causes an accident or injures a person, the consequences can be severe.

The Future of Robotics: A World of Possibilities

But despite the challenges, the future of robotics is bright. It's a future filled with possibilities, with opportunities to solve problems and improve lives. It's a future where robots can think, act, and interact just like we do, where they can assist us, entertain us, and protect us.

And it's a future that's already here. Every day, we're seeing new breakthroughs, new innovations, new ways of using robotics to make the world a better place. It's exciting, it's inspiring, and it's just the beginning.

So, my friends, as we journey through this magical world of robotics, let's remember the power and the potential that lies within. Let's remember the pioneers who came before us, the visionaries who dared to dream of a future where machines could think, act, and interact just like we do. And let's look forward to the exciting journey that lies ahead, as we continue to explore the boundless possibilities of artificial intelligence.

REAL-WORLD APPLICATIONS AND CASE STUDIES

Chapter 4: AI in Everyday Life: From Smartphones to Smart Homes

How AI Powers Your Favorite Apps and Gadgets

Introduction: The Magic Behind the Screens

Folks, gather 'round and let me spin you a yarn about the magical world of artificial intelligence and how it powers your favorite apps and gadgets. Now, I know what you're thinking: "AI? Sounds like something out of a science fiction novel." But fear not, my friends, for I'm here to make it all as clear as a summer's day. So, grab your favorite chair, pour yourself a glass of lemonade, and let's dive right in.

The Smartphone: Your Pocket-Sized Genius

Let's start with the gadget that's probably sitting in your pocket right now: the smartphone. This little device is a powerhouse of AI, packed with features that make your life easier, more convenient, and more fun.

Voice Assistants: Your Personal Helper

Ever wondered how Siri, Alexa, or Google Assistant understand what you're saying? It's all thanks to natural language processing (NLP) and machine learning. These voice assistants use AI to recognize your voice, interpret your words, and respond with the information you need. Think of it like having a personal assistant who's always ready to help, whether you need to set a reminder, send a message, or find out the weather.

Smart Cameras: Capturing the Perfect Shot

Ever noticed how your smartphone camera seems to know exactly when to take the perfect shot? That's AI at work, too. Modern smartphone cameras use computer vision and machine learning to recognize faces, adjust settings, and even suggest the best filters. It's like having a professional photographer in your pocket, always ready to capture those special moments.

Predictive Text: Typing Made Easy

Ever found yourself typing a message and having your smartphone suggest the next word before you even think of it? That's predictive text, powered by AI. Your smartphone uses machine learning to analyze your typing habits and suggest words and phrases that you're likely to use. It's like having a mind reader who knows exactly what you want to say.

Social Media: Connecting the World

Now, let's talk about social media. Whether you're scrolling through Facebook, Instagram, or Twitter, AI is working behind the scenes to make your experience better.

Personalized Feeds: Tailored Just for You

Ever wondered why your social media feed seems to know exactly what you like? It's all thanks to AI. Social media platforms use machine learning algorithms to analyze your behavior, understand your interests, and serve up content that you're most likely to enjoy. It's like having a personal curator who knows exactly what you want to see.

Face Recognition: Tagging Made Easy

Ever noticed how Facebook can automatically suggest tags for your friends in photos? That's face recognition, powered by AI.

Social media platforms use computer vision and machine learning to recognize faces in photos and suggest tags based on who's in the picture. It's like having a friend who knows everyone in your social circle.

Sentiment Analysis: Understanding the Mood

Ever wondered how social media platforms can gauge the mood of a post or a comment? It's all thanks to sentiment analysis, powered by AI. These platforms use natural language processing to analyze text and determine whether it's positive, negative, or neutral. It's like having a friend who can read between the lines and understand the emotions behind the words.

Streaming Services: Entertainment at Your Fingertips

Now, let's talk about streaming services. Whether you're watching Netflix, listening to Spotify, or playing games on Twitch, AI is working behind the scenes to make your experience better.

Recommendation Engines: Discovering New Favorites

Ever wondered how Netflix always seems to know exactly what you want to watch? It's all thanks to AI. Streaming services use machine learning algorithms to analyze your watching habits, understand your preferences, and suggest content that you're most likely to enjoy. It's like having a personal movie critic who knows exactly what you like.

Music Recommendations: Tunes Tailored to You

Ever noticed how Spotify always seems to know exactly what you want to listen to? That's AI at work, too. Music streaming services use machine learning to analyze your listening habits, understand your tastes, and suggest songs and playlists that you're most likely to enjoy. It's like having a personal DJ who knows exactly what you want to hear.

Live Chat and Support: Help When You Need It

Ever found yourself needing help with a streaming service and getting instant support through live chat? That's AI at work, too. Many streaming services use chatbots powered by AI to provide instant support and assistance, answering your questions and solving your problems in real-time. It's like having a customer service representative who's always available to help.

Smart Home Devices: Making Life Easier

Now, let's talk about smart home devices. Whether you're using a smart speaker, a smart thermostat, or a smart security camera, AI is working behind the scenes to make your life easier and more convenient.

Smart Speakers: Voice Control at Your Command

Ever wondered how smart speakers like Amazon Echo or Google Home understand what you're saying? It's all thanks to AI. These devices use natural language processing and machine learning to recognize your voice, interpret your commands, and perform actions like playing music, adjusting the lights, or answering questions. It's like having a personal assistant who's always ready to help.

Smart Thermostats: Comfort and Efficiency

Ever noticed how smart thermostats like Nest seem to know exactly when to adjust the temperature? That's AI at work, too. Smart thermostats use machine learning to analyze your habits, understand your preferences, and adjust the temperature to keep

Chapter 4: AI in Everyday Life: From Smartphones to Smart Homes

you comfortable and save energy. It's like having a personal climate control expert who knows exactly what you need.

Smart Security Cameras: Keeping You Safe

Ever wondered how smart security cameras can detect motion, recognize faces, and alert you to potential threats? It's all thanks to AI. These cameras use computer vision and machine learning to analyze video footage, detect unusual activity, and notify you when something suspicious happens. It's like having a personal security guard who's always on duty.

Health and Fitness: Staying in Shape

Now, let's talk about health and fitness. Whether you're tracking your steps, monitoring your heart rate, or getting personalized workout recommendations, AI is working behind the scenes to help you stay in shape.

Fitness Trackers: Monitoring Your Health

Ever wondered how fitness trackers like Fitbit or Apple Watch can monitor your steps, heart rate, and sleep patterns? It's all thanks to AI. These devices use machine learning algorithms to analyze your data, understand your habits, and provide insights and recommendations to help you stay healthy and fit. It's like having a personal trainer who's always with you.

Health Apps: Personalized Wellness

Ever noticed how health apps can provide personalized recommendations based on your data? That's AI at work, too. Health apps use machine learning to analyze your health information, understand your needs, and suggest actions that can improve your well-being. It's like having a personal wellness coach who knows exactly what you need.

Mental Health Support: Help When You Need It

Ever found yourself needing mental health support and getting instant help through an app? That's AI at work, too. Many mental health apps use chatbots powered by AI to provide instant support and assistance, offering guidance, encouragement, and resources to help you manage your mental health. It's like having a personal therapist who's always available to help.

The Future of AI: A World of Possibilities

But the power of AI doesngt stop with your favorite apps and gadgets. It's a future filled with possibilities, with opportunities to solve problems and improve lives. It's a future where AI can help us cure diseases, protect the environment, and build a better world.

And it's a future that's already here. Every day, we're seeing new breakthroughs, new innovations, new ways of using AI to make the world a better place. It's exciting, it's inspiring, and it's just the beginning.

So, my friends, as we journey through this magical world of AI, let's remember the power and the potential that lies within. Let's remember the pioneers who came before us, the visionaries who dared to dream of a future where machines could think, act, and interact just like we do. And let's look forward to the exciting journey that lies ahead, as we continue to explore the boundless possibilities of artificial intelligence.

The Future of Smart Homes: AI-Driven Convenience and Security

Introduction: The Home of Tomorrow

Folks, gather 'round and let me spin you a yarn about the magical world of smart homes. Now, I know what you're thinking: "Smart homes? Sounds like something out of a science fiction novel." But fear not, my friends, for I'm here to make it all as clear as a summer's day. So, grab your favorite chair, pour yourself a glass of lemonade, and let's dive right in.

The Evolution of the Home: From Simple to Smart

To understand where we're going, we gotta look at where we've been. Homes have come a long way from simple shelters to the sophisticated, tech-filled spaces we know today. But the future, my friends, is where things get really exciting.

From Stone Age to Smart Age

Think back to the days of our ancestors. They built homes from whatever they could find—stones, wood, mud. These homes were simple, but they served their purpose. Fast forward to the Industrial Revolution, and we see homes getting more complex, with electricity, plumbing, and other modern conveniences.

But it's the digital age that's really transformed our homes. With the advent of the internet, smartphones, and AI, our homes have become smarter, more connected, and more convenient than ever before.

The Building Blocks: Sensors, IoT, and AI

To understand smart homes, we gotta start with the building blocks: sensors, the Internet of Things (IoT), and AI. Just like a house is made of bricks, a smart home is made of these technological components.

Sensors: The Eyes and Ears of the Smart Home

Sensors are the eyes and ears of the smart home. They detect changes in the environment, like temperature, humidity, motion, and light. Think of them like little spies, always on the lookout, gathering information and reporting back to the central system.

IoT: The Nervous System of the Smart Home

The Internet of Things, or IoT for short, is the nervous system of the smart home. It connects all the devices and sensors together, allowing them to communicate and work in harmony. Think of it like a network of nerves, carrying signals back and forth, making sure everything runs smoothly.

AI: The Brain of the Smart Home

AI is the brain of the smart home. It takes all the data gathered by the sensors, analyzes it, and makes decisions based on that information. Think of it like a smart, invisible butler, always ready to help, always anticipating your needs.

The Magic of Convenience: AI-Driven Automation

Now, let's talk about the magic of convenience. AI-driven automation is what makes smart homes truly special. It's the ability of the home to anticipate your needs, to adjust to your preferences, and to make your life easier and more enjoyable.

Smart Lighting: Set the Mood

Ever wished your lights could adjust themselves based on the time of day, the weather, or your mood? With smart lighting, they can. AI-powered smart lights can learn your preferences and adjust the brightness, color, and intensity to create the perfect atmosphere. Think of it like having a personal lighting designer who knows exactly what you want.

Smart Thermostats: Comfort and Efficiency

Ever found yourself adjusting the thermostat multiple times a day to keep the temperature just right? With smart thermostats, those days are over. AI-powered thermostats can learn your habits, understand your preferences, and adjust the temperature automatically to keep you comfortable and save energy. It's like having a personal climate control expert who knows exactly what you need.

Smart Appliances: Cooking Made Easy

Ever wished your oven could preheat itself, or your fridge could order groceries when you're running low? With smart appliances, they can. AI-powered appliances can learn your routines, anticipate your needs, and perform tasks automatically, making cooking and cleaning a breeze. It's like having a personal chef and housekeeper rolled into one.

The Power of Security: AI-Driven Protection

But convenience aingt the only benefit of smart homes. Security is just as important, and AI is making our homes safer and more secure than ever before.

Smart Security Cameras: Keeping an Eye Out

Ever wished your security cameras could detect motion, recognize faces, and alert you to potential threats? With smart security cameras, they can. AI-powered cameras can analyze video footage, detect unusual activity, and notify you when something suspicious happens. It's like having a personal security guard who's always on duty.

Smart Locks: Peace of Mind

Ever found yourself worrying about whether you locked the door before leaving the house? With smart locks, those worries are a thing of the past. AI-powered locks can detect when you're leaving and lock the door automatically. They can also grant temporary access to visitors, track who comes and goes, and even alert you to attempted break-ins. It's like having a personal doorman who's always watching out for you.

Smart Alarms: Sound the Alert

Ever wished your alarm system could distinguish between a real threat and a false alarm? With smart alarms, they can. AI-powered alarm systems can analyze data from sensors, cameras, and other devices to determine whether a threat is real or not. They can also alert the authorities automatically, ensuring a quick response in case of an emergency. It's like having a personal emergency response team who's always ready to act.

The Human Touch: The Role of Engineers and Designers

But smart homes aingt just about technology. They're also about people. They're about the engineers and designers who are pushing the boundaries of what's possible. They're about the visionaries who are dreaming of a future where our homes can think, act, and interact just like we do.

Engineers and designers are a special breed. They're part inventor, part artist, part dreamer. They know how to design, build, and program smart homes. But more importantly, they know how to imagine, to innovate, and to create.

Think of it like this: an engineer is like a builder who can construct the systems we need to make smart homes a reality. A designer is like an artist who can envision the possibilities and the potentials of the future. Together, they're like a dynamic duo, working hand in hand to unlock the power of smart homes.

The Ethics of Smart Homes: Privacy, Security, and Responsibility

But with great power comes great responsibility. And when it comes to smart homes, that responsibility is enormous. You see, smart homes are powerful tools, but they're also potentially vulnerable. They can make our lives easier, but they can also expose us to risks if not used properly.

That's why it's so important to handle smart homes with care. It's why we need to think about privacy, security, and responsibility. It's why we need to be mindful of the ethical implications of our actions.

Take the example of data collection. Smart homes gather a lot of data about our habits, our preferences, and our lives. If that data falls into the wrong hands, it can be used for malicious purposes. That's why it's crucial to ensure that our smart homes are secure, that our data is protected, and that our privacy is respected.

The Future of Smart Homes: A World of Possibilities

But despite the challenges, the future of smart homes is bright. It's a future filled with possibilities, with opportunities to solve problems and improve lives. It's a future where our homes can think, act, and interact just like we do, where they can assist us, entertain us, and protect us.

And it's a future that's already here. Every day, we're seeing new breakthroughs, new innovations, new ways of using AI to make

our homes smarter, more convenient, and more secure. It's exciting, it's inspiring, and it's just the beginning.

So, my friends, as we journey through this magical world of smart homes, let's remember the power and the potential that lies within. Let's remember the pioneers who came before us, the visionaries who dared to dream of a future where our homes could think, act, and interact just like we do. And let's look forward to the exciting journey that lies ahead, as we continue to explore the boundless possibilities of artificial intelligence.

Case Study: Amazon Alexa and the Voice-Activated Revolution

Introduction: The Voice of the Future

Folks, gather 'round and let me spin you a yarn about the magical world of voice-activated technology and the revolution it's bringing to our daily lives. Now, I know what you're thinking: "Voice-activated technology? Sounds like something out of a science fiction novel." But fear not, my friends, for I'm here to make it all as clear as a summer's day. So, grab your favorite chair, pour yourself a glass of lemonade, and let's dive right in.

The Birth of Alexa: A Star is Born

To understand the impact of Amazon Alexa, we gotta go back to its beginnings. The story of Alexa starts in the hallowed halls of Amazon, where a team of brilliant engineers and scientists were dreaming up the future of voice technology.

The Vision: A Voice-Activated Assistant

The idea behind Alexa was simple yet revolutionary: create a voice-activated assistant that could understand and respond to human speech. Think of it like having a personal assistant who's always ready to help, whether you need to set a reminder, play some music, or get the latest news.

The Technology: Natural Language Processing and Machine Learning

But turning that vision into reality was no easy feat. The team at Amazon had to tackle some of the most complex challenges in natural language processing (NLP) and machine learning. They had to teach Alexa to recognize speech, understand context, and generate meaningful responses. It was like teaching a child to speak, listen, and think, all at the same time.

The Launch: Alexa Takes the Stage

After years of hard work and countless iterations, Alexa was finally ready to take the stage. In November 2014, Amazon unveiled the Echo, a sleek, cylindrical speaker that housed the voice-activated assistant. The world was about to change.

The Echo: A New Kind of Speaker

The Echo was more than just a speaker; it was a gateway to a whole new world of convenience and entertainment. With a simple voice command, users could play music, set alarms, check the weather, and even control other smart home devices. It was like having a genie in a bottle, always ready to grant your wishes.

The Response: A Hit with Consumers

The response to the Echo and Alexa was overwhelming. Consumers fell in love with the convenience and ease of use. Suddenly, people were talking to their speakers, asking for the weather, playing their favorite tunes, and even ordering pizza, all with just their voice. It was a revolution in the making.

The Evolution: Alexa Grows Up

But the story of Alexa doesngt stop with the Echo. Over the years, Amazon has continued to innovate and expand the capabilities of its voice-activated assistant. From new devices to advanced features, Alexa has grown and evolved, making our lives easier and more convenient.

New Devices: The Alexa Family Expands

One of the most exciting developments in the world of Alexa is the expansion of the device family. From the compact Echo Dot to the screen-equipped Echo Show, Amazon has introduced a range of devices designed to fit different needs and preferences. There's even an Echo for kids, complete with parental controls and educational content.

Advanced Features: Skills and Integrations

But it's not just about the hardware. Alexa's real power lies in its software, specifically its skills and integrations. Skills are like apps for Alexa, allowing it to perform a wide range of tasks, from ordering groceries to playing games. Integrations, on the other hand, allow Alexa to work seamlessly with other smart home devices, making it the hub of your connected home.

The Ecosystem: A World of Possibilities

Today, Alexa is more than just a voice-activated assistant; it's an ecosystem. With thousands of skills, countless integrations, and a growing family of devices, Alexa has become an integral part of our daily lives. It's like having a personal assistant, a DJ, a chef, and a teacher, all rolled into one.

The Impact: Changing the Way We Live

The impact of Alexa and voice-activated technology on our daily lives is profound. It's changing the way we interact with technology, the way we manage our homes, and even the way we communicate with each other.

Convenience: Simplifying Our Lives

One of the most obvious benefits of Alexa is convenience. With a simple voice command, we can control our smart home devices, set reminders, and even order groceries. It's like having a personal assistant who's always ready to help, making our lives easier and more efficient.

Entertainment: Enhancing Our Experiences

But Alexa isngt just about convenience; it's also about entertainment. With the ability to play music, tell jokes, and even play games, Alexa is transforming the way we enjoy our free time. It's like having a personal DJ, a comedian, and a game show host, all in one device.

Education: Learning and Growing

Alexa is also playing a crucial role in education. With skills that can teach languages, answer trivia questions, and even provide educational content for kids, Alexa is helping us learn and grow. It's like having a personal tutor who's always available to answer our questions and expand our knowledge.

The Challenges: Privacy and Security

But with great power comes great responsibility. And when it comes to voice-activated technology, that responsibility is enormous. You see, voice-activated assistants like Alexa are always listening, always ready to respond to our commands. But that also means they're always collecting data, data that can be sensitive and personal.

Privacy: Protecting Our Information

One of the biggest challenges with voice-activated technology is privacy. How do we ensure that our data is protected, that our conversations are kept private, and that our information is not misused? It's a complex issue, one that requires careful consideration and robust security measures.

Security: Keeping Our Homes Safe

But privacy isngt the only concern. Security is also a major issue. With voice-activated assistants controlling our smart home devices, there's a risk that unauthorized users could gain access to our homes. That's why it's crucial to have strong security measures in place, to protect our homes and our families from potential threats.

The Future: A World of Possibilities

But despite the challenges, the future of voice-activated technology is bright. It's a future filled with possibilities, with opportunities to solve problems and improve lives. It's a future where our homes can think, act, and interact just like we do, where they can assist us, entertain us, and protect us.

And it's a future that's already here. Every day, we're seeing new breakthroughs, new innovations, new ways of using voice-activated technology to make our lives better. It's exciting, it's inspiring, and it's just the beginning.

So, my friends, as we journey through this magical world of voice-activated technology, let's remember the power and the potential that lies within. Let's remember the pioneers who came before us, the visionaries who dared to dream of a future where our voices could control the world around us. And let's look forward to the exciting journey that lies ahead, as we continue to explore the boundless possibilities of artificial intelligence.

Chapter 5: AI in Healthcare: Saving Lives with Smart Technology

How AI is Transforming Medical Diagnostics and Treatment

Introduction: The Future of Medicine

Folks, gather 'round and let me spin you a yarn about the magical world of artificial intelligence and how it's transforming the way we diagnose and treat diseases. Now, I know what you're thinking: "AI in medicine? Sounds like something out of a science fiction novel." But fear not, my friends, for I'm here to make it all as clear as a summer's day. So, grab your favorite chair, pour yourself a glass of lemonade, and let's dive right in.

The Dawn of AI in Medicine: A New Era

To understand how AI is changing the game in medicine, we gotta go back to the beginning. For centuries, doctors have relied on their knowledge, experience, and intuition to diagnose and treat patients. But with the advent of AI, we're entering a new era, one where machines can assist doctors, making diagnoses more accurate and treatments more effective.

The Power of Data: The Backbone of AI in Medicine

At the heart of AI in medicine is data. Lots and lots of data. Think of it like this: data is the fuel that powers AI, the lifeblood that makes it all possible. In the medical world, this data comes from all sorts of sources—electronic health records, medical images, genetic information, and more.

Electronic Health Records: A Treasure Trove of Information

Electronic health records (EHRs) are like digital libraries, containing a wealth of information about patients' medical histories, symptoms, and treatments. By analyzing this data, AI can identify patterns, predict outcomes, and even suggest treatments. It's like having a medical detective who can sift through mountains of information to find the clues that matter most.

Medical Images: Seeing the Unseen

Medical images, like X-rays, MRIs, and CT scans, are another rich source of data. These images provide valuable insights into what's going on inside the body, but they can be complex and hard to interpret. That's where AI comes in. By using advanced algorithms, AI can analyze these images, detect anomalies, and even make diagnoses with astonishing accuracy. It's like having a pair of super-powered eyes that can see what the human eye might miss.

Genetic Information: The Blueprint of Life

Genetic information is perhaps the most powerful data of all. It's the blueprint of life, containing the instructions that make us who we are. By analyzing genetic data, AI can identify genetic mutations, predict the risk of diseases, and even tailor treatments to individual patients. It's like having a crystal ball that can peer into the future and show us the way forward.

AI in Diagnostics: Revolutionizing the Way We Detect Disease

One of the most exciting applications of AI in medicine is in diagnostics. By analyzing vast amounts of data, AI can help doctors make more accurate diagnoses, faster and more efficiently than ever before.

Cancer Detection: Early Intervention Saves Lives

Take cancer detection, for instance. Early detection is crucial for successful treatment, but it can be challenging to spot cancer in its early stages. That's where AI comes in. By analyzing medical images, AI can detect subtle changes that might indicate the presence of cancer, even before symptoms appear. It's like having a super-sensitive radar that can pick up the faintest signals, alerting doctors to potential problems before they become serious.

Heart Disease: Predicting the Future

Heart disease is another area where AI is making a big difference. By analyzing EHRs, AI can identify patterns that predict the risk of heart disease, allowing doctors to intervene early and prevent complications. It's like having a time machine that can show us the future, helping us make better decisions today.

Infectious Diseases: Staying Ahead of the Curve

Infectious diseases are a constant threat, but AI is helping us stay ahead of the curve. By analyzing data from outbreaks, AI can predict the spread of diseases, identify hotspots, and even suggest containment strategies. It's like having a global health monitor that can track the movement of diseases and help us respond quickly and effectively.

AI in Treatment: Personalizing Care for Better Outcomes

But AI isngt just about diagnostics; it's also about treatment. By analyzing patient data, AI can help doctors tailor treatments to individual patients, improving outcomes and enhancing the quality of care.

Personalized Medicine: Tailored to You

Chapter 5: AI in Healthcare: Saving Lives with Smart Technology

Personalized medicine is the future of healthcare, and AI is making it a reality. By analyzing genetic information, AI can identify the best treatments for individual patients, based on their unique genetic makeup. It's like having a custom-made treatment plan, designed just for you.

Drug Discovery: Accelerating the Process

Drug discovery is a long and complex process, but AI is speeding it up. By analyzing vast amounts of data, AI can identify potential drug candidates, predict their effectiveness, and even suggest new combinations of drugs. It's like having a super-powered researcher who can sift through mountains of information to find the next big breakthrough.

Clinical Trials: Optimizing the Search for Cures

Clinical trials are essential for testing new treatments, but they can be time-consuming and expensive. That's where AI comes in. By analyzing data from past trials, AI can identify the most promising treatments, optimizing the search for cures and accelerating the development of new therapies. It's like having a smart, invisible guide who can show us the way forward, helping us find the answers we need faster and more efficiently.

The Human Touch: The Role of Doctors and Scientists

But AI in medicine aingt just about technology. It's also about people. It's about the doctors and scientists who are pushing the boundaries of what's possible. It's about the visionaries who are dreaming of a future where AI can help us diagnose and treat diseases more effectively than ever before.

Doctors and scientists are a special breed. They're part healer, part researcher, part detective, and part dreamer. They know how to collect data, how to analyze data, and how to interpret data.

But more importantly, they know how to communicate their findings in a way that's clear and compelling.

Think of it like this: a doctor is like a healer who can use AI to make more accurate diagnoses and tailor treatments to individual patients. A scientist is like a researcher who can use AI to discover new treatments and accelerate the development of new therapies. Together, they're like a dynamic duo, working hand in hand to unlock the power of AI in medicine.

The Ethics of AI in Medicine: Privacy, Bias, and Fairness

But with great power comes great responsibility. And when it comes to AI in medicine, that responsibility is enormous. You see, medical data is personal. It's intimate. It's a reflection of who we are and what we're going through. And when we use AI to analyze this data, we're giving it access to some of the most sensitive and private aspects of our lives.

That's why it's so important to handle medical data with care. It's why we need to think about privacy, bias, and fairness. It's why we need to be mindful of the ethical implications of our actions.

Take the example of bias in AI. If the data used to train an AI model is biased, the model itself will be biased. This can lead to inaccurate diagnoses and unfair treatment, affecting the health and well-being of patients. That's why it's crucial to ensure that our data is diverse, representative, and free from bias.

The Future of AI in Medicine: A World of Possibilities

But despite the challenges, the future of AI in medicine is bright. It's a future filled with possibilities, with opportunities to solve problems and improve lives. It's a future where AI can help us diagnose and treat diseases more effectively than ever before, where it can help us discover new treatments and accelerate the development of new therapies.

And it's a future that's already here. Every day, we're seeing new breakthroughs, new innovations, new ways of using AI to make the world a better place. It's exciting, it's inspiring, and it's just the beginning.

So, my friends, as we journey through this magical world of AI in medicine, let's remember the power and the potential that lies within. Let's remember the pioneers who came before us, the visionaries who dared to dream of a future where AI could help us diagnose and treat diseases more effectively than ever before. And let's look forward to the exciting journey that lies ahead, as we continue to explore the boundless possibilities of artificial intelligence.

The Role of Machine Learning in Personalized Medicine

Introduction: The Future of Healthcare

Folks, gather 'round and let me spin you a yarn about the magical world of machine learning and how it's revolutionizing the field of personalized medicine. Now, I know what you're thinking: "Machine learning in medicine? Sounds like something out of a science fiction novel." But fear not, my friends, for I'm here to make it all as clear as a summer's day. So, grab your favorite chair, pour yourself a glass of lemonade, and let's dive right in.

The Dawn of Personalized Medicine: A New Era

To understand the role of machine learning in personalized medicine, we gotta go back to the beginning. For centuries, doctors have treated patients based on general guidelines and standard protocols. But every person is unique, with their own genetic makeup, lifestyle, and health history. That's where personalized medicine comes in—it's about tailoring treatments to the individual, making healthcare more effective and efficient.

The Power of Data: The Backbone of Personalized Medicine

At the heart of personalized medicine is data. Lots and lots of data. Think of it like this: data is the fuel that powers machine learning, the lifeblood that makes it all possible. In the medical world, this data comes from all sorts of sources—electronic health records, genetic information, wearable devices, and more.

Electronic Health Records: A Treasure Trove of Information

Electronic health records (EHRs) are like digital libraries, containing a wealth of information about patients' medical histories, symptoms, and treatments. By analyzing this data, machine learning algorithms can identify patterns, predict outcomes, and even suggest personalized treatments. It's like having a medical detective who can sift through mountains of information to find the clues that matter most.

Genetic Information: The Blueprint of Life

Genetic information is perhaps the most powerful data of all. It's the blueprint of life, containing the instructions that make us who we are. By analyzing genetic data, machine learning algorithms can identify genetic mutations, predict the risk of diseases, and even tailor treatments to individual patients. It's like having a crystal ball that can peer into the future and show us the way forward.

Wearable Devices: Tracking Every Move

Wearable devices, like smartwatches and fitness trackers, are another rich source of data. These devices collect information about our daily activities, heart rate, sleep patterns, and more. By analyzing this data, machine learning algorithms can provide insights into our health, help us make better lifestyle choices, and even detect early signs of disease. It's like having a personal health coach who's always with us, monitoring our every move.

Machine Learning in Diagnostics: Revolutionizing the Way We Detect Disease

One of the most exciting applications of machine learning in personalized medicine is in diagnostics. By analyzing vast amounts of data, machine learning algorithms can help doctors make more accurate diagnoses, faster and more efficiently than ever before.

Cancer Detection: Early Intervention Saves Lives

Take cancer detection, for instance. Early detection is crucial for successful treatment, but it can be challenging to spot cancer in its early stages. That's where machine learning comes in. By analyzing medical images, machine learning algorithms can detect subtle changes that might indicate the presence of cancer, even before symptoms appear. It's like having a super-sensitive radar that can pick up the faintest signals, alerting doctors to potential problems before they become serious.

Heart Disease: Predicting the Future

Heart disease is another area where machine learning is making a big difference. By analyzing EHRs, machine learning algorithms can identify patterns that predict the risk of heart disease, allowing doctors to intervene early and prevent complications. It's like having a time machine that can show us the future, helping us make better decisions today.

Infectious Diseases: Staying Ahead of the Curve

Infectious diseases are a constant threat, but machine learning is helping us stay ahead of the curve. By analyzing data from outbreaks, machine learning algorithms can predict the spread of diseases, identify hotspots, and even suggest containment strategies. It's like having a global health monitor that can track the movement of diseases and help us respond quickly and effectively.

Machine Learning in Treatment: Personalizing Care for Better Outcomes

But machine learning isngt just about diagnostics; it's also about treatment. By analyzing patient data, machine learning algorithms can help doctors tailor treatments to individual patients, improving outcomes and enhancing the quality of care.

Personalized Medicine: Tailored to You

Personalized medicine is the future of healthcare, and machine learning is making it a reality. By analyzing genetic information, machine learning algorithms can identify the best treatments for individual patients, based on their unique genetic makeup. It's like having a custom-made treatment plan, designed just for you.

Drug Discovery: Accelerating the Process

Drug discovery is a long and complex process, but machine learning is speeding it up. By analyzing vast amounts of data, machine learning algorithms can identify potential drug candidates, predict their effectiveness, and even suggest new combinations of drugs. It's like having a super-powered researcher who can sift through mountains of information to find the next big breakthrough.

Clinical Trials: Optimizing the Search for Cures

Clinical trials are essential for testing new treatments, but they can be time-consuming and expensive. That's where machine learning comes in. By analyzing data from past trials, machine learning algorithms can identify the most promising treatments, optimizing the search for cures and accelerating the development of new therapies. It's like having a smart, invisible guide who can show us the way forward, helping us find the answers we need faster and more efficiently.

The Human Touch: The Role of Doctors and Scientists

But machine learning in personalized medicine aingt just about technology. It's also about people. It's about the doctors and scientists who are pushing the boundaries of what's possible. It's about the visionaries who are dreaming of a future where machine learning can help us diagnose and treat diseases more effectively than ever before.

Doctors and scientists are a special breed. They're part healer, part researcher, part detective, and part dreamer. They know how to collect data, how to analyze data, and how to interpret data. But more importantly, they know how to communicate their findings in a way that's clear and compelling.

Think of it like this: a doctor is like a healer who can use machine learning to make more accurate diagnoses and tailor treatments to individual patients. A scientist is like a researcher who can use machine learning to discover new treatments and accelerate the development of new therapies. Together, they're like a dynamic duo, working hand in hand to unlock the power of machine learning in personalized medicine.

The Ethics of Machine Learning in Medicine: Privacy, Bias, and Fairness

But with great power comes great responsibility. And when it comes to machine learning in medicine, that responsibility is enormous. You see, medical data is personal. It's intimate. It's a reflection of who we are and what we're going through. And when we use machine learning to analyze this data, we're giving it access to some of the most sensitive and private aspects of our lives.

That's why it's so important to handle medical data with care. It's why we need to think about privacy, bias, and fairness. It's why we need to be mindful of the ethical implications of our actions.

Take the example of bias in machine learning. If the data used to train a machine learning model is biased, the model itself will be biased. This can lead to inaccurate diagnoses and unfair treatment, affecting the health and well-being of patients. That's why it's crucial to ensure that our data is diverse, representative, and free from bias.

The Future of Machine Learning in Personalized Medicine: A World of Possibilities

But despite the challenges, the future of machine learning in personalized medicine is bright. It's a future filled with possibilities, with opportunities to solve problems and improve lives. It's a future where machine learning can help us diagnose and treat diseases more effectively than ever before, where it can help us discover new treatments and accelerate the development of new therapies.

And it's a future that's already here. Every day, we're seeing new breakthroughs, new innovations, new ways of using machine learning to make the world a better place. It's exciting, it's inspiring, and it's just the beginning.

So, my friends, as we journey through this magical world of machine learning in personalized medicine, let's remember the power and the potential that lies within. Let's remember the pioneers who came before us, the visionaries who dared to dream of a future where machine learning could help us diagnose and treat diseases more effectively than ever before. And let's look forward to the exciting journey that lies ahead, as we continue to explore the boundless possibilities of artificial intelligence.

Case Study: IBM Watson and the Fight Against Cancer

Introduction: The Battle of a Lifetime

Folks, gather 'round and let me spin you a yarn about the magical world of artificial intelligence and how IBM Watson is taking on one of the toughest challenges of our time: the fight against cancer. Now, I know what you're thinking: "IBM Watson fighting cancer? Sounds like something out of a science fiction novel." But fear not, my friends, for I'm here to make it all as clear as a summer's day. So, grab your favorite chair, pour yourself a glass of lemonade, and let's dive right in.

The Birth of IBM Watson: A Star is Born

To understand the impact of IBM Watson in the fight against cancer, we gotta go back to its beginnings. The story of Watson starts in the hallowed halls of IBM, where a team of brilliant engineers and scientists were dreaming up the future of artificial intelligence.

The Vision: A Supercomputer with a Mission

The idea behind Watson was simple yet revolutionary: create a supercomputer that could understand and process natural language, analyze vast amounts of data, and make intelligent decisions. Think of it like having a super-smart assistant who can read, understand, and interpret information just like a human, but at a scale and speed that's beyond our comprehension.

The Technology: Natural Language Processing and Machine Learning

But turning that vision into reality was no easy feat. The team at IBM had to tackle some of the most complex challenges in natural language processing (NLP) and machine learning. They had to teach Watson to recognize speech, understand context, and generate meaningful responses. It was like teaching a child to speak, listen, and think, all at the same time.

The Launch: Watson Takes the Stage

After years of hard work and countless iterations, Watson was finally ready to take the stage. In 2011, IBM unveiled Watson to the world in a dramatic fashion: by having it compete on the popular game show "Jeopardy!" against two of the show's most successful contestants. The world watched in awe as Watson outperformed its human competitors, demonstrating its incredible ability to understand and process complex information.

The Response: A Hit with the Public

The response to Watsongs performance on "Jeopardy!" was overwhelming. People were amazed by the supercomputer's capabilities and excited about the potential it held for the future. Suddenly, the world was buzzing with possibilities, and IBM knew they had something special on their hands.

The Evolution: Watson Grows Up

But the story of Watson doesngt stop with its debut on "Jeopardy!" Over the years, IBM has continued to innovate and expand the capabilities of its supercomputer. From new applications to advanced features, Watson has grown and evolved, making our lives easier and more convenient.

New Applications: From Business to Healthcare

One of the most exciting developments in the world of Watson is its expansion into various industries, from business to healthcare. Watsongs ability to analyze vast amounts of data and make intelligent decisions has made it an invaluable tool for businesses looking to improve efficiency, enhance customer service, and drive innovation.

Advanced Features: The Power of AI

But it's not just about the applications. Watsongs real power lies in its advanced features, specifically its ability to analyze and interpret data. By using machine learning algorithms, Watson can identify patterns, predict outcomes, and even suggest actions based on that information. It's like having a super-smart, invisible assistant who can help you make better decisions, faster and more efficiently than ever before.

The Fight Against Cancer: Watsongs Greatest Challenge

Now, let's talk about the fight against cancer. Cancer is one of the most devastating diseases of our time, affecting millions of people worldwide. But with Watsongs advanced capabilities, we're seeing a new hope in the battle against this deadly disease.

The Power of Data: Unlocking the Secrets of Cancer

At the heart of Watsongs fight against cancer is data. Lots and lots of data. Think of it like this: data is the fuel that powers Watson, the lifeblood that makes it all possible. In the medical world, this data comes from all sorts of sources—electronic health records, genetic information, medical images, and more.

Electronic Health Records: A Treasure Trove of Information

Electronic health records (EHRs) are like digital libraries, containing a wealth of information about patients' medical histories, symptoms, and treatments. By analyzing this data, Watson can identify patterns, predict outcomes, and even suggest personalized treatments. It's like having a medical detective who

Chapter 5: AI in Healthcare: Saving Lives with Smart Technology

can sift through mountains of information to find the clues that matter most.

Genetic Information: The Blueprint of Life

Genetic information is perhaps the most powerful data of all. It's the blueprint of life, containing the instructions that make us who we are. By analyzing genetic data, Watson can identify genetic mutations, predict the risk of diseases, and even tailor treatments to individual patients. It's like having a crystal ball that can peer into the future and show us the way forward.

Medical Images: Seeing the Unseen

Medical images, like X-rays, MRIs, and CT scans, are another rich source of data. These images provide valuable insights into what's going on inside the body, but they can be complex and hard to interpret. That's where Watson comes in. By using advanced algorithms, Watson can analyze these images, detect anomalies, and even make diagnoses with astonishing accuracy. It's like having a pair of super-powered eyes that can see what the human eye might miss.

Watson in Action: Revolutionizing Cancer Care

One of the most exciting applications of Watson in the fight against cancer is its ability to revolutionize cancer care. By analyzing vast amounts of data, Watson can help doctors make more accurate diagnoses, develop personalized treatment plans, and even predict the likelihood of success.

Early Detection: Catching Cancer Before It's Too Late

Take early detection, for instance. Early detection is crucial for successful treatment, but it can be challenging to spot cancer in its early stages. That's where Watson comes in. By analyzing medical images, Watson can detect subtle changes that might indicate the presence of cancer, even before symptoms appear. It's like having a super-sensitive radar that can pick up the faintest signals, alerting doctors to potential problems before they become serious.

Personalized Treatment Plans: Tailored to You

Personalized treatment plans are another area where Watson is making a big difference. By analyzing genetic information, Watson can identify the best treatments for individual patients, based on their unique genetic makeup. It's like having a custom-made treatment plan, designed just for you.

Predictive Analytics: Looking into the Future

Predictive analytics is perhaps the most powerful tool in Watsongs arsenal. By analyzing data from past treatments, Watson can predict the likelihood of success for different treatment options. It's like having a time machine that can show us the future, helping us make better decisions today.

The Human Touch: The Role of Doctors and Scientists

But Watsongs fight against cancer aingt just about technology. It's also about people. It's about the doctors and scientists who are pushing the boundaries of what's possible. It's about the visionaries who are dreaming of a future where Watson can help us diagnose and treat cancer more effectively than ever before.

Doctors and scientists are a special breed. They're part healer, part researcher, part detective, and part dreamer. They know how to collect data, how to analyze data, and how to interpret data. But more importantly, they know how to communicate their findings in a way that's clear and compelling.

Think of it like this: a doctor is like a healer who can use Watson to make more accurate diagnoses and develop personalized treatment plans. A scientist is like a researcher who can use Watson to discover new treatments and accelerate the development of new therapies. Together, they're like a dynamic duo, working hand in hand to unlock the power of Watson in the fight against cancer.

The Ethics of AI in Medicine: Privacy, Bias, and Fairness

But with great power comes great responsibility. And when it comes to AI in medicine, that responsibility is enormous. You see, medical data is personal. It's intimate. It's a reflection of who we are and what we're going through. And when we use AI to analyze this data, we're giving it access to some of the most sensitive and private aspects of our lives.

That's why it's so important to handle medical data with care. It's why we need to think about privacy, bias, and fairness. It's why we need to be mindful of the ethical implications of our actions.

Take the example of bias in AI. If the data used to train a machine learning model is biased, the model itself will be biased. This can lead to inaccurate diagnoses and unfair treatment, affecting the health and well-being of patients. That's why it's crucial to ensure that our data is diverse, representative, and free from bias.

The Future of Watson in the Fight Against Cancer: A World of Possibilities

But despite the challenges, the future of Watson in the fight against cancer is bright. It's a future filled with possibilities, with opportunities to solve problems and improve lives. It's a future where Watson can help us diagnose and treat cancer more effectively than ever before, where it can help us discover new treatments and accelerate the development of new therapies.

And it's a future that's already here. Every day, we're seeing new breakthroughs, new innovations, new ways of using Watson to make the world a better place. It's exciting, it's inspiring, and it's just the beginning.

So, my friends, as we journey through this magical world of Watson and the fight against cancer, let's remember the power and the potential that lies within. Let's remember the pioneers who came before us, the visionaries who dared to dream of a future where Watson could help us diagnose and treat cancer more effectively than ever before. And let's look forward to the exciting journey that lies ahead, as we continue to explore the boundless possibilities of artificial intelligence.

Chapter 6: AI in Finance: Revolutionizing the Way We Handle Money

The Impact of AI on Banking and Investment

Introduction: The Future of Finance

Folks, gather 'round and let me spin you a yarn about the magical world of artificial intelligence and how it's transforming the way we bank and invest. Now, I know what you're thinking: "AI in banking and investment? Sounds like something out of a science fiction novel." But fear not, my friends, for I'm here to make it all as clear as a summer's day. So, grab your favorite chair, pour yourself a glass of lemonade, and let's dive right in.

The Evolution of Banking: From Bricks to Clicks

To understand the impact of AI on banking and investment, we gotta go back to the beginnings. Banking has come a long way from the days of brick-and-mortar branches and manual ledgers. With the advent of computers, the internet, and now AI, banking has become faster, more efficient, and more convenient than ever before.

From Bricks to Clicks: The Digital Transformation

The digital transformation of banking started with the introduction of computers and the internet. Suddenly, people could bank from the comfort of their own homes, making transactions, paying bills, and even applying for loans online. It was a revolution in the making.

The Rise of Mobile Banking: Banking on the Go

But the revolution didngt stop there. With the rise of smartphones, mobile banking became the new norm. People could now bank on the go, checking their balances, transferring funds, and even depositing checks with just a few taps on their phones. It was like having a bank in your pocket, always ready to serve you.

The Power of Data: The Backbone of AI in Finance

At the heart of AI in banking and investment is data. Lots and lots of data. Think of it like this: data is the fuel that powers AI, the lifeblood that makes it all possible. In the financial world, this data comes from all sorts of sources—transaction histories, market trends, customer behaviors, and more.

Transaction Histories: A Treasure Trove of Information

Transaction histories are like digital diaries, containing a wealth of information about customers' spending habits, financial behaviors, and preferences. By analyzing this data, AI can identify patterns, predict future behaviors, and even suggest personalized financial products and services. It's like having a financial detective who can sift through mountains of information to find the clues that matter most.

Market Trends: The Pulse of the Economy

Market trends are another rich source of data. These trends provide valuable insights into the health of the economy, the performance of different industries, and the behavior of investors. By analyzing this data, AI can predict market movements, identify investment opportunities, and even help investors make better decisions. It's like having a crystal ball that can peer into the future and show us the way forward.

Customer Behaviors: Understanding the Consumer

Customer behaviors are perhaps the most powerful data of all. By analyzing how customers interact with financial products and services, AI can identify their needs, preferences, and pain points. This information can then be used to develop new products, improve existing ones, and even tailor financial advice to individual customers. It's like having a personal financial advisor who knows exactly what you need and when you need it.

AI in Banking: Revolutionizing the Way We Manage Money

One of the most exciting applications of AI in banking is its ability to revolutionize the way we manage our money. By analyzing vast amounts of data, AI can help banks make better decisions, improve customer service, and even detect fraud.

Fraud Detection: Keeping Your Money Safe

Take fraud detection, for instance. Fraud is a constant threat in the financial world, but AI is helping banks stay ahead of the curve. By analyzing transaction histories, AI can identify unusual patterns that might indicate fraudulent activity. It's like having a super-sensitive radar that can pick up the faintest signals, alerting banks to potential threats before they become serious.

Personalized Financial Advice: Tailored to You

Personalized financial advice is another area where AI is making a big difference. By analyzing customer behaviors, AI can identify the best financial products and services for individual customers, based on their unique needs and preferences. It's like having a custom-made financial plan, designed just for you.

Customer Service: Always There to Help

Customer service is perhaps the most visible application of AI in banking. With the help of chatbots and virtual assistants, banks can now provide 24/7 customer support, answering questions, solving problems, and even offering financial advice. It's like having a personal banker who's always available to help, no matter the time or day.

AI in Investment: Making Smarter Decisions

But AI isngt just about banking; it's also about investment. By analyzing market trends, AI can help investors make smarter decisions, identifyng opportunities, and even predicting future movements.

Algorithmic Trading: The Future of Investment

Algorithmic trading is perhaps the most powerful application of AI in investment. By using advanced algorithms, AI can analyze vast amounts of market data, identify patterns, and even make trades automatically. It's like having a super-smart trader who can sift through mountains of information to find the best opportunities and act on them instantly.

Robo-Advisors: Your Personal Investment Guide

Robo-advisors are another exciting development in the world of AI and investment. These automated advisors use AI to analyze market trends, identify investment opportunities, and even manage portfolios. It's like having a personal investment guide who can help you make better decisions, faster and more efficiently than ever before.

Predictive Analytics: Looking into the Future

Predictive analytics is perhaps the most powerful tool in AI's arsenal. By analyzing market trends, AI can predict future movements, identifyng opportunities, and even help investors make better decisions. It's like having a time machine that can show us the future, helping us make better decisions today.

The Human Touch: The Role of Bankers and Investors

But AI in banking and investment aingt just about technology. It's also about people. It's about the bankers and investors who are pushing the boundaries of what's possible. It's about the visionaries who are dreaming of a future where AI can help us manage our money and make smarter investments more effectively than ever before.

Bankers and investors are a special breed. They're part financier, part analyst, part detective, and part dreamer. They know how to collect data, how to analyze data, and how to interpret data. But more importantly, they know how to communicate their findings in a way that's clear and compelling.

Think of it like this: a banker is like a financier who can use AI to make better decisions, improve customer service, and detect fraud. An investor is like an analyst who can use AI to identify opportunities, make smarter decisions, and even predict future movements. Together, they're like a dynamic duo, working hand in hand to unlock the power of AI in banking and investment.

The Ethics of AI in Finance: Privacy, Bias, and Fairness

But with great power comes great responsibility. And when it comes to AI in banking and investment, that responsibility is enormous. You see, financial data is personal. It's intimate. It's a reflection of who we are and what we're doing with our money. And when we use AI to analyze this data, we're giving it access to some of the most sensitive and private aspects of our lives.

That's why it's so important to handle financial data with care. It's why we need to think about privacy, bias, and fairness. It's why we need to be mindful of the ethical implications of our actions.

Take the example of bias in AI. If the data used to train a machine learning model is biased, the model itself will be biased. This can lead to unfair decisions, affecting the financial well-being of customers. That's why it's crucial to ensure that our data is diverse, representative, and free from bias.

The Future of AI in Banking and Investment: A World of Possibilities

But despite the challenges, the future of AI in banking and investment is bright. It's a future filled with possibilities, with opportunities to solve problems and improve lives. It's a future where AI can help us manage our money and make smarter investments more effectively than ever before, where it can help us detect fraud, improve customer service, and even predict future movements.

And it's a future that's already here. Every day, we're seeing new breakthroughs, new innovations, new ways of using AI to make the world a better place. It's exciting, it's inspiring, and it's just the beginning.

So, my friends, as we journey through this magical world of AI in banking and investment, let's remember the power and the potential that lies within. Let's remember the pioneers who came before us, the visionaries who dared to dream of a future where AI could help us manage our money and make smarter investments more effectively than ever before. And let's look forward to the exciting journey that lies ahead, as we continue to explore the boundless possibilities of artificial intelligence.

Chapter 6: AI in Finance: Revolutionizing the Way We Handle Money

Fraud Detection and Cybersecurity: AI as a Guardian

Introduction: The Guardians of the Digital Age

Folks, gather 'round and let me spin you a yarn about the magical world of artificial intelligence and how it's protecting us from fraud and cyber threats. Now, I know what you're thinking: "AI in fraud detection and cybersecurity? Sounds like something out of a science fiction novel." But fear not, my friends, for I'm here to make it all as clear as a summer's day. So, grab your favorite chair, pour yourself a glass of lemonade, and let's dive right in.

The Evolution of Fraud: From Pickpockets to Cybercriminals

To understand the role of AI in fraud detection and cybersecurity, we gotta go back to the beginnings. Fraud has been around since the dawn of civilization, evolving from simple pickpocketing to sophisticated cybercrimes. But with the advent of AI, we're seeing a new era, one where machines can help us detect and prevent fraud like never before.

From Pickpockets to Cybercriminals: The Evolution of Fraud

Fraud has come a long way from the days of pickpockets and con artists. With the rise of the internet and digital technologies, fraud has become more sophisticated and harder to detect. Cybercriminals now use advanced techniques to steal personal information, hack into accounts, and commit financial crimes. It's a constant battle, and the stakes are higher than ever.

The Rise of Cybersecurity: Protecting the Digital World

But the evolution of fraud didngt stop there. With the rise of cybersecurity, we're seeing a new frontier in the battle against fraud. Cybersecurity experts are now using advanced technologies to protect our digital world, making it safer and more secure than ever before. It's like having a digital fortress, always ready to defend us against the latest threats.

The Power of Data: The Backbone of AI in Fraud Detection and Cybersecurity

At the heart of AI in fraud detection and cybersecurity is data. Lots and lots of data. Think of it like this: data is the fuel that powers AI, the lifeblood that makes it all possible. In the digital world, this data comes from all sorts of sources—transaction histories, network logs, user behaviors, and more.

Transaction Histories: A Treasure Trove of Information

Transaction histories are like digital diaries, containing a wealth of information about customers' spending habits, financial behaviors, and preferences. By analyzing this data, AI can identify patterns, detect anomalies, and even predict future behaviors. It's like having a financial detective who can sift through mountains of information to find the clues that matter most.

Network Logs: The Pulse of the Digital World

Network logs are another rich source of data. These logs provide valuable insights into the health and security of our digital networks, revealing patterns of activity, detecting unusual behaviors, and even identifyng potential threats. By analyzing this data, AI can help us understand the pulse of the digital world, making it safer and more secure.

User Behaviors: Understanding the Consumer

User behaviors are perhaps the most powerful data of all. By analyzing how users interact with digital services, AI can identify their needs, preferences, and pain points. This information can then be used to develop new security measures, improve existing ones, and even tailor fraud detection strategies to individual users. It's like having a personal security guard who knows exactly what you need and when you need it.

AI in Fraud Detection: Revolutionizing the Way We Protect Our Money

One of the most exciting applications of AI in fraud detection is its ability to revolutionize the way we protect our money. By analyzing vast amounts of data, AI can help banks and financial institutions detect and prevent fraud more effectively than ever before.

Anomaly Detection: Spotting the Unusual

Take anomaly detection, for instance. Fraud often involves unusual or unexpected behaviors, and AI is particularly good at spotting these anomalies. By analyzing transaction histories, AI can identify patterns that deviate from the norm, alerting banks to potential fraudulent activities. It's like having a super-sensitive radar that can pick up the faintest signals, alerting us to potential threats before they become serious.

Real-Time Monitoring: Always on Guard

Real-time monitoring is another powerful tool in AI's arsenal. By continuously analyzing data as it comes in, AI can detect fraudulent activities in real-time, allowing banks to take immediate action. It's like having a digital watchdog who's always on guard, ready to bark at the first sign of trouble.

Predictive Analytics: Looking into the Future

Predictive analytics is perhaps the most powerful tool in AI's arsenal. By analyzing historical data, AI can predict future behaviors, identifyng potential risks, and even suggest preventive measures. It's like having a time machine that can show us the future, helping us make better decisions today.

AI in Cybersecurity: Protecting the Digital World

But AI isngt just about fraud detection; it's also about cybersecurity. By analyzing network logs, user behaviors, and other data, AI can help us protect our digital world from a wide range of threats, from malware to phishing attacks.

Intrusion Detection: Keeping the Bad Guys Out

Intrusion detection is one of the most exciting applications of AI in cybersecurity. By analyzing network logs, AI can identify unusual or suspicious activities, alerting security teams to potential intrusions. It's like having a digital sentry who's always on the lookout, ready to sound the alarm at the first sign of trouble.

Malware Detection: Fighting the Digital Viruses

Malware detection is another powerful tool in AI's arsenal. By analyzing the behavior of software and applications, AI can identify malicious activities, detecting and neutralizing malware before it can cause harm. It's like having a digital doctor who can diagnose and treat infections, keeping our digital world healthy and secure.

Phishing Detection: Protecting Against Scams

Phishing detection is perhaps the most important tool in AI's arsenal. By analyzing emails, messages, and other communications, AI can identify phishing attempts, alerting users to potential scams and protecting them from falling victim to cybercriminals. It's like having a digital bodyguard who's always by your side, ready to protect you from harm.

The Human Touch: The Role of Cybersecurity Experts

But AI in fraud detection and cybersecurity aingt just about technology. It's also about people. It's about the cybersecurity experts who are pushing the boundaries of what's possible. It's about the visionaries who are dreaming of a future where AI can help us protect our money and our digital world more effectively than ever before.

Cybersecurity experts are a special breed. They're part detective, part analyst, part engineer, and part dreamer. They know how to collect data, how to analyze data, and how to interpret data. But more importantly, they know how to communicate their findings in a way that's clear and compelling.

Think of it like this: a cybersecurity expert is like a detective who can use AI to identify unusual behaviors, detect potential threats, and even predict future risks. An engineer is like an analyst who can use AI to develop new security measures, improve existing ones, and even tailor fraud detection strategies to individual users. Together, they're like a dynamic duo, working hand in hand to unlock the power of AI in fraud detection and cybersecurity.

The Ethics of AI in Fraud Detection and Cybersecurity: Privacy, Bias, and Fairness

But with great power comes great responsibility. And when it comes to AI in fraud detection and cybersecurity, that responsibility is enormous. You see, financial and personal data is sensitive. It's intimate. It's a reflection of who we are and what we're doing with our money and our digital lives. And when we use AI to analyze this data, we're giving it access to some of the most private and personal aspects of our lives.

That's why it's so important to handle this data with care. It's why we need to think about privacy, bias, and fairness. It's why we need to be mindful of the ethical implications of our actions.

Take the example of bias in AI. If the data used to train a machine learning model is biased, the model itself will be biased. This can lead to unfair decisions, affecting the financial and digital well-being of users. That's why it's crucial to ensure that our data is diverse, representative, and free from bias.

The Future of AI in Fraud Detection and Cybersecurity: A World of Possibilities

But despite the challenges, the future of AI in fraud detection and cybersecurity is bright. It's a future filled with possibilities, with opportunities to solve problems and improve lives. It's a future where AI can help us protect our money and our digital world more effectively than ever before, where it can help us detect fraud, prevent cyber threats, and even predict future risks.

And it's a future that's already here. Every day, we're seeing new breakthroughs, new innovations, new ways of using AI to make the world a better place. It's exciting, it's inspiring, and it's just the beginning.

So, my friends, as we journey through this magical world of AI in fraud detection and cybersecurity, let's remember the power and the potential that lies within. Let's remember the pioneers who came before us, the visionaries who dared to dream of a future where AI could help us protect our money and our digital world more effectively than ever before. And let's look forward to the exciting journey that lies ahead, as we continue to explore the boundless possibilities of artificial intelligence.

Case Study: PayPal's AI-Driven Fraud Prevention System

Introduction: The Guardian of Digital Transactions

Folks, gather 'round and let me spin you a yarn about the magical world of artificial intelligence and how PayPal is using it to fight fraud. Now, I know what you're thinking: "AI in fraud prevention? Sounds like something out of a science fiction novel." But fear not, my friends, for I'm here to make it all as clear as a summer's day. So, grab your favorite chair, pour yourself a glass of lemonade, and let's dive right in.

The Birth of PayPal: A Revolution in Payments

To understand the impact of PayPal's AI-driven fraud prevention system, we gotta go back to its beginnings. The story of PayPal starts in the late 1990s, when a group of visionaries dreamed of creating a digital payment system that would make transactions faster, easier, and more secure.

The Vision: A Digital Wallet for the Modern World

The idea behind PayPal was simple yet revolutionary: create a digital wallet that would allow people to send and receive money online, securely and conveniently. Think of it like having a virtual bank account that you can access from anywhere, at any time.

The Technology: Innovation in Action

But turning that vision into reality was no easy feat. The team at PayPal had to tackle some of the most complex challenges in digital payments, from securing transactions to preventing fraud. They had to build a system that was not only fast and convenient but also secure and reliable.

The Launch: PayPal Takes the Stage

After years of hard work and countless iterations, PayPal was finally ready to take the stage. In 1998, PayPal was launched, and the world of digital payments was forever changed. Suddenly, people could send and receive money online with just a few clicks, making transactions faster, easier, and more convenient than ever before.

The Response: A Hit with the Public

The response to PayPal was overwhelming. People were amazed by the convenience and security of the digital payment system, and they flocked to it in droves. Suddenly, PayPal was everywhere, from online marketplaces to charitable donations, from peer-to-peer payments to business transactions. It was a revolution in the making.

The Evolution: PayPal Grows Up

But the story of PayPal doesngt stop with its launch. Over the years, PayPal has continued to innovate and expand, adding new features and improving its services. From mobile payments to international transactions, from business solutions to consumer protections, PayPal has grown and evolved, making our lives easier and more convenient.

New Features: Expanding the Horizons

One of the most exciting developments in the world of PayPal is its expansion into new markets and services. With the introduction of mobile payments, PayPal made it possible for people to send and receive money on the go, making transactions even faster and more convenient. And with the addition of international transactions, PayPal opened up a whole new world of possibilities, allowing people to send and receive money across borders with ease.

Improved Security: Protecting the Digital World

But it's not just about the features. PayPal's real power lies in its security. With the rise of digital payments, the risk of fraud has also increased, and PayPal has been at the forefront of the battle against it. By using advanced technologies and innovative solutions, PayPal has made its system more secure and reliable than ever before.

The Power of Data: The Backbone of AI in Fraud Prevention

At the heart of PayPal's AI-driven fraud prevention system is data. Lots and lots of data. Think of it like this: data is the fuel that powers AI, the lifeblood that makes it all possible. In the digital world, this data comes from all sorts of sources—transaction histories, user behaviors, network logs, and more.

Transaction Histories: A Treasure Trove of Information

Transaction histories are like digital diaries, containing a wealth of information about customers' spending habits, financial behaviors, and preferences. By analyzing this data, AI can identify patterns, detect anomalies, and even predict future behaviors. It's like having a financial detective who can sift through mountains of information to find the clues that matter most.

User Behaviors: Understanding the Consumer

User behaviors are perhaps the most powerful data of all. By analyzing how users interact with digital services, AI can identify their needs, preferences, and pain points. This information can then be used to develop new security measures, improve existing ones, and even tailor fraud prevention strategies to individual users. It's like having a personal security guard who knows exactly what you need and when you need it.

Network Logs: The Pulse of the Digital World

Network logs are another rich source of data. These logs provide valuable insights into the health and security of our digital networks, revealing patterns of activity, detecting unusual behaviors, and even identifyng potential threats. By analyzing this data, AI can help us understand the pulse of the digital world, making it safer and more secure.

AI in Fraud Prevention: Revolutionizing the Way We Protect Our Money

One of the most exciting applications of AI in fraud prevention is its ability to revolutionize the way we protect our money. By analyzing vast amounts of data, AI can help PayPal detect and prevent fraud more effectively than ever before.

Anomaly Detection: Spotting the Unusual

Take anomaly detection, for instance. Fraud often involves unusual or unexpected behaviors, and AI is particularly good at spotting these anomalies. By analyzing transaction histories, AI can identify patterns that deviate from the norm, alerting PayPal to potential fraudulent activities. It's like having a super-sensitive radar that can pick up the faintest signals, alerting us to potential threats before they become serious.

Real-Time Monitoring: Always on Guard

Real-time monitoring is another powerful tool in AI's arsenal. By continuously analyzing data as it comes in, AI can detect fraudulent activities in real-time, allowing PayPal to take immediate action. It's like having a digital watchdog who's always on guard, ready to bark at the first sign of trouble.

Predictive Analytics: Looking into the Future

Predictive analytics is perhaps the most powerful tool in AI's arsenal. By analyzing historical data, AI can predict future behaviors, identifyng potential risks, and even suggest preventive measures. It's like having a time machine that can show us the future, helping us make better decisions today.

The Human Touch: The Role of Cybersecurity Experts

But AI in fraud prevention aingt just about technology. It's also about people. It's about the cybersecurity experts who are pushing the boundaries of what's possible. It's about the visionaries who are dreaming of a future where AI can help us protect our money and our digital world more effectively than ever before.

Cybersecurity experts are a special breed. They're part detective, part analyst, part engineer, and part dreamer. They know how to collect data, how to analyze data, and how to interpret data. But more importantly, they know how to communicate their findings in a way that's clear and compelling.

Think of it like this: a cybersecurity expert is like a detective who can use AI to identify unusual behaviors, detect potential threats, and even predict future risks. An engineer is like an analyst who can use AI to develop new security measures, improve existing ones, and even tailor fraud prevention strategies to individual users. Together, they're like a dynamic duo, working hand in hand to unlock the power of AI in fraud prevention.

The Ethics of AI in Fraud Prevention: Privacy, Bias, and Fairness

But with great power comes great responsibility. And when it comes to AI in fraud prevention, that responsibility is enormous. You see, financial and personal data is sensitive. It's intimate. It's a reflection of who we are and what we're doing with our money and our digital lives. And when we use AI to analyze this data, we're giving it access to some of the most private and personal aspects of our lives.

That's why it's so important to handle this data with care. It's why we need to think about privacy, bias, and fairness. It's why we need to be mindful of the ethical implications of our actions.

Take the example of bias in AI. If the data used to train a machine learning model is biased, the model itself will be biased. This can lead to unfair decisions, affecting the financial and digital well-being of users. That's why it's crucial to ensure that our data is diverse, representative, and free from bias.

The Future of AI in Fraud Prevention: A World of Possibilities

But despite the challenges, the future of AI in fraud prevention is bright. It's a future filled with possibilities, with opportunities to solve problems and improve lives. It's a future where AI can help us protect our money and our digital world more effectively than ever before, where it can help us detect fraud, prevent cyber threats, and even predict future risks.

And it's a future that's already here. Every day, we're seeing new breakthroughs, new innovations, new ways of using AI to make the world a better place. It's exciting, it's inspiring, and it's just the beginning.

So, my friends, as we journey through this magical world of AI in fraud prevention, let's remember the power and the potential that lies within. Let's remember the pioneers who came before us, the visionaries who dared to dream of a future where AI could help us protect our money and our digital world more effectively than ever before. And let's look forward to the exciting journey that lies ahead, as we continue to explore the boundless possibilities of artificial intelligence.

THE IMPACT OF AI ON VARIOUS INDUSTRIES

Chapter 7: AI in Manufacturing: The Factory of the Future

Automation and the Rise of Smart Factories

Introduction: The Future of Manufacturing

Folks, gather 'round and let me spin you a yarn about the magical world of automation and how it's giving rise to smart factories. Now, I know what you're thinking: "Automation and smart factories? Sounds like something out of a science fiction novel." But fear not, my friends, for I'm here to make it all as clear as a summer's day. So, grab your favorite chair, pour yourself a glass of lemonade, and let's dive right in.

The Evolution of Manufacturing: From Crafts to Robots

To understand the impact of automation and the rise of smart factories, we gotta go back to the beginnings. Manufacturing has come a long way from the days of craftsmen and manual labor. With the advent of machines, the industrial revolution, and now AI, manufacturing has become faster, more efficient, and more precise than ever before.

From Crafts to Machines: The Industrial Revolution

The industrial revolution was a game-changer. It brought machines into the picture, making manufacturing faster and more efficient. Suddenly, factories could produce goods at a scale and speed that was unimaginable before. It was a revolution in the making.

Chapter 7: AI in Manufacturing: The Factory of the Future

From Machines to Robots: The Age of Automation

But the revolution didngt stop there. With the rise of automation, robots started taking over the factory floor. These robots could perform tasks faster, more accurately, and with less fatigue than human workers. It was like having an army of tireless, precise workers who never needed a break.

The Power of Data: The Backbone of Smart Factories

At the heart of smart factories is data. Lots and lots of data. Think of it like this: data is the fuel that powers automation, the lifeblood that makes it all possible. In the manufacturing world, this data comes from all sorts of sources—sensors, machines, production logs, and more.

Sensors: The Eyes and Ears of the Factory

Sensors are the eyes and ears of the smart factory. They detect changes in the environment, like temperature, humidity, motion, and light. Think of them like little spies, always on the lookout, gathering information and reporting back to the central system.

Machines: The Workhorses of the Factory

Machines are the workhorses of the smart factory. They perform the tasks, from cutting and shaping to assembling and packing. But unlike traditional machines, smart factory machines are connected, communicating with each other and with the central system. It's like having a team of workers who can talk to each other, coordinating their efforts to get the job done faster and more efficiently.

Production Logs: The Memory of the Factory

Production logs are the memory of the smart factory. They record everything that happens on the factory floor, from the start of production to the final product. By analyzing these logs, smart factories can identify patterns, detect anomalies, and even predict future behaviors. It's like having a historian who can tell you everything that's happened, helping you make better decisions today.

Automation in Action: The Magic of Smart Factories

One of the most exciting aspects of smart factories is automation in action. By using advanced technologies and innovative solutions, smart factories can perform tasks faster, more accurately, and with less waste than ever before.

Predictive Maintenance: Keeping the Machines Running

Take predictive maintenance, for instance. By analyzing sensor data, smart factories can predict when machines are likely to fail, allowing manufacturers to perform maintenance before problems occur. It's like having a crystal ball that can show us the future, helping us keep our machines running smoothly and efficiently.

Quality Control: Ensuring the Best Products

Quality control is another area where smart factories are making a big difference. By analyzing production data, smart factories can identify defects and anomalies, helping manufacturers ensure that their products meet the highest standards of quality. It's like having a super-sensitive inspector who can spot the tiniest flaws, making sure that only the best products make it to the market.

Supply Chain Management: Keeping the Goods Moving

Supply chain management is perhaps the most complex application of automation in smart factories. By analyzing logistics data, smart factories can optimize the flow of goods, from raw materials to finished products, helping manufacturers keep their supply chains running smoothly and efficiently. It's like having a master logistician who can manage the entire supply chain, making sure that everything runs like clockwork.

The Human Touch: The Role of Engineers and Technicians

But automation and smart factories aingt just about technology. It's also about people. It's about the engineers and technicians who are pushing the boundaries of what's possible. It's about the visionaries who are dreaming of a future where automation can help us transform manufacturing like never before.

Engineers and technicians are a special breed. They're part inventor, part scientist, part artist, and part dreamer. They know how to design, build, and program smart factories. But more importantly, they know how to imagine, to innovate, and to create.

Think of it like this: an engineer is like a builder who can construct the systems we need to make smart factories a reality. A technician is like an artist who can envision the possibilities and the potentials of the future. Together, they're like a dynamic duo, working hand in hand to unlock the power of automation and smart factories.

The Ethics of Automation: Privacy, Security, and Responsibility

But with great power comes great responsibility. And when it comes to automation and smart factories, that responsibility is enormous. You see, manufacturing data is sensitive. It's intimate. It's a reflection of how we make things, what we make, and who we make them for. And when we use automation to analyze this data, we're giving it access to some of the most sensitive and private aspects of our businesses.

That's why it's so important to handle manufacturing data with care. It's why we need to think about privacy, security, and responsibility. It's why we need to be mindful of the ethical implications of our actions.

Take the example of data security. If the data used to run a smart factory is compromised, it can lead to serious consequences, affecting the production, the quality, and even the safety of the products. That's why it's crucial to ensure that our data is secure, that our systems are protected, and that our processes are robust.

The Future of Automation and Smart Factories: A World of Possibilities

But despite the challenges, the future of automation and smart factories is bright. It's a future filled with possibilities, with opportunities to solve problems and improve lives. It's a future where automation can help us transform manufacturing like never before, where it can help us produce goods faster, more efficiently, and with less waste.

And it's a future that's already here. Every day, we're seeing new breakthroughs, new innovations, new ways of using automation to make the world a better place. It's exciting, it's inspiring, and it's just the beginning.

So, my friends, as we journey through this magical world of automation and smart factories, let's remember the power and the potential that lies within. Let's remember the pioneers who came before us, the visionaries who dared to dream of a future where automation could help us transform manufacturing like never before. And let's look forward to the exciting journey that lies ahead, as we continue to explore the boundless possibilities of artificial intelligence.

Chapter 7: AI in Manufacturing: The Factory of the Future

Predictive Maintenance: Keeping Machines Running Smoothly

Introduction: The Future of Machine Health

Folks, gather 'round and let me spin you a yarn about the magical world of predictive maintenance and how it's keeping our machines running smoothly. Now, I know what you're thinking: "Predictive maintenance? Sounds like something out of a science fiction novel." But fear not, my friends, for I'm here to make it all as clear as a summer's day. So, grab your favorite chair, pour yourself a glass of lemonade, and let's dive right in.

The Evolution of Maintenance: From Reactive to Proactive

To understand the impact of predictive maintenance, we gotta go back to the beginnings. Maintenance has come a long way from the days of reactive repairs, where machines were fixed only after they broke down. With the advent of technology, maintenance has become more proactive, preventing problems before they happen.

From Reactive to Proactive: A Shift in Mindset

Reactive maintenance was the norm for centuries. Machines were fixed only after they broke down, leading to downtime, reduced productivity, and increased costs. But with the rise of technology, maintenance became more proactive. Scheduled maintenance and regular check-ups became the new norm, helping to prevent problems before they occurred.

The Rise of Predictive Maintenance: A New Era

But the evolution didngt stop there. With the advent of artificial intelligence and machine learning, predictive maintenance emerged as a new era in machine health. By analyzing data from sensors and other sources, predictive maintenance can anticipate when machines are likely to fail, allowing for timely repairs and minimizing downtime. It's like having a crystal ball that can show us the future, helping us keep our machines running smoothly and efficiently.

The Power of Data: The Backbone of Predictive Maintenance

At the heart of predictive maintenance is data. Lots and lots of data. Think of it like this: data is the fuel that powers predictive maintenance, the lifeblood that makes it all possible. In the industrial world, this data comes from all sorts of sources—sensors, machines, production logs, and more.

Sensors: The Eyes and Ears of the Factory

Sensors are the eyes and ears of the factory. They detect changes in the environment, like temperature, humidity, motion, and light. Think of them like little spies, always on the lookout, gathering information and reporting back to the central system. By analyzing this data, predictive maintenance can identify patterns, detect anomalies, and even predict future behaviors.

Machines: The Workhorses of the Factory

Machines are the workhorses of the factory. They perform the tasks, from cutting and shaping to assembling and packing. But unlike traditional machines, smart factory machines are connected, communicating with each other and with the central system. It's like having a team of workers who can talk to each other, coordinating their efforts to get the job done faster and more efficiently.

Production Logs: The Memory of the Factory

Production logs are the memory of the factory. They record everything that happens on the factory floor, from the start of production to the final product. By analyzing these logs, predictive maintenance can identify patterns, detect anomalies, and even predict future behaviors. It's like having a historian who can tell you everything that's happened, helping you make better decisions today.

Predictive Maintenance in Action: The Magic of Keeping Machines Running

One of the most exciting aspects of predictive maintenance is seeing it in action. By using advanced technologies and innovative solutions, predictive maintenance can keep machines running smoothly, minimizing downtime and maximizing productivity.

Predictive Analytics: Looking into the Future

Predictive analytics is perhaps the most powerful tool in the arsenal of predictive maintenance. By analyzing historical data, predictive analytics can identify patterns, detect anomalies, and even predict future behaviors. It's like having a time machine that can show us the future, helping us make better decisions today.

Real-Time Monitoring: Always on Guard

Real-time monitoring is another powerful tool in predictive maintenance. By continuously analyzing data as it comes in, real-time monitoring can detect issues in real-time, allowing for immediate action. It's like having a digital watchdog who's always on guard, ready to bark at the first sign of trouble.

Condition-Based Maintenance: Fixing Things Before They Break

Condition-based maintenance is perhaps the most proactive application of predictive maintenance. By analyzing the condition

Chapter 7: AI in Manufacturing: The Factory of the Future

of machines in real-time, condition-based maintenance can identify when machines are likely to fail, allowing for timely repairs before problems occur. It's like having a super-sensitive mechanic who can spot the tiniest issues, fixing them before they become serious.

The Human Touch: The Role of Engineers and Technicians

But predictive maintenance aingt just about technology. It's also about people. It's about the engineers and technicians who are pushing the boundaries of what's possible. It's about the visionaries who are dreaming of a future where predictive maintenance can help us keep our machines running smoothly and efficiently.

Engineers and technicians are a special breed. They're part inventor, part scientist, part artist, and part dreamer. They know how to design, build, and program predictive maintenance systems. But more importantly, they know how to imagine, to innovate, and to create.

Think of it like this: an engineer is like a builder who can construct the systems we need to make predictive maintenance a reality. A technician is like an artist who can envision the possibilities and the potentials of the future. Together, they're like a dynamic duo, working hand in hand to unlock the power of predictive maintenance.

The Ethics of Predictive Maintenance: Privacy, Security, and Responsibility

But with great power comes great responsibility. And when it comes to predictive maintenance, that responsibility is enormous. You see, industrial data is sensitive. It's intimate. It's a reflection of how we make things, what we make, and who we make them for.

And when we use predictive maintenance to analyze this data, we're giving it access to some of the most sensitive and private aspects of our businesses.

That's why it's so important to handle industrial data with care. It's why we need to think about privacy, security, and responsibility. It's why we need to be mindful of the ethical implications of our actions.

Take the example of data security. If the data used to run a predictive maintenance system is compromised, it can lead to serious consequences, affecting the production, the quality, and even the safety of the products. That's why it's crucial to ensure that our data is secure, that our systems are protected, and that our processes are robust.

The Future of Predictive Maintenance: A World of Possibilities

But despite the challenges, the future of predictive maintenance is bright. It's a future filled with possibilities, with opportunities to solve problems and improve lives. It's a future where predictive maintenance can help us keep our machines running smoothly and efficiently, minimizing downtime and maximizing productivity.

And it's a future that's already here. Every day, we're seeing new breakthroughs, new innovations, new ways of using predictive maintenance to make the world a better place. It's exciting, it's inspiring, and it's just the beginning.

So, my friends, as we journey through this magical world of predictive maintenance, let's remember the power and the potential that lies within. Let's remember the pioneers who came before us, the visionaries who dared to dream of a future where predictive maintenance could help us keep our machines running smoothly and efficiently. And let's look forward to the exciting journey that lies ahead, as we continue to explore the boundless possibilities of artificial intelligence.

Chapter 7: AI in Manufacturing: The Factory of the Future

Case Study: Tesla's AI-Driven Manufacturing Innovations

Introduction: The Future of Automotive Manufacturing

Folks, gather 'round and let me spin you a yarn about the magical world of Tesla and how their AI-driven manufacturing innovations are revolutionizing the automotive industry. Now, I know what you're thinking: "Tesla and AI-driven manufacturing? Sounds like something out of a science fiction novel." But fear not, my friends, for I'm here to make it all as clear as a summer's day. So, grab your favorite chair, pour yourself a glass of lemonade, and let's dive right in.

The Birth of Tesla: A Vision of the Future

To understand the impact of Tesla's AI-driven manufacturing innovations, we gotta go back to the beginnings. The story of Tesla starts with a visionary named Elon Musk, who dreamed of creating a sustainable future through electric vehicles and clean energy.

The Vision: A Sustainable Future

Elon Musk's vision was simple yet revolutionary: create electric vehicles that were not only environmentally friendly but also high-performance and stylish. Think of it like having a supercar that's also good for the planet. It was a bold vision, and it required innovations in every aspect of the automotive industry, from design to manufacturing.

The Technology: Innovation in Action

But turning that vision into reality was no easy feat. Tesla had to tackle some of the most complex challenges in automotive manufacturing, from developing advanced battery technology to

Chapter 7: AI in Manufacturing: The Factory of the Future

creating efficient production lines. They had to build a system that was not only innovative but also scalable and reliable.

The Launch: Tesla Takes the Stage

After years of hard work and countless iterations, Tesla was finally ready to take the stage. In 2008, Tesla launched its first electric vehicle, the Roadster, and the world of automotive manufacturing was forever changed. Suddenly, people could drive cars that were not only environmentally friendly but also high-performance and stylish. It was a revolution in the making.

The Response: A Hit with the Public

The response to Tesla's Roadster was overwhelming. People were amazed by the performance and style of the electric vehicle, and they flocked to it in droves. Suddenly, Tesla was everywhere, from highways to racetracks, from urban streets to rural roads. It was a revolution in the making.

The Evolution: Tesla Grows Up

But the story of Tesla doesngt stop with the Roadster. Over the years, Tesla has continued to innovate and expand, adding new models and improving its manufacturing processes. From the Model S to the Model X, from the Model 3 to the Model Y, Tesla has grown and evolved, making electric vehicles more accessible and more efficient than ever before.

New Models: Expanding the Horizons

One of the most exciting developments in the world of Tesla is its expansion into new models. With the introduction of the Model S, Tesla brought luxury and performance to the electric vehicle market. And with the Model 3, Tesla made electric vehicles more affordable and accessible than ever before. It was like having a supercar for the masses.

Improved Manufacturing: Streamlining the Process

But it's not just about the models. Tesla's real power lies in its manufacturing innovations. By using advanced technologies and innovative solutions, Tesla has made its production lines faster, more efficient, and more reliable than ever before. It's like having a super-efficient factory that can produce cars at a scale and speed that was unimaginable before.

The Power of Data: The Backbone of AI-Driven Manufacturing

At the heart of Tesla's AI-driven manufacturing innovations is data. Lots and lots of data. Think of it like this: data is the fuel that powers AI, the lifeblood that makes it all possible. In the automotive world, this data comes from all sorts of sources—sensors, machines, production logs, and more.

Sensors: The Eyes and Ears of the Factory

Sensors are the eyes and ears of the Tesla factory. They detect changes in the environment, like temperature, humidity, motion, and light. Think of them like little spies, always on the lookout, gathering information and reporting back to the central system. By analyzing this data, Tesla can identify patterns, detect anomalies, and even predict future behaviors.

Machines: The Workhorses of the Factory

Machines are the workhorses of the Tesla factory. They perform the tasks, from cutting and shaping to assembling and packing. But unlike traditional machines, Tesla's machines are connected, communicating with each other and with the central system. It's like having a team of workers who can talk to each other, coordinating their efforts to get the job done faster and more efficiently.

Production Logs: The Memory of the Factory

Production logs are the memory of the Tesla factory. They record everything that happens on the factory floor, from the start of production to the final product. By analyzing these logs, Tesla can identify patterns, detect anomalies, and even predict future behaviors. It's like having a historian who can tell you everything that's happened, helping you make better decisions today.

AI-Driven Manufacturing in Action: The Magic of Tesla

One of the most exciting aspects of Tesla's AI-driven manufacturing innovations is seeing them in action. By using advanced technologies and innovative solutions, Tesla can produce cars faster, more efficiently, and with less waste than ever before.

Predictive Maintenance: Keeping the Machines Running

Take predictive maintenance, for instance. By analyzing sensor data, Tesla can predict when machines are likely to fail, allowing for timely repairs before problems occur. It's like having a crystal ball that can show us the future, helping us keep our machines running smoothly and efficiently.

Quality Control: Ensuring the Best Products

Quality control is another area where Tesla's AI-driven manufacturing innovations are making a big difference. By analyzing production data, Tesla can identify defects and anomalies, helping to ensure that their vehicles meet the highest standards of quality. It's like having a super-sensitive inspector who can spot the tiniest flaws, making sure that only the best products make it to the market.

Supply Chain Management: Keeping the Goods Moving

Supply chain management is perhaps the most complex application of AI-driven manufacturing in Tesla. By analyzing logistics data, Tesla can optimize the flow of goods, from raw materials to finished products, helping to keep their supply chains running smoothly and efficiently. It's like having a master logistician who can manage the entire supply chain, making sure that everything runs like clockwork.

The Human Touch: The Role of Engineers and Technicians

But Tesla's AI-driven manufacturing innovations aingt just about technology. It's also about people. It's about the engineers and technicians who are pushing the boundaries of what's possible. It's about the visionaries who are dreaming of a future where AI can help us transform automotive manufacturing like never before.

Engineers and technicians are a special breed. They're part inventor, part scientist, part artist, and part dreamer. They know how to design, build, and program AI-driven manufacturing systems. But more importantly, they know how to imagine, to innovate, and to create.

Think of it like this: an engineer is like a builder who can construct the systems we need to make AI-driven manufacturing a reality. A technician is like an artist who can envision the possibilities and the potentials of the future. Together, they're like a dynamic duo, working hand in hand to unlock the power of AI-driven manufacturing.

The Ethics of AI-Driven Manufacturing: Privacy, Security, and Responsibility

But with great power comes great responsibility. And when it comes to AI-driven manufacturing, that responsibility is enormous. You see, manufacturing data is sensitive. It's intimate. It's a reflection of how we make things, what we make, and who we make them for. And when we use AI to analyze this data, we're giving it access to some of the most sensitive and private aspects of our businesses.

That's why it's so important to handle manufacturing data with care. It's why we need to think about privacy, security, and responsibility. It's why we need to be mindful of the ethical implications of our actions.

Take the example of data security. If the data used to run an AI-driven manufacturing system is compromised, it can lead to serious consequences, affecting the production, the quality, and even the safety of the products. That's why it's crucial to ensure that our data is secure, that our systems are protected, and that our processes are robust.

The Future of AI-Driven Manufacturing: A World of Possibilities

But despite the challenges, the future of AI-driven manufacturing is bright. It's a future filled with possibilities, with opportunities to solve problems and improve lives. It's a future where AI can help us transform automotive manufacturing like never before, where it can help us produce cars faster, more efficiently, and with less waste.

And it's a future that's already here. Every day, we're seeing new breakthroughs, new innovations, new ways of using AI to make

the world a better place. It's exciting, it's inspiring, and it's just the beginning.

So, my friends, as we journey through this magical world of Tesla's AI-driven manufacturing innovations, let's remember the power and the potential that lies within. Let's remember the pioneers who came before us, the visionaries who dared to dream of a future where AI could help us transform automotive manufacturing like never before. And let's look forward to the exciting journey that lies ahead, as we continue to explore the boundless possibilities of artificial intelligence.

Chapter 8: AI in Retail: Personalizing the Shopping Experience

How AI is Changing the Way We Shop

Introduction: The Future of Retail

Folks, gather 'round and let me spin you a yarn about the magical world of artificial intelligence and how it's changing the way we shop. Now, I know what you're thinking: "AI and shopping? Sounds like something out of a science fiction novel." But fear not, my friends, for I'm here to make it all as clear as a summer's day. So, grab your favorite chair, pour yourself a glass of lemonade, and let's dive right in.

The Evolution of Shopping: From Brick-and-Mortar to Clicks

To understand how AI is changing the way we shop, we gotta go back to the beginnings. Shopping has come a long way from the days of brick-and-mortar stores and manual transactions. With the advent of the internet and digital technologies, shopping has become faster, more convenient, and more personalized than ever before.

From Brick-and-Mortar to Clicks: The Digital Transformation

The digital transformation of shopping started with the introduction of the internet. Suddenly, people could shop from the comfort of their own homes, making transactions, browsing products, and even comparing prices online. It was a revolution in the making.

The Rise of Mobile Shopping: Shopping on the Go

But the revolution didngt stop there. With the rise of smartphones, mobile shopping became the new norm. People could now shop on the go, checking prices, reading reviews, and even making purchases with just a few taps on their phones. It was like having a shopping mall in your pocket, always ready to serve you.

The Power of Data: The Backbone of AI in Retail

At the heart of AI in retail is data. Lots and lots of data. Think of it like this: data is the fuel that powers AI, the lifeblood that makes it all possible. In the retail world, this data comes from all sorts of sources—customer behaviors, purchase histories, browsing patterns, and more.

Customer Behaviors: Understanding the Consumer

Customer behaviors are perhaps the most powerful data of all. By analyzing how customers interact with products and services, AI can identify their needs, preferences, and pain points. This information can then be used to develop new marketing strategies, improve existing ones, and even tailor shopping experiences to individual customers. It's like having a personal shopper who knows exactly what you need and when you need it.

Purchase Histories: A Treasure Trove of Information

Purchase histories are like digital diaries, containing a wealth of information about customers' spending habits, preferences, and behaviors. By analyzing this data, AI can identify patterns, predict future behaviors, and even suggest personalized products and services. It's like having a financial detective who can sift through mountains of information to find the clues that matter most.

Browsing Patterns: The Digital Footprint

Browsing patterns are another rich source of data. These patterns provide valuable insights into what customers are looking for, what they're interested in, and what they might be willing to buy. By analyzing this data, AI can tailor shopping experiences to individual customers, making it more personalized and more enjoyable. It's like having a digital guide who can show you the way to the products you're most likely to love.

AI in Action: Revolutionizing the Shopping Experience

One of the most exciting aspects of AI in retail is seeing it in action. By using advanced technologies and innovative solutions, AI can transform the shopping experience, making it faster, more convenient, and more personalized than ever before.

Personalized Recommendations: Tailored to You

Take personalized recommendations, for instance. By analyzing customer behaviors, AI can identify the best products for individual customers, based on their unique needs and preferences. It's like having a personal shopper who knows exactly what you need and when you need it.

Virtual Try-On: Seeing Before You Buy

Virtual try-on is another exciting application of AI in retail. By using augmented reality (AR) and AI, customers can now try on products virtually, seeing how they look and feel before making a purchase. It's like having a digital mirror that can show you exactly what you'll look like in that new outfit or with that new makeup.

Chatbots and Virtual Assistants: Always There to Help

Chatbots and virtual assistants are perhaps the most visible application of AI in retail. With the help of these digital helpers, retailers can now provide 24/7 customer support, answering questions, solving problems, and even offering shopping advice. It's like having a personal shopper who's always available to help, no matter the time or day.

The Human Touch: The Role of Retailers and Marketers

But AI in retail aingt just about technology. It's also about people. It's about the retailers and marketers who are pushing the boundaries of what's possible. It's about the visionaries who are dreaming of a future where AI can help us transform the shopping experience like never before.

Retailers and marketers are a special breed. They're part salesperson, part analyst, part artist, and part dreamer. They know how to collect data, how to analyze data, and how to interpret data. But more importantly, they know how to communicate their findings in a way that's clear and compelling.

Think of it like this: a retailer is like a salesperson who can use AI to identify the best products for individual customers, based on their unique needs and preferences. A marketer is like an analyst who can use AI to develop new marketing strategies, improve existing ones, and even tailor shopping experiences to individual customers. Together, they're like a dynamic duo, working hand in hand to unlock the power of AI in retail.

The Ethics of AI in Retail: Privacy, Bias, and Fairness

But with great power comes great responsibility. And when it comes to AI in retail, that responsibility is enormous. You see, customer data is sensitive. It's intimate. It's a reflection of who we are and what we're doing with our money and our time. And when we use AI to analyze this data, we're giving it access to some of the most private and personal aspects of our lives.

That's why it's so important to handle customer data with care. It's why we need to think about privacy, bias, and fairness. It's why we need to be mindful of the ethical implications of our actions.

Take the example of bias in AI. If the data used to train a machine learning model is biased, the model itself will be biased. This can lead to unfair decisions, affecting the shopping experience and even the well-being of customers. That's why it's crucial to ensure that our data is diverse, representative, and free from bias.

The Future of AI in Retail: A World of Possibilities

But despite the challenges, the future of AI in retail is bright. It's a future filled with possibilities, with opportunities to solve problems and improve lives. It's a future where AI can help us transform the shopping experience like never before, where it can help us make shopping faster, more convenient, and more personalized.

And it's a future that's already here. Every day, we're seeing new breakthroughs, new innovations, new ways of using AI to make the world a better place. It's exciting, it's inspiring, and it's just the beginning.

So, my friends, as we journey through this magical world of AI in retail, let's remember the power and the potential that lies within. Let's remember the pioneers who came before us, the visionaries who dared to dream of a future where AI could help us transform the shopping experience like never before. And let's look forward to the exciting journey that lies ahead, as we continue to explore the boundless possibilities of artificial intelligence.

Personalized Recommendations and Targeted Marketing

Introduction: The Future of Shopping

Folks, gather 'round and let me spin you a yarn about the magical world of personalized recommendations and targeted marketing. Now, I know what you're thinking: "Personalized recommendations and targeted marketing? Sounds like something out of a science fiction novel." But fear not, my friends, for I'm here to make it all as clear as a summer's day. So, grab your favorite chair, pour yourself a glass of lemonade, and let's dive right in.

The Evolution of Marketing: From Broadcast to Personal

To understand the impact of personalized recommendations and targeted marketing, we gotta go back to the beginnings. Marketing has come a long way from the days of broadcast advertising and mass mailings. With the advent of digital technologies and AI, marketing has become more personalized, more targeted, and more effective than ever before.

From Broadcast to Personal: The Shift in Mindset

Broadcast advertising was the norm for decades. Companies would blast their messages to the masses, hoping to reach as many people as possible. But with the rise of digital technologies, marketing became more personal. Companies started collecting data on their customers, understanding their needs and preferences, and tailoring their messages accordingly. It was a shift in mindset, from broadcast to personal.

The Rise of Digital Marketing: The New Norm

Chapter 8: AI in Retail: Personalizing the Shopping Experience

But the evolution didngt stop there. With the rise of digital marketing, companies started using advanced technologies to reach their customers more effectively. They started using email marketing, social media marketing, and even mobile marketing to deliver personalized messages to their customers. It was like having a personal marketer who could talk to each customer individually, understanding their needs and preferences, and delivering messages that resonated with them.

The Power of Data: The Backbone of Personalized Recommendations and Targeted Marketing

At the heart of personalized recommendations and targeted marketing is data. Lots and lots of data. Think of it like this: data is the fuel that powers AI, the lifeblood that makes it all possible. In the marketing world, this data comes from all sorts of sources—customer behaviors, purchase histories, browsing patterns, and more.

Customer Behaviors: Understanding the Consumer

Customer behaviors are perhaps the most powerful data of all. By analyzing how customers interact with products and services, AI can identify their needs, preferences, and pain points. This information can then be used to develop new marketing strategies, improve existing ones, and even tailor shopping experiences to individual customers. It's like having a personal shopper who knows exactly what you need and when you need it.

Purchase Histories: A Treasure Trove of Information

Purchase histories are like digital diaries, containing a wealth of information about customers' spending habits, preferences, and behaviors. By analyzing this data, AI can identify patterns, predict future behaviors, and even suggest personalized products and services. It's like having a financial detective who can sift through mountains of information to find the clues that matter most.

Browsing Patterns: The Digital Footprint

Browsing patterns are another rich source of data. These patterns provide valuable insights into what customers are looking for, what they're interested in, and what they might be willing to buy. By analyzing this data, AI can tailor shopping experiences to individual customers, making it more personalized and more enjoyable. It's like having a digital guide who can show you the way to the products you're most likely to love.

Personalized Recommendations: Tailored to You

One of the most exciting aspects of AI in marketing is personalized recommendations. By analyzing customer behaviors, AI can identify the best products for individual customers, based on their unique needs and preferences. It's like having a personal shopper who knows exactly what you need and when you need it.

The Magic of Algorithms: Making Sense of Data

The magic of personalized recommendations lies in the algorithms. These algorithms analyze customer data, identifyng patterns, and making sense of the information. They can predict what products a customer is likely to buy, based on their past behaviors, preferences, and even their browsing patterns. It's like having a super-smart assistant who can read your mind and suggest the perfect products for you.

Collaborative Filtering: Learning from Others

Collaborative filtering is another powerful tool in the arsenal of personalized recommendations. This technique uses the behaviors of similar customers to make recommendations. For example, if a customer likes a particular product, the algorithm might recommend similar products that other customers who liked the same product also liked. It's like having a community of shoppers who can share their experiences and help each other find the best products.

Content-Based Filtering: Understanding the Product

Content-based filtering is yet another tool in the arsenal of personalized recommendations. This technique uses the characteristics of the products themselves to make recommendations. For example, if a customer likes a particular type of product, the algorithm might recommend other products with similar characteristics. It's like having a product expert who can understand the features and benefits of each product and suggest the best ones for you.

Targeted Marketing: Hitting the Bullseye

But personalized recommendations aingt just about suggesting products. It's also about targeted marketing. By analyzing customer data, AI can deliver personalized messages to individual customers, hitting the bullseye every time.

Segmentation: Divide and Conquer

Segmentation is a key tool in targeted marketing. By dividing customers into different groups based on their behaviors, preferences, and demographics, companies can deliver more personalized messages to each group. It's like having a marketer who can talk to each customer individually, understanding their needs and preferences, and delivering messages that resonate with them.

Retargeting: The Second Chance

Retargeting is another powerful tool in targeted marketing. By tracking customers' browsing behaviors, companies can deliver ads to customers who have shown interest in their products but havengt made a purchase yet. It's like having a second chance to convince the customer to buy, reminding them of the products they were interested in and encouraging them to take action.

Dynamic Content: Making It Personal

Dynamic content is perhaps the most personalized tool in targeted marketing. By using AI to analyze customer data, companies can deliver content that is tailored to each individual customer. For example, a company might send an email to a customer with a personalized message, recommending products based on their past behaviors and preferences. It's like having a personal marketer who can talk to each customer individually, understanding their needs and preferences, and delivering messages that resonate with them.

The Human Touch: The Role of Marketers and Data Scientists

But personalized recommendations and targeted marketing aingt just about technology. It's also about people. It's about the marketers and data scientists who are pushing the boundaries of what's possible. It's about the visionaries who are dreaming of a future where AI can help us transform the shopping experience like never before.

Marketers and data scientists are a special breed. They're part salesperson, part analyst, part artist, and part dreamer. They know how to collect data, how to analyze data, and how to interpret data. But more importantly, they know how to communicate their findings in a way that's clear and compelling.

Think of it like this: a marketer is like a salesperson who can use AI to identify the best products for individual customers, based on their unique needs and preferences. A data scientist is like an analyst who can use AI to develop new marketing strategies, improve existing ones, and even tailor shopping experiences to individual customers. Together, they're like a dynamic duo, working hand in hand to unlock the power of personalized recommendations and targeted marketing.

The Ethics of Personalized Recommendations and Targeted Marketing: Privacy, Bias, and Fairness

But with great power comes great responsibility. And when it comes to personalized recommendations and targeted marketing, that responsibility is enormous. You see, customer data is sensitive. It's intimate. It's a reflection of who we are and what we're doing with our money and our time. And when we use AI to analyze this data, we're giving it access to some of the most private and personal aspects of our lives.

That's why it's so important to handle customer data with care. It's why we need to think about privacy, bias, and fairness. It's why we need to be mindful of the ethical implications of our actions.

Take the example of bias in AI. If the data used to train a machine learning model is biased, the model itself will be biased. This can lead to unfair decisions, affecting the shopping experience and even the well-being of customers. That's why it's crucial to ensure that our data is diverse, representative, and free from bias.

The Future of Personalized Recommendations and Targeted Marketing: A World of Possibilities

But despite the challenges, the future of personalized recommendations and targeted marketing is bright. It's a future filled with possibilities, with opportunities to solve problems and improve lives. It's a future where AI can help us transform the shopping experience like never before, where it can help us make shopping faster, more convenient, and more personalized.

And it's a future that's already here. Every day, we're seeing new breakthroughs, new innovations, new ways of using AI to make the world a better place. It's exciting, it's inspiring, and it's just the beginning.

So, my friends, as we journey through this magical world of personalized recommendations and targeted marketing, let's remember the power and the potential that lies within. Let's remember the pioneers who came before us, the visionaries who dared to dream of a future where AI could help us transform the shopping experience like never before. And let's look forward to the exciting journey that lies ahead, as we continue to explore the boundless possibilities of artificial intelligence.

Case Study: Netflix's Recommendation Engine

Introduction: The Magic of Personalized Entertainment

Folks, gather 'round and let me spin you a yarn about the magical world of Netflix and its recommendation engine. Now, I know what you're thinking: "Netflix and its recommendation engine? Sounds like something out of a science fiction novel." But fear not, my friends, for I'm here to make it all as clear as a summer's day. So, grab your favorite chair, pour yourself a glass of lemonade, and let's dive right in.

The Birth of Netflix: A Revolution in Entertainment

To understand the impact of Netflix's recommendation engine, we gotta go back to the beginnings. The story of Netflix starts with a visionary named Reed Hastings, who dreamed of creating a new way to rent movies. Instead of driving to the video store, he wanted people to be able to rent movies online and have them delivered right to their doorstep.

The Vision: Movies at Your Doorstep

Reed Hastings' vision was simple yet revolutionary: create a service that allowed people to rent movies online and have them delivered by mail. Think of it like having a video store that comes to you, instead of you going to it. It was a bold vision, and it required innovations in every aspect of the movie rental business, from logistics to technology.

The Technology: Innovation in Action

But turning that vision into reality was no easy feat. Netflix had to tackle some of the most complex challenges in the movie rental business, from building an efficient delivery system to creating a user-friendly website. They had to build a system that was not only innovative but also scalable and reliable.

The Launch: Netflix Takes the Stage

After years of hard work and countless iterations, Netflix was finally ready to take the stage. In 1998, Netflix launched its online movie rental service, and the world of entertainment was forever changed. Suddenly, people could rent movies from the comfort of their own homes, without ever having to leave the house. It was a revolution in the making.

The Response: A Hit with the Public

The response to Netflix was overwhelming. People were amazed by the convenience and ease of the online movie rental service, and they flocked to it in droves. Suddenly, Netflix was everywhere, from living rooms to bedrooms, from urban apartments to rural homes. It was a revolution in the making.

The Evolution: Netflix Grows Up

But the story of Netflix doesngt stop with its launch. Over the years, Netflix has continued to innovate and expand, adding new features and improving its services. From DVD rentals to streaming, from original content to personalized recommendations, Netflix has grown and evolved, making entertainment more accessible and more enjoyable than ever before.

New Features: Expanding the Horizons

One of the most exciting developments in the world of Netflix is its expansion into new features. With the introduction of streaming, Netflix brought instant entertainment to the masses, allowing people to watch movies and TV shows on demand, anytime, anywhere. And with the addition of original content, Netflix started producing its own movies and TV shows, offering unique and exclusive entertainment to its subscribers. It was like having a movie studio and a TV network all rolled into one.

Improved Services: Streamlining the Experience

But it's not just about the features. Netflix's real power lies in its services. By using advanced technologies and innovative solutions, Netflix has made its platform faster, more efficient, and more enjoyable than ever before. It's like having a super-efficient entertainment hub that can deliver the best content to you, whenever and wherever you want it.

The Power of Data: The Backbone of Netflix's Recommendation Engine

At the heart of Netflix's recommendation engine is data. Lots and lots of data. Think of it like this: data is the fuel that powers the recommendation engine, the lifeblood that makes it all possible. In the world of Netflix, this data comes from all sorts of sources—viewing histories, ratings, browsing patterns, and more.

Viewing Histories: A Treasure Trove of Information

Viewing histories are like digital diaries, containing a wealth of information about subscribers' watching habits, preferences, and behaviors. By analyzing this data, Netflix can identify patterns, predict future behaviors, and even suggest personalized content. It's like having a digital detective who can sift through mountains of information to find the clues that matter most.

Ratings: The Voice of the Viewer

Ratings are another rich source of data. These ratings provide valuable insights into what subscribers think about the content they're watching. By analyzing this data, Netflix can identify the most popular and highly-rated content, helping to inform its recommendations and even its original productions. It's like having a focus group that's always available, ready to share their opinions and help shape the future of entertainment.

Browsing Patterns: The Digital Footprint

Browsing patterns are yet another source of data. These patterns provide valuable insights into what subscribers are looking for, what they're interested in, and what they might be willing to watch. By analyzing this data, Netflix can tailor its recommendations to individual subscribers, making it more personalized and more enjoyable. It's like having a digital guide who can show you the way to the content you're most likely to love.

The Recommendation Engine in Action: The Magic of Personalized Entertainment

One of the most exciting aspects of Netflix's recommendation engine is seeing it in action. By using advanced technologies and innovative solutions, Netflix can transform the entertainment experience, making it faster, more convenient, and more personalized than ever before.

Collaborative Filtering: Learning from Others

Collaborative filtering is one of the most powerful tools in Netflix's recommendation engine. This technique uses the behaviors of similar subscribers to make recommendations. For example, if a subscriber likes a particular movie, the algorithm might recommend similar movies that other subscribers who liked the same movie also liked. It's like having a community of viewers who can share their experiences and help each other find the best content.

Content-Based Filtering: Understanding the Content

Content-based filtering is another powerful tool in Netflix's recommendation engine. This technique uses the characteristics of the content itself to make recommendations. For example, if a subscriber likes a particular type of movie, the algorithm might recommend other movies with similar characteristics. It's like having a content expert who can understand the features and benefits of each piece of content and suggest the best ones for you.

Hybrid Systems: The Best of Both Worlds

Hybrid systems combine the best of both collaborative filtering and content-based filtering. By using a combination of these techniques, Netflix can make even more accurate and personalized recommendations. It's like having a super-smart assistant who can understand both the behaviors of other subscribers and the characteristics of the content, suggesting the perfect entertainment for you.

The Human Touch: The Role of Data Scientists and Engineers

But Netflix's recommendation engine aingt just about technology. It's also about people. It's about the data scientists and engineers who are pushing the boundaries of what's possible. It's about the visionaries who are dreaming of a future where AI can help us transform the entertainment experience like never before.

Data scientists and engineers are a special breed. They're part analyst, part inventor, part artist, and part dreamer. They know how to collect data, how to analyze data, and how to interpret data. But more importantly, they know how to communicate their findings in a way that's clear and compelling.

Think of it like this: a data scientist is like an analyst who can use AI to identify the best content for individual subscribers, based on their unique needs and preferences. An engineer is like an inventor who can use AI to develop new recommendation algorithms, improve existing ones, and even tailor entertainment experiences to individual subscribers. Together, they're like a dynamic duo, working hand in hand to unlock the power of Netflix's recommendation engine.

The Ethics of Netflix's Recommendation Engine: Privacy, Bias, and Fairness

But with great power comes great responsibility. And when it comes to Netflix's recommendation engine, that responsibility is enormous. You see, subscriber data is sensitive. It's intimate. It's a reflection of who we are and what we're doing with our time and our entertainment. And when we use AI to analyze this data, we're giving it access to some of the most private and personal aspects of our lives.

That's why it's so important to handle subscriber data with care. It's why we need to think about privacy, bias, and fairness. It's why we need to be mindful of the ethical implications of our actions.

Take the example of bias in AI. If the data used to train a machine learning model is biased, the model itself will be biased. This can lead to unfair decisions, affecting the entertainment experience and even the well-being of subscribers. That's why it's crucial to ensure that our data is diverse, representative, and free from bias.

The Future of Netflix's Recommendation Engine: A World of Possibilities

But despite the challenges, the future of Netflix's recommendation engine is bright. It's a future filled with possibilities, with opportunities to solve problems and improve lives. It's a future where AI can help us transform the entertainment experience like never before, where it can help us make entertainment faster, more convenient, and more personalized.

And it's a future that's already here. Every day, we're seeing new breakthroughs, new innovations, new ways of using AI to make the world a better place. It's exciting, it's inspiring, and it's just the beginning.

So, my friends, as we journey through this magical world of Netflix's recommendation engine, let's remember the power and the potential that lies within. Let's remember the pioneers who came before us, the visionaries who dared to dream of a future where AI could help us transform the entertainment experience like never before. And let's look forward to the exciting journey that lies ahead, as we continue to explore the boundless possibilities of artificial intelligence.

Chapter 9: AI in Transportation: The Road to Autonomous Vehicles

The Evolution of Self-Driving Cars

Introduction: The Future of Transportation

Folks, gather 'round and let me spin you a yarn about the magical world of self-driving cars. Now, I know what you're thinking: "Self-driving cars? Sounds like something out of a science fiction novel." But fear not, my friends, for I'm here to make it all as clear as a summer's day. So, grab your favorite chair, pour yourself a glass of lemonade, and let's dive right in.

The Birth of Self-Driving Cars: A Vision of the Future

To understand the impact of self-driving cars, we gotta go back to the beginnings. The story of self-driving cars starts with a vision of a future where cars can drive themselves, making transportation safer, more efficient, and more convenient than ever before.

The Vision: Cars That Drive Themselves

The vision of self-driving cars was simple yet revolutionary: create cars that can drive themselves, without the need for human intervention. Think of it like having a chauffeur who never gets tired, never makes mistakes, and always knows the best route to take. It was a bold vision, and it required innovations in every aspect of the automotive industry, from sensors to software, from hardware to AI.

The Technology: Innovation in Action

But turning that vision into reality was no easy feat. Self-driving cars had to tackle some of the most complex challenges in the automotive industry, from developing advanced sensors to creating sophisticated algorithms. They had to build a system that was not only innovative but also reliable and safe.

The Early Days: The Pioneers of Self-Driving Cars

The early days of self-driving cars were filled with pioneers and visionaries who dared to dream of a future where cars could drive themselves. These pioneers laid the foundation for the self-driving cars we see today, experimenting with new technologies and pushing the boundaries of what was possible.

The DARPA Grand Challenge: The Race to Innovation

One of the most exciting developments in the early days of self-driving cars was the DARPA Grand Challenge. Sponsored by the Defense Advanced Research Projects Agency (DARPA), this competition challenged teams to build autonomous vehicles that could navigate a 150-mile course through the Mojave Desert. It was a race to innovation, and it sparked a wave of creativity and experimentation in the field of self-driving cars.

The Stanford Racing Team: The Winners

The Stanford Racing Team, led by Sebastian Thrun, was one of the pioneers of the DARPA Grand Challenge. Their vehicle, Stanley, was a modified Volkswagen Touareg equipped with advanced sensors and algorithms. Stanley successfully navigated the course, winning the competition and cementing its place in the history of self-driving cars. It was a triumph of innovation and a testament to the power of human ingenuity.

The Rise of Self-Driving Cars: From Experiments to Reality

But the story of self-driving cars doesngt stop with the DARPA Grand Challenge. Over the years, self-driving cars have continued to evolve, moving from experiments to reality. Companies like Google, Tesla, and Waymo have taken the lead, developing advanced technologies and bringing self-driving cars to the masses.

Google's Self-Driving Car Project: The Pioneers

Google's Self-Driving Car Project, now known as Waymo, was one of the pioneers in the field of self-driving cars. Led by Sebastian Thrun, the project aimed to develop a fully autonomous vehicle that could navigate the complexities of urban driving. Waymo's vehicles were equipped with advanced sensors, including LIDAR, radar, and cameras, and sophisticated algorithms that could analyze the data and make decisions in real-time. It was a groundbreaking achievement, and it paved the way for the self-driving cars we see today.

Tesla's Autopilot: The Mainstream

Tesla's Autopilot was another groundbreaking development in the field of self-driving cars. Unlike Waymo's fully autonomous vehicles, Tesla's Autopilot was designed to assist drivers, rather than replace them. Autopilot used a combination of sensors and algorithms to provide features like adaptive cruise control, lane keeping assist, and even automatic lane changing. It was a step towards mainstream adoption, and it brought self-driving technology to the masses.

The Power of Data: The Backbone of Self-Driving Cars

At the heart of self-driving cars is data. Lots and lots of data. Think of it like this: data is the fuel that powers self-driving cars, the lifeblood that makes it all possible. In the world of self-driving cars, this data comes from all sorts of sources—sensors, cameras, LIDAR, radar, and more.

Sensors: The Eyes and Ears of the Car

Sensors are the eyes and ears of the self-driving car. They detect changes in the environment, like the presence of other vehicles, pedestrians, and obstacles. Think of them like little spies, always on the lookout, gathering information and reporting back to the central system. By analyzing this data, self-driving cars can make decisions in real-time, navigating the complexities of the road and keeping passengers safe.

Cameras: The Visual Aid

Cameras are another crucial component of self-driving cars. They provide visual information about the environment, helping the car to understand its surroundings and make decisions accordingly. By analyzing this data, self-driving cars can identify traffic signs, recognize lane markings, and even detect pedestrians and other vehicles. It's like having a super-sensitive observer who can see everything and understand its significance.

LIDAR and Radar: The Distance Detectors

LIDAR and radar are the distance detectors of the self-driving car. They use light and radio waves to measure the distance to objects, helping the car to understand its surroundings and navigate safely. By analyzing this data, self-driving cars can detect obstacles, avoid collisions, and even plan their routes more efficiently. It's like having a super-sensitive navigator who can see through the fog and guide the car safely to its destination.

The Evolution of Self-Driving Cars: From Assistance to Autonomy

One of the most exciting aspects of self-driving cars is their evolution from assistance to autonomy. Over the years, self-driving cars have become more sophisticated, more capable, and more independent, moving from simple driver assistance systems to fully autonomous vehicles.

Driver Assistance Systems: The First Steps

Driver assistance systems were the first steps towards self-driving cars. These systems used sensors and algorithms to provide features like adaptive cruise control, lane keeping assist, and even automatic emergency braking. They were designed to assist drivers, rather than replace them, making driving safer and more convenient. It was a step towards autonomy, and it paved the way for the self-driving cars we see today.

Partial Autonomy: The Middle Ground

Partial autonomy was the next step in the evolution of self-driving cars. These systems were designed to take over some of the driving tasks, like steering, accelerating, and braking, but still required human intervention in certain situations. They were a middle ground between driver assistance systems and fully autonomous vehicles, offering a taste of the future while still maintaining a level of human control.

Full Autonomy: The Future

Full autonomy is the ultimate goal of self-driving cars. These vehicles are designed to drive themselves, without the need for human intervention. They use advanced sensors and algorithms to navigate the complexities of the road, making decisions in real-time and keeping passengers safe. It's a vision of the future, and it's already becoming a reality.

The Human Touch: The Role of Engineers and Scientists

But self-driving cars aingt just about technology. It's also about people. It's about the engineers and scientists who are pushing the boundaries of what's possible. It's about the visionaries who are dreaming of a future where self-driving cars can transform transportation like never before.

Engineers and scientists are a special breed. They're part inventor, part analyst, part artist, and part dreamer. They know how to design, build, and program self-driving cars. But more importantly, they know how to imagine, to innovate, and to create.

Think of it like this: an engineer is like a builder who can construct the systems we need to make self-driving cars a reality. A scientist is like an analyst who can understand the complexities of the technology and develop new solutions. Together, they're like a dynamic duo, working hand in hand to unlock the power of self-driving cars.

The Ethics of Self-Driving Cars: Safety, Privacy, and Responsibility

But with great power comes great responsibility. And when it comes to self-driving cars, that responsibility is enormous. You see, self-driving cars are complex machines that operate in the real world, interacting with other vehicles, pedestrians, and even the environment. And when we use AI to control these machines, we're giving it access to some of the most sensitive and critical aspects of our lives.

That's why it's so important to handle self-driving cars with care. It's why we need to think about safety, privacy, and responsibility. It's why we need to be mindful of the ethical implications of our actions.

Take the example of safety in self-driving cars. If the algorithms used to control a self-driving car are flawed, it can lead to serious consequences, affecting the safety of passengers, other drivers, and even pedestrians. That's why it's crucial to ensure that our algorithms are robust, reliable, and safe.

The Future of Self-Driving Cars: A World of Possibilities

But despite the challenges, the future of self-driving cars is bright. It's a future filled with possibilities, with opportunities to solve problems and improve lives. It's a future where self-driving cars can transform transportation like never before, making it safer, more efficient, and more convenient.

And it's a future that's already here. Every day, we're seeing new breakthroughs, new innovations, new ways of using AI to make the world a better place. It's exciting, it's inspiring, and it's just the beginning.

So, my friends, as we journey through this magical world of self-driving cars, let's remember the power and the potential that lies within. Let's remember the pioneers who came before us, the visionaries who dared to dream of a future where self-driving cars could transform transportation like never before. And let's look forward to the exciting journey that lies ahead, as we continue to explore the boundless possibilities of artificial intelligence.

AI in Logistics and Supply Chain Management

Introduction: The Future of Supply Chains

Folks, gather 'round and let me spin you a yarn about the magical world of artificial intelligence in logistics and supply chain management. Now, I know what you're thinking: "AI in logistics and supply chain management? Sounds like something out of a science fiction novel." But fear not, my friends, for I'm here to make it all as clear as a summer's day. So, grab your favorite chair, pour yourself a glass of lemonade, and let's dive right in.

The Evolution of Supply Chains: From Manual to Automated

To understand the impact of AI in logistics and supply chain management, we gotta go back to the beginnings. Supply chains have come a long way from the days of manual processes and paper-based systems. With the advent of technology and AI, supply chains have become faster, more efficient, and more reliable than ever before.

From Manual to Automated: A Shift in Mindset

Manual processes and paper-based systems were the norm for decades. Companies relied on human labor to manage their supply chains, from ordering supplies to delivering products. But with the rise of technology, supply chains became more automated. Companies started using computers and software to manage their operations, making them faster and more efficient. It was a shift in mindset, from manual to automated.

The Rise of AI: The New Norm

But the evolution didngt stop there. With the rise of AI, supply chains became even more sophisticated. Companies started using advanced technologies and innovative solutions to optimize their operations, from predictive analytics to autonomous vehicles, from robotics to machine learning. It was like having a super-smart assistant who could manage the entire supply chain, making it more efficient and more reliable.

The Power of Data: The Backbone of AI in Logistics and Supply Chain Management

At the heart of AI in logistics and supply chain management is data. Lots and lots of data. Think of it like this: data is the fuel that powers AI, the lifeblood that makes it all possible. In the world of logistics and supply chain management, this data comes from all sorts of sources—sensors, GPS devices, IoT devices, and more.

Sensors: The Eyes and Ears of the Supply Chain

Sensors are the eyes and ears of the supply chain. They detect changes in the environment, like temperature, humidity, motion, and light. Think of them like little spies, always on the lookout, gathering information and reporting back to the central system. By analyzing this data, AI can identify patterns, detect anomalies, and even predict future behaviors. It's like having a super-sensitive observer who can see everything and understand its significance.

GPS Devices: The Navigators

GPS devices are the navigators of the supply chain. They provide real-time information about the location of vehicles, shipments, and even individual items. By analyzing this data, AI can optimize routes, reduce travel times, and even predict delays. It's like having a super-smart navigator who can guide the supply chain safely and efficiently to its destination.

IoT Devices: The Connectors

IoT devices are the connectors of the supply chain. They connect all sorts of devices, from sensors to GPS devices, from vehicles to warehouses, from machines to people. By analyzing this data, AI can create a seamless and integrated supply chain, making it more efficient and more reliable. It's like having a super-smart network that can connect everything and make it work together.

AI in Action: Revolutionizing Logistics and Supply Chain Management

One of the most exciting aspects of AI in logistics and supply chain management is seeing it in action. By using advanced technologies and innovative solutions, AI can transform the supply chain, making it faster, more efficient, and more reliable than ever before.

Predictive Analytics: Looking into the Future

Predictive analytics is perhaps the most powerful tool in the arsenal of AI in logistics and supply chain management. By analyzing historical data, predictive analytics can identify patterns, detect anomalies, and even predict future behaviors. It's like having a time machine that can show us the future, helping us make better decisions today.

Autonomous Vehicles: The Future of Transportation

Autonomous vehicles are another exciting application of AI in logistics and supply chain management. By using advanced sensors and AI algorithms, autonomous vehicles can navigate the roads safely and efficiently, without the need for human drivers. It's like having a super-smart chauffeur who can get you where you need to go, without the risk of human error.

Robotics: The Workhorses of the Warehouse

Robotics are the workhorses of the warehouse. By using advanced sensors and AI algorithms, robots can perform tasks faster, more accurately, and with less fatigue than human workers. It's like having an army of tireless, precise workers who never need a break.

Machine Learning: The Brains of the Operation

Machine learning is the brains of the operation. By analyzing data and learning from it, machine learning algorithms can improve over time, making the supply chain more efficient and more reliable. It's like having a super-smart assistant who can learn from experience and get better and better at their job.

The Human Touch: The Role of Logisticians and Data Scientists

But AI in logistics and supply chain management aingt just about technology. It's also about people. It's about the logisticians and data scientists who are pushing the boundaries of what's possible. It's about the visionaries who are dreaming of a future where AI can help us transform the supply chain like never before.

Logisticians and data scientists are a special breed. They're part planner, part analyst, part inventor, and part dreamer. They know how to design, build, and program AI systems. But more importantly, they know how to imagine, to innovate, and to create.

Think of it like this: a logistician is like a planner who can use AI to optimize the supply chain, making it more efficient and more reliable. A data scientist is like an analyst who can use AI to develop new solutions, improve existing ones, and even tailor supply chain operations to individual needs. Together, they're like a dynamic duo, working hand in hand to unlock the power of AI in logistics and supply chain management.

The Ethics of AI in Logistics and Supply Chain Management: Privacy, Security, and Responsibility

But with great power comes great responsibility. And when it comes to AI in logistics and supply chain management, that responsibility is enormous. You see, supply chain data is sensitive. It's intimate. It's a reflection of how we move goods, what we move, and who we move them for. And when we use AI to analyze this data, we're giving it access to some of the most sensitive and private aspects of our businesses.

That's why it's so important to handle supply chain data with care. It's why we need to think about privacy, security, and responsibility. It's why we need to be mindful of the ethical implications of our actions.

Take the example of data security. If the data used to run an AI system in logistics and supply chain management is compromised, it can lead to serious consequences, affecting the efficiency, the reliability, and even the safety of the supply chain. That's why it's crucial to ensure that our data is secure, that our systems are protected, and that our processes are robust.

The Future of AI in Logistics and Supply Chain Management: A World of Possibilities

But despite the challenges, the future of AI in logistics and supply chain management is bright. It's a future filled with possibilities, with opportunities to solve problems and improve lives. It's a future where AI can help us transform the supply chain like never before, making it faster, more efficient, and more reliable.

And it's a future that's already here. Every day, we're seeing new breakthroughs, new innovations, new ways of using AI to make

the world a better place. It's exciting, it's inspiring, and it's just the beginning.

So, my friends, as we journey through this magical world of AI in logistics and supply chain management, let's remember the power and the potential that lies within. Let's remember the pioneers who came before us, the visionaries who dared to dream of a future where AI could help us transform the supply chain like never before. And let's look forward to the exciting journey that lies ahead, as we continue to explore the boundless possibilities of artificial intelligence.

Case Study: Waymo and the Future of Autonomous Driving

Introduction: The Future of Transportation

Folks, gather 'round and let me spin you a yarn about the magical world of Waymo and the future of autonomous driving. Now, I know what you're thinking: "Waymo and autonomous driving? Sounds like something out of a science fiction novel." But fear not, my friends, for I'm here to make it all as clear as a summer's day. So, grab your favorite chair, pour yourself a glass of lemonade, and let's dive right in.

The Birth of Waymo: A Vision of the Future

To understand the impact of Waymo on the future of autonomous driving, we gotta go back to the beginnings. The story of Waymo starts with a vision of a future where cars can drive themselves, making transportation safer, more efficient, and more convenient than ever before.

The Vision: Cars That Drive Themselves

The vision of Waymo was simple yet revolutionary: create cars that can drive themselves, without the need for human intervention. Think of it like having a chauffeur who never gets tired, never makes mistakes, and always knows the best route to take. It was a bold vision, and it required innovations in every aspect of the automotive industry, from sensors to software, from hardware to AI.

The Technology: Innovation in Action

But turning that vision into reality was no easy feat. Waymo had to tackle some of the most complex challenges in the automotive industry, from developing advanced sensors to creating sophisticated algorithms. They had to build a system that was not only innovative but also reliable and safe.

The Early Days: The Pioneers of Autonomous Driving

The early days of Waymo were filled with pioneers and visionaries who dared to dream of a future where cars could drive themselves. These pioneers laid the foundation for the autonomous driving technology we see today, experimenting with new technologies and pushing the boundaries of what was possible.

The DARPA Grand Challenge: The Race to Innovation

One of the most exciting developments in the early days of autonomous driving was the DARPA Grand Challenge. Sponsored by the Defense Advanced Research Projects Agency (DARPA), this competition challenged teams to build autonomous vehicles that could navigate a 150-mile course through the Mojave Desert. It was a race to innovation, and it sparked a wave of creativity and experimentation in the field of autonomous driving.

The Stanford Racing Team: The Winners

The Stanford Racing Team, led by Sebastian Thrun, was one of the pioneers of the DARPA Grand Challenge. Their vehicle, Stanley, was a modified Volkswagen Touareg equipped with advanced sensors and algorithms. Stanley successfully navigated the course, winning the competition and cementing its place in the history of autonomous driving. It was a triumph of innovation and a testament to the power of human ingenuity.

The Rise of Waymo: From Experiments to Reality

But the story of Waymo doesngt stop with the DARPA Grand Challenge. Over the years, Waymo has continued to evolve, moving from experiments to reality. Waymo, originally known as the Google Self-Driving Car Project, has taken the lead in developing advanced technologies and bringing autonomous driving to the masses.

Google's Self-Driving Car Project: The Pioneers

Google's Self-Driving Car Project, now known as Waymo, was one of the pioneers in the field of autonomous driving. Led by Sebastian Thrun, the project aimed to develop a fully autonomous vehicle that could navigate the complexities of urban driving. Waymo's vehicles were equipped with advanced sensors, including LIDAR, radar, and cameras, and sophisticated algorithms that could analyze the data and make decisions in real-time. It was a groundbreaking achievement, and it paved the way for the autonomous driving technology we see today.

The Firefly: The Cute Little Car

One of the most exciting developments in the rise of Waymo was the introduction of the Firefly. This cute little car was designed from the ground up to be fully autonomous, with no steering wheel, no pedals, and no need for human intervention. The Firefly was equipped with advanced sensors and algorithms, and it was designed to be safe, efficient, and convenient. It was a step towards mainstream adoption, and it brought autonomous driving technology to the masses.

The Power of Data: The Backbone of Waymo's Autonomous Driving Technology

At the heart of Waymo's autonomous driving technology is data. Lots and lots of data. Think of it like this: data is the fuel that powers Waymo's autonomous driving technology, the lifeblood that makes it all possible. In the world of Waymo, this data comes from all sorts of sources—sensors, cameras, LIDAR, radar, and more.

Sensors: The Eyes and Ears of the Car

Sensors are the eyes and ears of the Waymo car. They detect changes in the environment, like the presence of other vehicles, pedestrians, and obstacles. Think of them like little spies, always on the lookout, gathering information and reporting back to the central system. By analyzing this data, Waymo's autonomous driving technology can make decisions in real-time, navigating the complexities of the road and keeping passengers safe.

Cameras: The Visual Aid

Cameras are another crucial component of Waymo's autonomous driving technology. They provide visual information about the environment, helping the car to understand its surroundings and make decisions accordingly. By analyzing this data, Waymo's autonomous driving technology can identify traffic signs, recognize lane markings, and even detect pedestrians and other vehicles. It's like having a super-sensitive observer who can see everything and understand its significance.

LIDAR and Radar: The Distance Detectors

LIDAR and radar are the distance detectors of the Waymo car. They use light and radio waves to measure the distance to objects, helping the car to understand its surroundings and navigate safely. By analyzing this data, Waymo's autonomous driving technology can detect obstacles, avoid collisions, and even plan its routes more efficiently. It's like having a super-sensitive navigator who can see through the fog and guide the car safely to its destination.

Waymo in Action: Revolutionizing Autonomous Driving

Chapter 9: AI in Transportation: The Road to Autonomous Vehicles

One of the most exciting aspects of Waymo's autonomous driving technology is seeing it in action. By using advanced technologies and innovative solutions, Waymo can transform the transportation experience, making it faster, more convenient, and more personalized than ever before.

Predictive Analytics: Looking into the Future

Predictive analytics is perhaps the most powerful tool in the arsenal of Waymo's autonomous driving technology. By analyzing historical data, predictive analytics can identify patterns, detect anomalies, and even predict future behaviors. It's like having a time machine that can show us the future, helping us make better decisions today.

Autonomous Vehicles: The Future of Transportation

Autonomous vehicles are the future of transportation. By using advanced sensors and AI algorithms, autonomous vehicles can navigate the roads safely and efficiently, without the need for human drivers. It's like having a super-smart chauffeur who can get you where you need to go, without the risk of human error.

Robotics: The Workhorses of the Warehouse

Robotics are the workhorses of the warehouse. By using advanced sensors and AI algorithms, robots can perform tasks faster, more accurately, and with less fatigue than human workers. It's like having an army of tireless, precise workers who never need a break.

Machine Learning: The Brains of the Operation

Machine learning is the brains of the operation. By analyzing data and learning from it, machine learning algorithms can improve over time, making the autonomous driving technology more efficient and more reliable. It's like having a super-smart assistant who can learn from experience and get better and better at their job.

The Human Touch: The Role of Engineers and Scientists

But Waymo's autonomous driving technology aingt just about technology. It's also about people. It's about the engineers and scientists who are pushing the boundaries of what's possible. It's about the visionaries who are dreaming of a future where AI can help us transform the transportation experience like never before.

Engineers and scientists are a special breed. They're part inventor, part analyst, part artist, and part dreamer. They know how to design, build, and program autonomous driving systems. But more importantly, they know how to imagine, to innovate, and to create.

Think of it like this: an engineer is like a builder who can construct the systems we need to make autonomous driving a reality. A scientist is like an analyst who can understand the complexities of the technology and develop new solutions. Together, they're like a dynamic duo, working hand in hand to unlock the power of Waymo's autonomous driving technology.

The Ethics of Waymo's Autonomous Driving Technology: Safety, Privacy, and Responsibility

But with great power comes great responsibility. And when it comes to Waymo's autonomous driving technology, that responsibility is enormous. You see, autonomous driving data is sensitive. It's intimate. It's a reflection of how we move, what we move, and who we move for. And when we use AI to analyze this data, we're giving it access to some of the most sensitive and private aspects of our lives.

That's why it's so important to handle autonomous driving data with care. It's why we need to think about safety, privacy, and responsibility. It's why we need to be mindful of the ethical implications of our actions.

Take the example of safety in autonomous driving. If the algorithms used to control an autonomous vehicle are flawed, it can lead to serious consequences, affecting the safety of passengers, other drivers, and even pedestrians. That's why it's crucial to ensure that our algorithms are robust, reliable, and safe.

The Future of Waymo's Autonomous Driving Technology: A World of Possibilities

But despite the challenges, the future of Waymo's autonomous driving technology is bright. It's a future filled with possibilities, with opportunities to solve problems and improve lives. It's a future where AI can help us transform the transportation experience like never before, where it can help us make transportation safer, more efficient, and more convenient.

And it's a future that's already here. Every day, we're seeing new breakthroughs, new innovations, new ways of using AI to make the world a better place. It's exciting, it's inspiring, and it's just the beginning.

So, my friends, as we journey through this magical world of Waymo and the future of autonomous driving, let's remember the power and the potential that lies within. Let's remember the pioneers who came before us, the visionaries who dared to dream of a future where AI could help us transform the transportation experience like never before. And let's look forward to the exciting journey that lies ahead, as we continue to explore the boundless possibilities of artificial intelligence.

ETHICAL CONSIDERATIONS AND CHALLENGES

Chapter 10: The Ethics of AI: Navigating the Moral Maze

Bias in AI: The Dangers of Unintended Discrimination

Introduction: The Dark Side of AI

Folks, gather 'round and let me spin you a yarn about the dark side of artificial intelligence—bias. Now, I know what you're thinking: "Bias in AI? Sounds like something out of a science fiction novel." But fear not, my friends, for I'm here to make it all as clear as a summer's day. So, grab your favorite chair, pour yourself a glass of lemonade, and let's dive right in.

The Promise of AI: A Revolution in the Making

Artificial intelligence is revolutionizing the world as we know it. From healthcare to finance, from transportation to entertainment, AI is transforming industries and improving lives. It's like having a super-smart assistant who can analyze data, make decisions, and even predict the future. It's a revolution in the making, and it's already changing the way we live and work.

But with great power comes great responsibility. And when it comes to AI, that responsibility is enormous. You see, AI is a double-edged sword. It has the power to do immense good, but it also has the potential to cause significant harm. That's why it's so important to consider the ethical implications of AI and to address the challenges that come with it.

The Problem of Bias: The Hidden Danger

Chapter 10: The Ethics of AI: Navigating the Moral Maze

One of the biggest ethical challenges in AI is bias. Think of it like this: AI systems are only as good as the data they're trained on. If the data is biased, the AI system will be biased too. And this bias can lead to unfair decisions, discriminatory practices, and even social injustice.

Garbage In, Garbage Out: The Data Dilemma

The data dilemma is a classic case of "garbage in, garbage out." If the data used to train an AI system is biased, the system itself will be biased. This can lead to all sorts of problems, from unfair lending practices to discriminatory hiring decisions. It's a hidden danger, and it's one that requires vigilance and careful scrutiny.

The Case of Amazongs Recruiting Tool: A Lesson in Bias

The case of Amazongs recruiting tool is a lesson in bias. In 2018, it was revealed that Amazongs AI-powered recruiting tool was biased against women. The tool was trained on historical data, which was predominantly male, and as a result, it favored male candidates over female candidates. It was a wake-up call about the dangers of bias in AI and the importance of fairness and equality.

The Roots of Bias: Where It All Begins

Bias in AI doesngt just appear out of thin air. It has roots, and it's important to understand where it comes from.

Historical Data: The Past Haunts the Present

Historical data is one of the main sources of bias in AI. If the data used to train an AI system reflects historical biases and inequalities, the system itself will perpetuate those biases. It's like having a time machine that brings the past into the present, with all its flaws and imperfections.

The Case of Facial Recognition: A Tale of Two Faces

The case of facial recognition is a tale of two faces. Facial recognition systems are often trained on datasets that are predominantly white and male. As a result, these systems are less accurate when it comes to recognizing faces of people of color, particularly women of color. It's a stark reminder of the dangers of bias in AI and the importance of diversity and inclusion.

The Consequences of Bias: The Real-World Impact

Bias in AI isngt just a theoretical problem. It has real-world consequences, and they can be severe.

Discriminatory Practices: The Unfair Advantage

Discriminatory practices are one of the most serious consequences of bias in AI. If an AI system is biased, it can lead to unfair decisions that disadvantage certain groups of people. This can manifest in many ways, from unfair lending practices to discriminatory hiring decisions. It's a real-world impact, and it's one that can have lasting consequences.

The Case of COMPAS: A Lesson in Fairness

The case of COMPAS is a lesson in fairness. COMPAS is an AI-powered risk assessment tool used in the criminal justice system to predict the likelihood of a defendant reoffending. However, it has been criticized for its potential bias against African Americans. It's a stark reminder of the real-world impact of bias in AI and the importance of fairness and equality.

The Human Touch: The Role of Ethicists and Data Scientists

But bias in AI aingt just about technology. It's also about people. It's about the ethicists and data scientists who are pushing the boundaries of what's possible. It's about the visionaries who are dreaming of a future where AI can help us transform the world like never before.

Ethicists and data scientists are a special breed. They're part philosopher, part analyst, part advocate, and part dreamer. They know how to identify ethical issues, how to analyze ethical dilemmas, and how to develop ethical solutions. But more importantly, they know how to communicate their findings in a way that's clear and compelling.

Think of it like this: an ethicist is like a philosopher who can use AI to identify ethical issues and develop ethical solutions. A data scientist is like an analyst who can use AI to develop new solutions, improve existing ones, and even tailor ethical guidelines to individual needs. Together, they're like a dynamic duo, working hand in hand to unlock the power of ethical AI.

The Future of Ethical AI: A World of Possibilities

But despite the challenges, the future of ethical AI is bright. It's a future filled with possibilities, with opportunities to solve problems and improve lives. It's a future where AI can help us transform the world like never before, where it can help us make the world a better, fairer, and more just place.

And it's a future that's already here. Every day, we're seeing new breakthroughs, new innovations, new ways of using AI to make the world a better place. It's exciting, it's inspiring, and it's just the beginning.

So, my friends, as we journey through this magical world of bias in AI and the dangers of unintended discrimination, let's remember the power and the potential that lies within. Let's remember the pioneers who came before us, the visionaries who dared to dream of a future where AI could help us transform the world like never before. And let's look forward to the exciting journey that lies ahead, as we continue to explore the boundless possibilities of artificial intelligence.

Privacy Concerns: Balancing Innovation and Personal Data

Introduction: The Double-Edged Sword of AI

Folks, gather 'round and let me spin you a yarn about the magical world of artificial intelligence and the privacy concerns that come with it. Now, I know what you're thinking: "Privacy concerns? Sounds like something out of a spy novel." But fear not, my friends, for I'm here to make it all as clear as a summer's day. So, grab your favorite chair, pour yourself a glass of lemonade, and let's dive right in.

The Promise of AI: A Revolution in the Making

Artificial intelligence is revolutionizing the world as we know it. From healthcare to finance, from transportation to entertainment, AI is transforming industries and improving lives. It's like having a super-smart assistant who can analyze data, make decisions, and even predict the future. It's a revolution in the making, and it's already changing the way we live and work.

But with great power comes great responsibility. And when it comes to AI, that responsibility is enormous. You see, AI is a double-edged sword. It has the power to do immense good, but it also has the potential to cause significant harm. That's why it's so important to consider the ethical implications of AI and to address the challenges that come with it.

The Power of Data: The Lifeblood of AI

At the heart of AI is data. Lots and lots of data. Think of it like this: data is the fuel that powers AI, the lifeblood that makes it all possible. In the world of AI, this data comes from all sorts of sources—sensors, cameras, IoT devices, and more.

Sensors: The Eyes and Ears of the System

Sensors are the eyes and ears of the AI system. They detect changes in the environment, like temperature, humidity, motion, and light. Think of them like little spies, always on the lookout, gathering information and reporting back to the central system. By analyzing this data, AI can identify patterns, detect anomalies, and even predict future behaviors. It's like having a super-sensitive observer who can see everything and understand its significance.

Cameras: The Visual Aid

Cameras are another crucial component of AI systems. They provide visual information about the environment, helping the system to understand its surroundings and make decisions accordingly. By analyzing this data, AI can identify objects, recognize faces, and even detect emotions. It's like having a super-sensitive observer who can see everything and understand its significance.

IoT Devices: The Connectors

IoT devices are the connectors of the AI system. They connect all sorts of devices, from sensors to cameras, from vehicles to wearables, from machines to people. By analyzing this data, AI can create a seamless and integrated system, making it more efficient and more reliable. It's like having a super-smart network that can connect everything and make it work together.

The Privacy Dilemma: Balancing Innovation and Personal Data

But with all this data comes a big dilemma—privacy. Think of it like this: AI relies on data, lots and lots of data. And much of this data is personal, sensitive, and intimate. It's a reflection of who we are, what we do, and how we live our lives. And when we use

AI to analyze this data, we're giving it access to some of the most private and personal aspects of our lives.

The Data Dilemma: Balancing Privacy and Utility

The data dilemma is a balancing act between privacy and utility. On one hand, we want to use AI to analyze data and gain insights that can improve our lives. On the other hand, we want to protect our privacy and ensure that our personal information is kept safe and secure. It's a delicate balance, and it's one that requires careful consideration and thoughtful solutions.

The Case of Cambridge Analytica: A Cautionary Tale

The case of Cambridge Analytica is a cautionary tale about the dangers of data misuse. In 2018, it was revealed that Cambridge Analytica had harvested the personal data of millions of Facebook users without their consent. This data was then used to target political advertising and influence elections. It was a scandal that rocked the world and highlighted the importance of data privacy and the ethical use of AI.

The Roots of Privacy Concerns: Where It All Begins

Privacy concerns in AI dongt just appear out of thin air. They have roots, and it's important to understand where they come from.

Data Collection: The Starting Point

Data collection is the starting point of privacy concerns in AI. When companies collect data, they need to ensure that they have the consent of the individuals whose data they're collecting. They also need to be transparent about how the data will be used and who will have access to it. It's a matter of trust, and it's one that requires careful consideration and thoughtful solutions.

The Case of Google Street View: A Lesson in Transparency

The case of Google Street View is a lesson in transparency. When Google first launched its Street View service, it faced criticism for collecting and publishing images of people's homes and private property without their consent. It was a reminder of the importance of transparency and the need for companies to be open and honest about their data collection practices.

The Consequences of Privacy Breaches: The Real-World Impact

Privacy breaches in AI arengt just a theoretical problem. They have real-world consequences, and they can be severe.

Identity Theft: The Nightmare Scenario

Identity theft is one of the most serious consequences of privacy breaches in AI. If personal data is compromised, it can be used to steal identities, commit fraud, and even cause financial ruin. It's a nightmare scenario, and it's one that requires vigilance and careful scrutiny.

The Case of Equifax: A Lesson in Security

The case of Equifax is a lesson in security. In 2017, it was revealed that Equifax, one of the largest credit reporting agencies in the US, had suffered a massive data breach. The breach compromised the personal data of over 147 million people, including their names, addresses, Social Security numbers, and even driver's license numbers. It was a wake-up call about the importance of data security and the need for companies to protect the personal information of their customers.

The Human Touch: The Role of Ethicists and Data Scientists

But privacy concerns in AI aingt just about technology. It's also about people. It's about the ethicists and data scientists who are pushing the boundaries of what's possible. It's about the visionaries who are dreaming of a future where AI can help us transform the world like never before.

Ethicists and data scientists are a special breed. They're part philosopher, part analyst, part advocate, and part dreamer. They know how to identify ethical issues, how to analyze ethical dilemmas, and how to develop ethical solutions. But more importantly, they know how to communicate their findings in a way that's clear and compelling.

Think of it like this: an ethicist is like a philosopher who can use AI to identify ethical issues and develop ethical solutions. A data scientist is like an analyst who can use AI to develop new solutions, improve existing ones, and even tailor ethical guidelines to individual needs. Together, they're like a dynamic duo, working hand in hand to unlock the power of ethical AI.

The Future of Ethical AI: A World of Possibilities

But despite the challenges, the future of ethical AI is bright. It's a future filled with possibilities, with opportunities to solve problems and improve lives. It's a future where AI can help us transform the world like never before, where it can help us make the world a better, fairer, and more just place.

And it's a future that's already here. Every day, we're seeing new breakthroughs, new innovations, new ways of using AI to make the world a better place. It's exciting, it's inspiring, and it's just the beginning.

So, my friends, as we journey through this magical world of privacy concerns and the balancing act between innovation and personal data, let's remember the power and the potential that lies within. Let's remember the pioneers who came before us, the visionaries who dared to dream of a future where AI could help us transform the world like never before. And let's look forward to the exciting journey that lies ahead, as we continue to explore the boundless possibilities of artificial intelligence.

The Debate Over AI Regulation and Governance

Introduction: The Wild West of AI

Folks, gather 'round and let me spin you a yarn about the wild and woolly world of artificial intelligence and the great debate over its regulation and governance. Now, I know what you're thinking: "AI regulation and governance? Sounds like something out of a political thriller." But fear not, my friends, for I'm here to make it all as clear as a summer's day. So, grab your favorite chair, pour yourself a glass of lemonade, and let's dive right in.

The Promise of AI: A Revolution in the Making

Artificial intelligence is revolutionizing the world as we know it. From healthcare to finance, from transportation to entertainment, AI is transforming industries and improving lives. It's like having a super-smart assistant who can analyze data, make decisions, and even predict the future. It's a revolution in the making, and it's already changing the way we live and work.

But with great power comes great responsibility. And when it comes to AI, that responsibility is enormous. You see, AI is a double-edged sword. It has the power to do immense good, but it also has the potential to cause significant harm. That's why it's so important to consider the ethical implications of AI and to address the challenges that come with it.

The Need for Regulation: Taming the Beast

As AI continues to grow and evolve, so does the need for regulation. Think of it like this: AI is like a wild beast, powerful and unpredictable. Without proper regulation, it can run amok, causing all sorts of trouble. But with the right rules and guidelines, it can be tamed, harnessed, and put to good use.

Chapter 10: The Ethics of AI: Navigating the Moral Maze

The Case of Autonomous Vehicles: A Lesson in Safety

The case of autonomous vehicles is a lesson in safety. Autonomous vehicles have the potential to revolutionize transportation, making it safer, more efficient, and more convenient. But they also come with significant risks, from technical malfunctions to ethical dilemmas. That's why it's so important to have regulations in place, to ensure that these vehicles are safe, reliable, and responsible.

The Case of Facial Recognition: A Tale of Two Faces

The case of facial recognition is a tale of two faces. Facial recognition technology can be a powerful tool for law enforcement, helping to identify criminals and prevent crime. But it also comes with significant risks, from privacy concerns to racial bias. That's why it's so important to have regulations in place, to ensure that this technology is used responsibly and ethically.

The Debate Over Governance: Who's in Charge?

But regulation is just one piece of the puzzle. Governance is another crucial aspect of AI. Think of it like this: AI is like a complex machine, with many moving parts and interconnected systems. Without proper governance, it can become chaotic, unmanageable, and even dangerous. But with the right structures and processes in place, it can be controlled, coordinated, and directed towards the greater good.

The Role of Government: The Guardians of the Public Interest

The role of government in AI governance is to act as the guardians of the public interest. Governments have the power to set policies, enforce regulations, and ensure that AI is used for the benefit of all. They can provide the oversight and accountability needed to keep AI in check and prevent it from causing harm.

The Role of Industry: The Innovators and Pioneers

The role of industry in AI governance is to act as the innovators and pioneers. Companies have the expertise, the resources, and the motivation to develop and deploy AI technologies. They can drive innovation, push the boundaries of what's possible, and create new opportunities for growth and prosperity.

The Role of Civil Society: The Advocates and Watchdogs

The role of civil society in AI governance is to act as the advocates and watchdogs. Non-governmental organizations, advocacy groups, and concerned citizens can provide the scrutiny, the transparency, and the accountability needed to ensure that AI is used responsibly and ethically. They can raise awareness, mobilize support, and hold both governments and industries accountable for their actions.

The Challenges of Regulation and Governance: Navigating the Minefield

But regulation and governance of AI aingt easy. It's like navigating a minefield, full of pitfalls, obstacles, and hidden dangers.

The Pace of Innovation: Keeping Up with the Joneses

The pace of innovation in AI is staggering. New technologies, new applications, and new discoveries are emerging every day. Keeping up with this rapid pace of change is a challenge in itself, and it requires agile, adaptive, and forward-thinking policies.

The Global Nature of AI: A Worldwide Phenomenon

The global nature of AI is another challenge. AI is a worldwide phenomenon, transcending borders, cultures, and jurisdictions. Developing effective regulation and governance requires international cooperation, coordination, and collaboration. It's a complex and daunting task, but one that's crucial for the future of AI.

The Balance Between Innovation and Regulation: Walking the Tightrope

The balance between innovation and regulation is a delicate one. Too much regulation can stifle innovation, hinder progress, and prevent AI from realizing its full potential. But too little regulation can lead to chaos, harm, and unintended consequences. It's like walking a tightrope, and it requires careful consideration, thoughtful solutions, and a keen sense of balance.

The Human Touch: The Role of Ethicists, Policymakers, and Advocates

But regulation and governance of AI aingt just about technology. It's also about people. It's about the ethicists, policymakers, and advocates who are pushing the boundaries of what's possible. It's about the visionaries who are dreaming of a future where AI can help us transform the world like never before.

Ethicists, policymakers, and advocates are a special breed. They're part philosopher, part analyst, part advocate, and part dreamer. They know how to identify ethical issues, how to analyze ethical dilemmas, and how to develop ethical solutions. But more importantly, they know how to communicate their findings in a way that's clear and compelling.

Think of it like this: an ethicist is like a philosopher who can use AI to identify ethical issues and develop ethical solutions. A policymaker is like an analyst who can use AI to develop new regulations, improve existing ones, and even tailor ethical guidelines to individual needs. An advocate is like a watchdog who can use AI to raise awareness, mobilize support, and hold both governments and industries accountable for their actions. Together, they're like a dynamic trio, working hand in hand to unlock the power of ethical AI.

The Future of AI Regulation and Governance: A World of Possibilities

But despite the challenges, the future of AI regulation and governance is bright. It's a future filled with possibilities, with opportunities to solve problems and improve lives. It's a future where AI can help us transform the world like never before, where it can help us make the world a better, fairer, and more just place.

And it's a future that's already here. Every day, we're seeing new breakthroughs, new innovations, new ways of using AI to make the world a better place. It's exciting, it's inspiring, and it's just the beginning.

So, my friends, as we journey through this wild and woolly world of AI regulation and governance, let's remember the power and the potential that lies within. Let's remember the pioneers who came before us, the visionaries who dared to dream of a future where AI could help us transform the world like never before. And let's look forward to the exciting journey that lies ahead, as we continue to explore the boundless possibilities of artificial intelligence.

Chapter 11: The Dark Side of AI: Cybersecurity and Misuse

The Threat of AI-Powered Cyber Attacks

Introduction: The Dark Side of AI

Folks, gather 'round and let me spin you a yarn about the dark side of artificial intelligence—the threat of AI-powered cyber attacks. Now, I know what you're thinking: "AI-powered cyber attacks? Sounds like something out of a spy novel." But fear not, my friends, for I'm here to make it all as clear as a summer's day. So, grab your favorite chair, pour yourself a glass of lemonade, and let's dive right in.

The Promise of AI: A Revolution in the Making

Artificial intelligence is revolutionizing the world as we know it. From healthcare to finance, from transportation to entertainment, AI is transforming industries and improving lives. It's like having a super-smart assistant who can analyze data, make decisions, and even predict the future. It's a revolution in the making, and it's already changing the way we live and work.

But with great power comes great responsibility. And when it comes to AI, that responsibility is enormous. You see, AI is a double-edged sword. It has the power to do immense good, but it also has the potential to cause significant harm. That's why it's so important to consider the ethical implications of AI and to address the challenges that come with it.

The Rise of Cyber Attacks: A Growing Threat

Cyber attacks are a growing threat in today's digital world. From data breaches to ransomware, from phishing to malware, cyber attacks are becoming more sophisticated, more frequent, and more dangerous. And with the rise of AI, these threats are only getting worse.

The Case of WannaCry: A Global Epidemic

The case of WannaCry is a global epidemic. In 2017, the WannaCry ransomware attack infected hundreds of thousands of computers worldwide, encrypting their data and demanding payment in Bitcoin. The attack caused widespread disruption, affecting hospitals, businesses, and even governments. It was a wake-up call about the dangers of cyber attacks and the need for robust cybersecurity measures.

The Power of AI: A Double-Edged Sword

AI has the power to revolutionize cybersecurity, making it more effective, more efficient, and more reliable. But it also has the power to make cyber attacks more sophisticated, more targeted, and more dangerous. Think of it like this: AI is like a super-smart weapon, capable of both protecting and attacking. It's a double-edged sword, and it's one that requires careful consideration and thoughtful solutions.

AI-Powered Cybersecurity: The Guardian Angel

AI-powered cybersecurity is like a guardian angel, watching over our digital lives and protecting us from harm. By using advanced algorithms and machine learning techniques, AI can detect anomalies, identify threats, and even predict future attacks. It's like having a super-smart sentinel who can see everything and understand its significance.

AI-Powered Cyber Attacks: The Invisible Enemy

AI-powered cyber attacks are like an invisible enemy, lurking in the shadows and striking when we least expect it. By using advanced algorithms and machine learning techniques, AI can create more sophisticated, more targeted, and more dangerous attacks. It's like having a super-smart adversary who can outwit, outmaneuver, and outsmart us.

The Threat of AI-Powered Cyber Attacks: The Dark Side of Innovation

The threat of AI-powered cyber attacks is the dark side of innovation. As AI continues to grow and evolve, so does its potential for misuse. Think of it like this: AI is like a powerful tool, capable of both creating and destroying. In the wrong hands, it can be used to cause significant harm, from data breaches to infrastructure attacks, from financial fraud to political manipulation.

The Case of Deepfakes: A Disturbing Trend

The case of deepfakes is a disturbing trend. Deepfakes are AI-generated videos that can mimic the appearance and voice of real people, creating convincing but fake content. They can be used to spread misinformation, manipulate public opinion, and even commit fraud. It's a stark reminder of the dark side of AI and the need for vigilance and careful scrutiny.

The Case of AI-Powered Phishing: A New Level of Deception

The case of AI-powered phishing is a new level of deception. By using advanced algorithms and natural language processing techniques, AI can create more convincing, more personalized, and more effective phishing attacks. It can mimic the writing style of real people, craft believable messages, and even adapt to the

Chapter 11: The Dark Side of AI: Cybersecurity and Misuse

behavior of its targets. It's a chilling example of the power of AI and the need for robust cybersecurity measures.

The Human Touch: The Role of Cybersecurity Experts and Ethicists

But the threat of AI-powered cyber attacks aingt just about technology. It's also about people. It's about the cybersecurity experts and ethicists who are pushing the boundaries of what's possible. It's about the visionaries who are dreaming of a future where AI can help us transform the world like never before.

Cybersecurity experts and ethicists are a special breed. They're part detective, part analyst, part advocate, and part dreamer. They know how to identify threats, how to analyze vulnerabilities, and how to develop solutions. But more importantly, they know how to communicate their findings in a way that's clear and compelling.

Think of it like this: a cybersecurity expert is like a detective who can use AI to identify threats and develop solutions. An ethicist is like an analyst who can use AI to develop ethical guidelines, improve existing ones, and even tailor cybersecurity measures to individual needs. Together, they're like a dynamic duo, working hand in hand to unlock the power of ethical AI.

The Future of Cybersecurity: A World of Possibilities

But despite the challenges, the future of cybersecurity is bright. It's a future filled with possibilities, with opportunities to solve problems and improve lives. It's a future where AI can help us transform the world like never before, where it can help us make the world a safer, more secure, and more resilient place.

And it's a future that's already here. Every day, we're seeing new breakthroughs, new innovations, new ways of using AI to make

the world a better place. It's exciting, it's inspiring, and it's just the beginning.

So, my friends, as we journey through this dark and dangerous world of AI-powered cyber attacks, let's remember the power and the potential that lies within. Let's remember the pioneers who came before us, the visionaries who dared to dream of a future where AI could help us transform the world like never before. And let's look forward to the exciting journey that lies ahead, as we continue to explore the boundless possibilities of artificial intelligence.

Chapter 11: The Dark Side of AI: Cybersecurity and Misuse

Deepfakes and the Erosion of Trust in Digital Media

Introduction: The Unseen Enemy

Folks, gather 'round and let me spin you a yarn about the unseen enemy lurking in the shadows of digital media—deepfakes. Now, I know what you're thinking: "Deepfakes? Sounds like something out of a science fiction novel." But fear not, my friends, for I'm here to make it all as clear as a summer's day. So, grab your favorite chair, pour yourself a glass of lemonade, and let's dive right in.

The Promise of AI: A Revolution in the Making

Artificial intelligence is revolutionizing the world as we know it. From healthcare to finance, from transportation to entertainment, AI is transforming industries and improving lives. It's like having a super-smart assistant who can analyze data, make decisions, and even predict the future. It's a revolution in the making, and it's already changing the way we live and work.

But with great power comes great responsibility. And when it comes to AI, that responsibility is enormous. You see, AI is a double-edged sword. It has the power to do immense good, but it also has the potential to cause significant harm. That's why it's so important to consider the ethical implications of AI and to address the challenges that come with it.

The Rise of Deepfakes: A Disturbing Trend

Deepfakes are a disturbing trend in the world of digital media. These AI-generated videos can mimic the appearance and voice of real people, creating convincing but fake content. Think of it like this: deepfakes are like digital doppelgangers, capable of deceiving the eye and the ear, making it hard to tell what's real and what's not.

The Technology Behind Deepfakes: A Double-Edged Sword

The technology behind deepfakes is a double-edged sword. On one hand, it's a testament to the power of AI, showing how advanced algorithms and machine learning techniques can create incredibly realistic and convincing content. On the other hand, it's a tool that can be used for deception, manipulation, and even harm.

The Case of the Fake Obama Video: A Wake-Up Call

The case of the fake Obama video is a wake-up call. In 2018, a deepfake video of former President Barack Obama surfaced online. The video showed Obama making statements he never actually made. It was a shocking example of the power of deepfakes and the potential for misuse. The video was created by BuzzFeed and filmmaker Jordan Peele to raise awareness about the dangers of deepfakes and the need for vigilance and careful scrutiny.

The Erosion of Trust: A Crisis of Confidence

The rise of deepfakes is leading to an erosion of trust in digital media. Think of it like this: in a world where deepfakes can create convincing but fake content, how can we trust what we see and hear? How can we distinguish between what's real and what's not? It's a crisis of confidence, and it's one that requires careful consideration and thoughtful solutions.

The Impact on Journalism: A Battle for Credibility

The impact of deepfakes on journalism is a battle for credibility. Journalists rely on the trust of their audience to report the news accurately and fairly. But with the rise of deepfakes, that trust is being eroded. Fake news, misinformation, and disinformation are spreading like wildfire, making it harder for journalists to do their jobs and for the public to trust what they're reporting.

The Case of the Fake Pelosi Video: A Lesson in Vigilance

The case of the fake Pelosi video is a lesson in vigilance. In 2019, a doctored video of House Speaker Nancy Pelosi surfaced online. The video was slowed down to make Pelosi appear drunk or impaired. It was a blatant attempt to spread misinformation and manipulate public opinion. The video was quickly debunked, but it highlighted the importance of vigilance and the need for critical thinking and careful scrutiny.

The Human Touch: The Role of Journalists, Ethicists, and Technologists

But the erosion of trust in digital media aingt just about technology. It's also about people. It's about the journalists, ethicists, and technologists who are pushing the boundaries of what's possible. It's about the visionaries who are dreaming of a future where AI can help us transform the world like never before.

Journalists, ethicists, and technologists are a special breed. They're part detective, part analyst, part advocate, and part dreamer. They know how to identify threats, how to analyze vulnerabilities, and how to develop solutions. But more importantly, they know how to communicate their findings in a way that's clear and compelling.

Think of it like this: a journalist is like a detective who can use AI to identify threats and develop solutions. An ethicist is like an analyst who can use AI to develop ethical guidelines, improve existing ones, and even tailor digital media measures to individual needs.

A technologist is like an innovator who can use AI to create new tools, improve existing ones, and even develop countermeasures to deepfakes. Together, they're like a dynamic trio, working hand in hand to unlock the power of ethical AI.

The Future of Digital Media: A World of Possibilities

But despite the challenges, the future of digital media is bright. It's a future filled with possibilities, with opportunities to solve problems and improve lives. It's a future where AI can help us transform the world like never before, where it can help us make the world a safer, more secure, and more resilient place.

And it's a future that's already here. Every day, we're seeing new breakthroughs, new innovations, new ways of using AI to make the world a better place. It's exciting, it's inspiring, and it's just the beginning.

So, my friends, as we journey through this disturbing world of deepfakes and the erosion of trust in digital media, let's remember the power and the potential that lies within. Let's remember the pioneers who came before us, the visionaries who dared to dream of a future where AI could help us transform the world like never before. And let's look forward to the exciting journey that lies ahead, as we continue to explore the boundless possibilities of artificial intelligence.

Case Study: The Cambridge Analytica Scandal

Introduction: The Unraveling of a Scandal

Folks, gather 'round and let me spin you a yarn about one of the most infamous scandals in the world of data privacy—the Cambridge Analytica scandal. Now, I know what you're thinking: "Cambridge Analytica? Sounds like something out of a spy novel." But fear not, my friends, for I'm here to make it all as clear as a summer's day. So, grab your favorite chair, pour yourself a glass of lemonade, and let's dive right in.

The Birth of Cambridge Analytica: A Vision of Power

To understand the Cambridge Analytica scandal, we gotta go back to the beginnings. Cambridge Analytica was a British political consulting firm that specialized in data mining, data analysis, and strategic communication. Their vision was simple yet powerful: use data to influence elections and shape public opinion. Think of it like having a crystal ball that could predict the future and a magic wand that could change it.

The Founders: The Masterminds Behind the Curtain

The founders of Cambridge Analytica were a group of masterminds, each bringing their unique skills and expertise to the table. Among them were Alexander Nix, the CEO, and Christopher Wylie, the whistleblower who later exposed the company's unethical practices. Together, they formed a powerful team, ready to take on the world of politics and data.

The Rise of Data-Driven Politics: A New Era

The rise of data-driven politics marked a new era in the world of elections and public opinion. With the advent of social media and advanced data analytics, political campaigns could now target voters with unprecedented precision. It was like having a super-smart assistant who could analyze data, identify trends, and even predict voter behavior.

The Power of Data: The Lifeblood of Influence

Data is the lifeblood of influence in the world of politics. By collecting and analyzing vast amounts of data, political campaigns could gain insights into voter preferences, behaviors, and even emotions. This data could then be used to craft targeted messages, tailor advertisements, and even sway public opinion. It was a powerful tool, and it was one that Cambridge Analytica knew how to wield.

The Scandal Unfolds: The Dark Side of Data

But with great power comes great responsibility. And when it comes to data, that responsibility is enormous. You see, data is a double-edged sword. It has the power to do immense good, but it also has the potential to cause significant harm. That's why it's so important to consider the ethical implications of data collection and use.

The Data Breach: The Unseen Enemy

The Cambridge Analytica scandal began with a data breach. In 2014, Cambridge Analytica obtained the personal data of millions of Facebook users without their consent. This data was collected through a personality quiz app called "This Is Your Digital Life," developed by a researcher named Aleksandr Kogan. The app not only collected data from the users who took the quiz but also from their Facebook friends, resulting in a massive data breach that affected over 87 million people worldwide.

The Misuse of Data: The Weapon of Influence

The misuse of data was the weapon of influence in the Cambridge Analytica scandal. With the stolen data in hand, Cambridge Analytica used advanced algorithms and machine learning techniques to analyze voter preferences, behaviors, and emotions. This information was then used to craft targeted advertisements and influence voters in key elections, including the 2016 US presidential election and the UK's Brexit referendum.

The Whistleblower: The Voice of Truth

The whistleblower in the Cambridge Analytica scandal was Christopher Wylie, a former employee of the company. Wylie exposed the unethical practices of Cambridge Analytica, revealing how the company had obtained and misused the personal data of millions of Facebook users. His revelations sparked a global outcry and led to investigations by governments and regulatory bodies around the world.

The Impact of the Scandal: A Shockwave of Distrust

The impact of the Cambridge Analytica scandal was a shockwave of distrust. The revelations about the misuse of personal data shook the foundations of trust in social media platforms and data-driven politics. People began to question the integrity of elections, the ethics of data collection, and the role of technology in shaping public opinion. It was a wake-up call about the dangers of data misuse and the need for robust data privacy regulations.

The Aftermath: The Fallout and the Lessons Learned

The aftermath of the Cambridge Analytica scandal was a fallout of epic proportions. The company faced legal investigations, regulatory scrutiny, and a barrage of negative publicity. Facebook, the platform through which the data was obtained, also faced significant backlash and was forced to implement stricter data privacy measures.

The Lessons Learned: The Path to Ethical Data Use

The lessons learned from the Cambridge Analytica scandal are a path to ethical data use. The scandal highlighted the importance of data privacy, transparency, and accountability. It showed the need for robust regulations and oversight to prevent the misuse of personal data and ensure that data-driven technologies are used responsibly and ethically.

The Human Touch: The Role of Ethicists, Policymakers, and Advocates

But the Cambridge Analytica scandal aingt just about technology. It's also about people. It's about the ethicists, policymakers, and advocates who are pushing the boundaries of what's possible. It's about the visionaries who are dreaming of a future where data can be used responsibly and ethically to improve lives and strengthen democracy.

Ethicists, policymakers, and advocates are a special breed. They're part philosopher, part analyst, part advocate, and part dreamer. They know how to identify ethical issues, how to analyze ethical dilemmas, and how to develop ethical solutions. But more importantly, they know how to communicate their findings in a way that's clear and compelling.

Think of it like this: an ethicist is like a philosopher who can use data to identify ethical issues and develop ethical solutions. A policymaker is like an analyst who can use data to develop new regulations, improve existing ones, and even tailor ethical guidelines to individual needs. An advocate is like a watchdog who can use data to raise awareness, mobilize support, and hold both governments and industries accountable for their actions. Together, they're like a dynamic trio, working hand in hand to unlock the power of ethical data use.

The Future of Data Privacy: A World of Possibilities

But despite the challenges, the future of data privacy is bright. It's a future filled with possibilities, with opportunities to solve problems and improve lives. It's a future where data can be used responsibly and ethically to strengthen democracy, protect individual rights, and build a more just and equitable society.

And it's a future that's already here. Every day, we're seeing new breakthroughs, new innovations, new ways of using data to make the world a better place. It's exciting, it's inspiring, and it's just the beginning.

So, my friends, as we journey through this shocking world of the Cambridge Analytica scandal and the dark side of data, let's remember the power and the potential that lies within. Let's remember the pioneers who came before us, the visionaries who dared to dream of a future where data could be used responsibly and ethically to transform the world like never before. And let's look forward to the exciting journey that lies ahead, as we continue to explore the boundless possibilities of artificial intelligence and data privacy.

Chapter 12: AI and the Future of Work: Opportunities and Challenges

The Impact of Automation on Jobs and the Economy

Introduction: The March of Progress

Folks, gather 'round and let me spin you a yarn about the march of progress—the impact of automation on jobs and the economy. Now, I know what you're thinking: "Automation? Sounds like something out of a science fiction novel." But fear not, my friends, for I'm here to make it all as clear as a summer's day. So, grab your favorite chair, pour yourself a glass of lemonade, and let's dive right in.

The Promise of Automation: A Revolution in the Making

Automation is revolutionizing the world as we know it. From factories to offices, from farms to hospitals, automation is transforming industries and improving lives. It's like having a super-smart assistant who can perform tasks faster, more accurately, and with less fatigue than human workers. It's a revolution in the making, and it's already changing the way we live and work.

But with great power comes great responsibility. And when it comes to automation, that responsibility is enormous. You see, automation is a double-edged sword. It has the power to do immense good, but it also has the potential to cause significant harm. That's why it's so important to consider the ethical implications of automation and to address the challenges that come with it.

The History of Automation: From Steam Engines to Robots

Chapter 12: AI and the Future of Work: Opportunities and Challenges

To understand the impact of automation on jobs and the economy, we gotta go back to the beginnings. The history of automation is a long and winding road, filled with innovations, transformations, and revolutions.

The Industrial Revolution: The Birth of Automation

The Industrial Revolution was the birth of automation. In the late 18th and early 19th centuries, the invention of the steam engine and the mechanization of production processes transformed the world of work. Factories sprang up, machines replaced manual labor, and productivity soared. It was a revolution that changed the face of the economy and the nature of work forever.

The Assembly Line: The Rise of Mass Production

The assembly line was the rise of mass production. In the early 20th century, Henry Ford introduced the assembly line to the automotive industry, revolutionizing the way cars were manufactured. The assembly line allowed for the mass production of goods, making them more affordable and accessible to the general public. It was a game-changer, and it paved the way for the modern era of automation.

The Digital Revolution: The Age of Computers

The digital revolution was the age of computers. In the late 20th and early 21st centuries, the advent of computers and digital technology transformed the world of work once again. Automated systems replaced manual processes, data became the new currency, and the internet connected the world like never before. It was a revolution that changed the way we live, work, and communicate.

The Impact on Jobs: The Double-Edged Sword

The impact of automation on jobs is a double-edged sword. On one hand, automation can create new opportunities, increase productivity, and improve working conditions. On the other hand, it can displace workers, eliminate jobs, and cause economic disruption. It's a complex and nuanced issue, and it requires careful consideration and thoughtful solutions.

Job Creation: The Silver Lining

Job creation is the silver lining of automation. While automation can eliminate certain jobs, it also creates new ones. Think of it like this: as machines take over repetitive and mundane tasks, human workers are freed up to focus on more creative, more complex, and more valuable activities. New jobs are created in fields like data analysis, robotics, and artificial intelligence, offering exciting opportunities for those with the right skills and knowledge.

The Case of Amazon: A Lesson in Adaptation

The case of Amazon is a lesson in adaptation. As the e-commerce giant has grown, it has invested heavily in automation, from warehouse robots to delivery drones. While these technologies have eliminated some jobs, they have also created new ones, from software engineers to data scientists. Amazon has shown that by embracing automation and investing in retraining and upskilling, companies can adapt to the changing landscape of work and create new opportunities for their employees.

Job Displacement: The Dark Cloud

Job displacement is the dark cloud of automation. As machines become more capable and more efficient, they can replace human workers in a wide range of industries, from manufacturing to retail, from transportation to healthcare. This displacement can lead to unemployment, economic hardship, and social unrest. It's

Chapter 12: AI and the Future of Work: Opportunities and Challenges

a serious challenge, and it requires innovative solutions and proactive policies.

The Case of the Self-Driving Car: A Cautionary Tale

The case of the self-driving car is a cautionary tale. As autonomous vehicles become more advanced and more widespread, they have the potential to displace millions of drivers, from taxi drivers to truck drivers, from delivery drivers to bus drivers. This displacement could have significant economic and social consequences, affecting not only the displaced workers but also their families, their communities, and the broader economy.

The Impact on the Economy: The Ripple Effect

The impact of automation on the economy is a ripple effect. As automation transforms industries and displaces workers, it has far-reaching consequences for the broader economy. Think of it like this: automation is like a stone thrown into a pond, creating ripples that spread out in all directions.

Productivity Gains: The Engine of Growth

Productivity gains are the engine of growth in the economy. Automation can increase productivity by making production processes more efficient, more reliable, and more cost-effective. This increased productivity can lead to higher output, lower prices, and greater economic growth. It's a powerful force, and it's one that can drive innovation, competitiveness, and prosperity.

The Case of the Textile Industry: A Lesson in Efficiency

The case of the textile industry is a lesson in efficiency. In the 19th century, the invention of the power loom revolutionized the textile industry, making it possible to produce cloth faster, cheaper, and in greater quantities than ever before. This increased productivity led to a boom in the textile industry, creating new jobs, stimulating economic growth, and improving living standards for millions of people.

Economic Disruption: The Storm Cloud

Economic disruption is the storm cloud of automation. As automation displaces workers and transforms industries, it can cause significant economic disruption, from unemployment to income inequality, from social unrest to political instability. It's a serious challenge, and it requires proactive policies and innovative solutions.

The Case of the Rust Belt: A Lesson in Transition

The case of the Rust Belt is a lesson in transition. In the mid-20th century, the Rust Belt was the heart of American manufacturing, home to thriving industries like steel, automotive, and machinery. But as automation and globalization transformed these industries, many of the jobs that had sustained the region disappeared, leaving behind a legacy of unemployment, poverty, and economic decline. The Rust Belt is a stark reminder of the challenges of economic transition and the need for proactive policies and innovative solutions.

The Human Touch: The Role of Policymakers, Educators, and Innovators

But the impact of automation on jobs and the economy aingt just about technology. It's also about people. It's about the policymakers, educators, and innovators who are pushing the boundaries of what's possible. It's about the visionaries who are dreaming of a future where automation can help us transform the world like never before.

Chapter 12: AI and the Future of Work: Opportunities and Challenges

Policymakers, educators, and innovators are a special breed. They're part strategist, part analyst, part advocate, and part dreamer. They know how to identify challenges, how to analyze solutions, and how to develop policies. But more importantly, they know how to communicate their findings in a way that's clear and compelling.

Think of it like this: a policymaker is like a strategist who can use automation to identify challenges and develop policies. An educator is like an analyst who can use automation to develop new curricula, improve existing ones, and even tailor educational programs to individual needs. An innovator is like a dreamer who can use automation to create new technologies, improve existing ones, and even develop solutions to the challenges of job displacement and economic disruption. Together, they're like a dynamic trio, working hand in hand to unlock the power of ethical automation.

The Future of Automation: A World of Possibilities

But despite the challenges, the future of automation is bright. It's a future filled with possibilities, with opportunities to solve problems and improve lives. It's a future where automation can help us transform the world like never before, where it can help us make the world a safer, more efficient, and more prosperous place.

And it's a future that's already here. Every day, we're seeing new breakthroughs, new innovations, new ways of using automation to make the world a better place. It's exciting, it's inspiring, and it's just the beginning.

So, my friends, as we journey through this march of progress—the impact of automation on jobs and the economy—let's remember the power and the potential that lies within. Let's remember the pioneers who came before us, the visionaries who dared to dream of a future where automation could help us transform the world like never before. And let's look forward to the exciting journey that lies ahead, as we continue to explore the boundless possibilities of artificial intelligence and automation.

Upskilling and Reskilling: Preparing for the AI-Driven Workforce

Introduction: The Winds of Change

Folks, gather 'round and let me spin you a yarn about the winds of change—upskilling and reskilling for the AI-driven workforce. Now, I know what you're thinking: "Upskilling and reskilling? Sounds like something out of a self-help book." But fear not, my friends, for I'm here to make it all as clear as a summer's day. So, grab your favorite chair, pour yourself a glass of lemonade, and let's dive right in.

The Promise of AI: A Revolution in the Making

Artificial intelligence is revolutionizing the world as we know it. From healthcare to finance, from transportation to entertainment, AI is transforming industries and improving lives. It's like having a super-smart assistant who can analyze data, make decisions, and even predict the future. It's a revolution in the making, and it's already changing the way we live and work.

But with great power comes great responsibility. And when it comes to AI, that responsibility is enormous. You see, AI is a double-edged sword. It has the power to do immense good, but it also has the potential to cause significant harm. That's why it's so important to consider the ethical implications of AI and to address the challenges that come with it.

The Changing Nature of Work: The AI-Driven Workforce

The changing nature of work is the AI-driven workforce. As AI continues to grow and evolve, it's transforming the way we work, the jobs we do, and the skills we need. Think of it like this: AI is like a powerful engine, driving the world of work forward, creating new opportunities, and demanding new skills.

The Rise of Automation: The New Normal

The rise of automation is the new normal. From factories to offices, from farms to hospitals, automation is transforming industries and improving lives. It's like having a super-smart assistant who can perform tasks faster, more accurately, and with less fatigue than human workers. It's a revolution in the making, and it's already changing the way we live and work.

The Case of Amazon: A Lesson in Adaptation

The case of Amazon is a lesson in adaptation. As the e-commerce giant has grown, it has invested heavily in automation, from warehouse robots to delivery drones. While these technologies have eliminated some jobs, they have also created new ones, from software engineers to data scientists. Amazon has shown that by embracing automation and investing in retraining and upskilling, companies can adapt to the changing landscape of work and create new opportunities for their employees.

The Need for Upskilling and Reskilling: The Path to Success

The need for upskilling and reskilling is the path to success in the AI-driven workforce. As AI continues to transform industries and demand new skills, workers need to adapt, learn, and grow. Think of it like this: upskilling and reskilling are like the keys to the kingdom, unlocking new opportunities, new careers, and new paths to success.

Upskilling: The Art of Improving

Upskilling is the art of improving. It's about learning new skills, enhancing existing ones, and staying ahead of the curve. Think of it like this: upskilling is like sharpening your tools, making them more effective, more efficient, and more valuable. It's about embracing change, adapting to new technologies, and preparing for the future.

The Case of IBM: A Lesson in Lifelong Learning

The case of IBM is a lesson in lifelong learning. IBM has invested heavily in upskilling its workforce, offering a wide range of training programs, from online courses to in-person workshops, from technical skills to soft skills. The company has shown that by investing in the continuous learning and development of its employees, it can stay ahead of the curve, adapt to new technologies, and prepare for the future.

Reskilling: The Art of Reinventing

Reskilling is the art of reinventing. It's about learning new skills, transitioning to new careers, and embracing new opportunities. Think of it like this: reskilling is like reinventing yourself, transforming your career, and preparing for a new future. It's about adapting to change, embracing new technologies, and seizing new opportunities.

The Case of AT&T: A Lesson in Career Transformation

The case of AT&T is a lesson in career transformation. AT&T has invested heavily in reskilling its workforce, offering a wide range of training programs, from online courses to in-person workshops, from technical skills to soft skills. The company has shown that by investing in the continuous learning and development of its employees, it can help them transition to new careers, adapt to new technologies, and prepare for the future.

The Role of Education: The Foundation of Success

The role of education is the foundation of success in the AI-driven workforce. As AI continues to transform industries and demand new skills, education plays a crucial role in preparing workers for the future. Think of it like this: education is like the cornerstone of a building, supporting the entire structure, providing the foundation for success.

The Importance of STEM Education: The Building Blocks of the Future

The importance of STEM education is the building blocks of the future. STEM—science, technology, engineering, and mathematics—is the foundation of the AI-driven workforce. By investing in STEM education, we can prepare the next generation of workers for the challenges and opportunities of the future. It's about building a strong foundation, equipping workers with the skills they need to succeed, and preparing them for the AI-driven workforce.

The Case of Code.org: A Lesson in Early Education

The case of Code.org is a lesson in early education. Code.org is a non-profit organization that aims to expand access to computer science education, particularly for underrepresented groups. The organization has shown that by investing in early education, we can prepare the next generation of workers for the challenges and opportunities of the AI-driven workforce. It's about building a strong foundation, equipping workers with the skills they need to succeed, and preparing them for the future.

The Role of Government: The Guardians of the Future

The role of government is the guardians of the future in the AI-driven workforce. As AI continues to transform industries and demand new skills, governments play a crucial role in supporting workers, investing in education, and preparing for the future. Think of it like this: governments are like the guardians of the future, protecting workers, supporting education, and preparing for the AI-driven workforce.

The Importance of Public Policy: The Framework for Success

The importance of public policy is the framework for success in the AI-driven workforce. By developing and implementing effective public policies, governments can support workers, invest in education, and prepare for the future. It's about creating a supportive environment, encouraging continuous learning and development, and preparing workers for the AI-driven workforce.

The Case of Singapore: A Lesson in Government Support

The case of Singapore is a lesson in government support. The Singaporean government has invested heavily in upskilling and reskilling its workforce, offering a wide range of training programs, from online courses to in-person workshops, from technical skills to soft skills. The government has shown that by investing in the continuous learning and development of its citizens, it can support workers, prepare for the future, and create a thriving AI-driven workforce.

The Role of Business: The Drivers of Innovation

The role of business is the drivers of innovation in the AI-driven workforce. As AI continues to transform industries and demand new skills, businesses play a crucial role in investing in upskilling and reskilling, supporting workers, and preparing for the future. Think of it like this: businesses are like the drivers of innovation, pushing the boundaries of what's possible, investing in upskilling and reskilling, and preparing for the AI-driven workforce.

The Importance of Corporate Training: The Engine of Growth

The importance of corporate training is the engine of growth in the AI-driven workforce. By investing in upskilling and reskilling, businesses can support workers, adapt to new technologies, and prepare for the future. It's about creating a supportive environment, encouraging continuous learning and development, and preparing workers for the AI-driven workforce.

The Case of Microsoft: A Lesson in Corporate Investment

The case of Microsoft is a lesson in corporate investment. Microsoft has invested heavily in upskilling and reskilling its workforce, offering a wide range of training programs, from online courses to in-person workshops, from technical skills to soft skills. The company has shown that by investing in the continuous learning and development of its employees, it can support workers, adapt to new technologies, and prepare for the future.

The Human Touch: The Role of Educators, Policymakers, and Business Leaders

But upskilling and reskilling for the AI-driven workforce aingt just about technology. It's also about people. It's about the educators, policymakers, and business leaders who are pushing the boundaries of what's possible. It's about the visionaries who are dreaming of a future where AI can help us transform the world like never before.

Educators, policymakers, and business leaders are a special breed. They're part teacher, part strategist, part advocate, and part dreamer. They know how to identify challenges, how to analyze solutions, and how to develop policies. But more importantly, they know how to communicate their findings in a way that's clear and compelling.

Think of it like this: an educator is like a teacher who can use AI to identify challenges and develop solutions. A policymaker is like a strategist who can use AI to develop new policies, improve existing ones, and even tailor educational programs to individual needs. A business leader is like a dreamer who can use AI to create new technologies, improve existing ones, and even develop solutions to the challenges of upskilling and reskilling. Together, they're like a dynamic trio, working hand in hand to unlock the power of ethical AI.

The Future of the AI-Driven Workforce: A World of Possibilities

But despite the challenges, the future of the AI-driven workforce is bright. It's a future filled with possibilities, with opportunities to solve problems and improve lives. It's a future where AI can help us transform the world like never before, where it can help us make the world a safer, more efficient, and more prosperous place.

And it's a future that's already here. Every day, we're seeing new breakthroughs, new innovations, new ways of using AI to make the world a better place. It's exciting, it's inspiring, and it's just the beginning.

So, my friends, as we journey through this wind of change—upskilling and reskilling for the AI-driven workforce—let's remember the power and the potential that lies within. Let's remember the pioneers who came before us, the visionaries who dared to dream of a future where AI could help us transform the world like never before. And let's look forward to the exciting journey that lies ahead, as we continue to explore the boundless possibilities of artificial intelligence and the AI-driven workforce.

Case Study: The Gig Economy and the Role of AI

Introduction: The New Frontier of Work

Folks, gather 'round and let me spin you a yarn about the new frontier of work—the gig economy and the role of AI. Now, I know what you're thinking: "Gig economy and AI? Sounds like something out of a futuristic novel." But fear not, my friends, for I'm here to make it all as clear as a summer's day. So, grab your favorite chair, pour yourself a glass of lemonade, and let's dive right in.

The Birth of the Gig Economy: A New Way of Working

The gig economy is a new way of working, where freelancers, independent contractors, and temporary workers take on short-term jobs or "gigs." Think of it like this: instead of having a traditional 9-to-5 job, folks in the gig economy work on a project-by-project basis, choosing their own hours and working for multiple clients. It's a flexible, dynamic, and often unpredictable way of earning a living.

The Rise of Platforms: The Backbone of the Gig Economy

The rise of platforms is the backbone of the gig economy. Companies like Uber, Lyft, Airbnb, and Upwork have created digital platforms that connect freelancers with clients, making it easier than ever to find work and get paid. These platforms use advanced algorithms and AI to match workers with jobs, manage schedules, and even set prices. It's like having a super-smart matchmaker who can find you the perfect gig in the blink of an eye.

The Role of AI: The Brains of the Operation

AI plays a crucial role in the gig economy, acting as the brains of the operation. From matching workers with jobs to optimizing schedules, AI is the invisible force that keeps the gig economy humming along. Think of it like this: AI is like the conductor of an orchestra, coordinating all the different instruments to create a harmonious symphony of work.

Matching Workers with Jobs: The Art of Algorithms

Matching workers with jobs is the art of algorithms. AI-powered platforms use sophisticated algorithms to analyze data about workers and jobs, finding the best matches based on skills, availability, and preferences. It's like having a super-smart assistant who can sift through thousands of job postings and find the perfect one for you.

The Case of Uber: A Lesson in Efficiency

The case of Uber is a lesson in efficiency. Uber uses AI to match drivers with passengers, optimizing routes and minimizing wait times. The company's algorithms analyze data about driver availability, passenger demand, and traffic conditions to create the most efficient matches possible. It's a powerful tool that helps Uber provide a seamless and reliable service to its customers.

Optimizing Schedules: The Science of Timing

Optimizing schedules is the science of timing. AI-powered platforms use advanced algorithms to analyze data about worker availability, job requirements, and customer demand, creating optimized schedules that maximize efficiency and minimize downtime. It's like having a super-smart planner who can juggle multiple tasks and deadlines with ease.

The Case of Instacart: A Lesson in Timing

The case of Instacart is a lesson in timing. Instacart uses AI to optimize the schedules of its shoppers, matching them with grocery orders and creating efficient delivery routes. The company's algorithms analyze data about shopper availability, order volume, and delivery times to create the most efficient schedules possible. It's a powerful tool that helps Instacart provide a fast and reliable service to its customers.

The Benefits of the Gig Economy: Flexibility and Freedom

The benefits of the gig economy are flexibility and freedom. Workers in the gig economy have the freedom to choose their own hours, work for multiple clients, and even set their own prices. It's a liberating way of working that allows folks to balance their professional and personal lives, pursue their passions, and even travel the world.

The Case of Digital Nomads: A Lesson in Freedom

The case of digital nomads is a lesson in freedom. Digital nomads are workers in the gig economy who use technology to work remotely, traveling the world while earning a living. They take advantage of the flexibility and freedom of the gig economy to explore new places, meet new people, and experience new cultures. It's a liberating way of life that allows folks to combine work and adventure in a way that was never possible before.

The Challenges of the Gig Economy: Uncertainty and Insecurity

But the gig economy aingt all sunshine and roses. It also comes with its share of challenges, from uncertainty to insecurity. Workers in the gig economy often face unpredictable income, lack of benefits, and even job insecurity. It's a tough and often unforgiving way of working that requires resilience, adaptability, and a strong support network.

Chapter 12: AI and the Future of Work: Opportunities and Challenges

The Case of Job Insecurity: A Lesson in Resilience

The case of job insecurity is a lesson in resilience. Workers in the gig economy often face the constant threat of job loss, as clients come and go and projects end. They must be resilient, adaptable, and always on the lookout for new opportunities. It's a challenging way of working that requires a strong support network and a positive attitude.

The Role of AI in Addressing Challenges: Innovation and Solutions

AI plays a crucial role in addressing the challenges of the gig economy, offering innovative solutions and improving the lives of workers. Think of it like this: AI is like a super-smart problem solver, finding creative ways to tackle the toughest challenges and making the gig economy a better place for everyone.

Predicting Income: The Power of Data

Predicting income is the power of data. AI-powered platforms can use data to predict future income for workers in the gig economy, helping them plan their finances and make informed decisions. It's like having a super-smart financial advisor who can see into the future and guide you through the ups and downs of the gig economy.

The Case of Upwork: A Lesson in Prediction

The case of Upwork is a lesson in prediction. Upwork uses AI to predict future income for freelancers on its platform, helping them plan their finances and make informed decisions. The company's algorithms analyze data about job postings, client demand, and freelancer performance to create accurate and reliable income predictions. It's a powerful tool that helps freelancers navigate the uncertainties of the gig economy with confidence.

Providing Benefits: The Promise of Security

Providing benefits is the promise of security. AI-powered platforms can use data to identify workers in the gig economy who are eligible for benefits, such as health insurance, retirement plans, and even paid time off. It's like having a super-smart HR department that can ensure workers have the support and security they need to thrive in the gig economy.

The Case of Stride Health: A Lesson in Benefits

The case of Stride Health is a lesson in benefits. Stride Health uses AI to help gig workers find affordable health insurance, retirement plans, and other benefits. The company's algorithms analyze data about worker eligibility, plan options, and market trends to create personalized recommendations for each worker. It's a powerful tool that helps gig workers access the benefits they need to stay healthy, secure, and productive.

The Human Touch: The Role of Advocates, Policymakers, and Innovators

But the gig economy and the role of AI aingt just about technology. It's also about people. It's about the advocates, policymakers, and innovators who are pushing the boundaries of what's possible. It's about the visionaries who are dreaming of a future where the gig economy can help us transform the world like never before.

Advocates, policymakers, and innovators are a special breed. They're part champion, part strategist, part dreamer, and part problem solver. They know how to identify challenges, how to analyze solutions, and how to develop policies. But more importantly, they know how to communicate their findings in a way that's clear and compelling.

Think of it like this: an advocate is like a champion who can use AI to identify challenges and develop solutions. A policymaker is like a strategist who can use AI to develop new policies, improve existing ones, and even tailor benefits to individual needs. An innovator is like a dreamer who can use AI to create new technologies, improve existing ones, and even develop solutions to the challenges of the gig economy. Together, they're like a dynamic trio, working hand in hand to unlock the power of ethical AI.

The Future of the Gig Economy: A World of Possibilities

But despite the challenges, the future of the gig economy is bright. It's a future filled with possibilities, with opportunities to solve problems and improve lives. It's a future where AI can help us transform the world like never before, where it can help us make the world a safer, more efficient, and more prosperous place.

And it's a future that's already here. Every day, we're seeing new breakthroughs, new innovations, new ways of using AI to make the world a better place. It's exciting, it's inspiring, and it's just the beginning.

So, my friends, as we journey through this new frontier of work—the gig economy and the role of AI—let's remember the power and the potential that lies within. Let's remember the pioneers who came before us, the visionaries who dared to dream of a future where AI could help us transform the world like never before. And let's look forward to the exciting journey that lies ahead, as we continue to explore the boundless possibilities of artificial intelligence and the gig economy.

Practical Tips for Implementing AI in Businesses

Introduction: The AI Revolution

Folks, gather 'round and let me spin you a yarn about the AI revolution—practical tips for implementing AI in businesses. Now, I know what you're thinking: "AI in businesses? Sounds like something out of a futuristic novel." But fear not, my friends, for I'm here to make it all as clear as a summer's day. So, grab your favorite chair, pour yourself a glass of lemonade, and let's dive right in.

Understanding the Basics: The ABCs of AI

Before we dive into the nitty-gritty of implementing AI in your business, let's get a handle on the basics. AI, or artificial intelligence, is like having a super-smart assistant who can analyze data, make decisions, and even predict the future. It's a powerful tool that can transform industries and improve lives.

Machine Learning: The Brains Behind AI

Machine learning is the brains behind AI. It's like teaching a computer to think and learn from data. Think of it like this: machine learning is like a super-smart student who can analyze patterns, identify trends, and make predictions based on the data it's given. It's a powerful tool that can help businesses make better decisions, improve efficiency, and even create new opportunities.

Deep Learning: The Next Level

Deep learning is the next level of machine learning. It's like giving your super-smart student a PhD in data analysis. Deep learning uses complex algorithms and neural networks to analyze data at a deeper level, making it possible to solve even more complex

Chapter 12: AI and the Future of Work: Opportunities and Challenges

problems. It's a powerful tool that can help businesses push the boundaries of what's possible and achieve even greater success.

Identifying the Right Use Cases: Where AI Can Shine

The first step in implementing AI in your business is identifyng the right use cases. Think of it like this: AI is like a super-smart tool, and you gotta know where to use it to get the best results.

Customer Service: The Personal Touch

Customer service is one area where AI can shine. Think of it like this: AI can help you provide a more personalized and efficient customer experience. From chatbots that can answer customer questions 24/7 to personalized recommendations based on customer data, AI can help you build stronger relationships with your customers and improve their overall experience.

The Case of Amazon: A Lesson in Personalization

The case of Amazon is a lesson in personalization. Amazon uses AI to analyze customer data and provide personalized recommendations based on their browsing and purchase history. This personalized approach helps Amazon build stronger relationships with its customers and improve their overall experience. It's a powerful tool that can help businesses of all sizes provide a more personalized and efficient customer service.

Operational Efficiency: The Streamlined Approach

Operational efficiency is another area where AI can shine. Think of it like this: AI can help you streamline your operations, making them more efficient and cost-effective. From automating repetitive tasks to optimizing supply chains, AI can help you reduce costs, improve efficiency, and even increase productivity.

The Case of Walmart: A Lesson in Efficiency

The case of Walmart is a lesson in efficiency. Walmart uses AI to optimize its supply chain, predicting demand and adjusting inventory levels in real-time. This approach helps Walmart reduce costs, improve efficiency, and even increase sales. It's a powerful tool that can help businesses of all sizes streamline their operations and achieve greater success.

Gathering the Right Data: The Fuel for AI

The next step in implementing AI in your business is gathering the right data. Think of it like this: data is the fuel that powers AI. Without the right data, your AI wongt be able to make accurate predictions or provide valuable insights.

Quality Over Quantity: The Importance of Good Data

Quality over quantity is the importance of good data. Think of it like this: it's better to have a small amount of high-quality data than a large amount of low-quality data. High-quality data is accurate, complete, and relevant to your business goals. It's the kind of data that can help your AI make accurate predictions and provide valuable insights.

The Case of Google: A Lesson in Data Quality

The case of Google is a lesson in data quality. Google uses high-quality data to power its search engine, making it possible to provide accurate and relevant search results to its users. This approach helps Google maintain its position as the world's leading search engine and continue to provide value to its users. It's a powerful reminder of the importance of gathering high-quality data for your AI.

Data Privacy: The Ethical Consideration

Data privacy is the ethical consideration. Think of it like this: when you gather data, you gotta make sure you're doing it ethically and responsibly. That means getting consent from your customers, being transparent about how you're using their data, and protecting their privacy at all times. It's a crucial aspect of implementing AI in your business and one that cangt be overlooked.

The Case of GDPR: A Lesson in Privacy

The case of GDPR is a lesson in privacy. GDPR, or the General Data Protection Regulation, is a set of rules designed to protect the privacy of EU citizens. It requires businesses to be transparent about how they're collecting and using data, and to obtain consent from their customers before doing so. It's a powerful reminder of the importance of data privacy and the need to implement ethical data practices in your business.

Building the Right Team: The Experts You Need

The next step in implementing AI in your business is building the right team. Think of it like this: AI is a complex and ever-changing field, and you need a team of experts who can help you navigate the challenges and opportunities it presents.

Data Scientists: The Analysts

Data scientists are the analysts. They're the folks who can analyze data, identify patterns, and make predictions based on the insights they uncover. Think of it like this: data scientists are like detectives, sifting through mountains of data to find the clues that can help you make better decisions and achieve greater success.

The Case of Netflix: A Lesson in Data Science

The case of Netflix is a lesson in data science. Netflix uses data scientists to analyze viewer data and make personalized recommendations based on their watching history. This approach helps Netflix build stronger relationships with its viewers and improve their overall experience. It's a powerful reminder of the importance of having a team of data scientists who can help you make the most of your data.

AI Engineers: The Builders

AI engineers are the builders. They're the folks who can design, develop, and implement AI systems that meet your business needs. Think of it like this: AI engineers are like architects, designing and building the systems that can help you achieve your business goals and drive greater success.

The Case of Tesla: A Lesson in AI Engineering

The case of Tesla is a lesson in AI engineering. Tesla uses AI engineers to design and develop the autonomous driving systems that power its vehicles. This approach helps Tesla push the boundaries of what's possible and achieve even greater success in the automotive industry. It's a powerful reminder of the importance of having a team of AI engineers who can help you build the systems you need to succeed.

Choosing the Right Tools: The Technology You Need

The next step in implementing AI in your business is choosing the right tools. Think of it like this: AI is a complex and ever-changing field, and you need the right tools to help you navigate the challenges and opportunities it presents.

Cloud Platforms: The Foundation

Cloud platforms are the foundation. They provide the infrastructure and resources you need to build, deploy, and manage your AI systems. Think of it like this: cloud platforms are like the foundation of a building, supporting the entire structure and providing the stability you need to succeed.

The Case of AWS: A Lesson in Cloud Computing

The case of AWS is a lesson in cloud computing. AWS, or Amazon Web Services, provides a range of cloud-based tools and services that can help you build, deploy, and manage your AI systems. This approach helps businesses of all sizes take advantage of the power of AI and achieve even greater success. It's a powerful reminder of the importance of choosing the right cloud platform for your business.

AI Frameworks: The Building Blocks

AI frameworks are the building blocks. They provide the tools and libraries you need to develop and deploy your AI systems. Think of it like this: AI frameworks are like the building blocks of a structure, providing the components you need to create something powerful and effective.

The Case of TensorFlow: A Lesson in AI Frameworks

The case of TensorFlow is a lesson in AI frameworks. TensorFlow is an open-source AI framework developed by Google that provides a range of tools and libraries for developing and deploying AI systems. This approach helps businesses of all sizes take advantage of the power of AI and achieve even greater success. It's a powerful reminder of the importance of choosing the right AI framework for your business.

Measuring Success: The Metrics That Matter

The next step in implementing AI in your business is measuring success. Think of it like this: AI is a powerful tool, but you gotta know how to measure its impact to understand its true value.

Key Performance Indicators (KPIs): The Metrics That Matter

Key performance indicators, or KPIs, are the metrics that matter. They help you measure the impact of your AI systems and understand their true value. Think of it like this: KPIs are like the scorecard of a game, telling you how well you're doing and where you need to improve.

The Case of Uber: A Lesson in KPIs

The case of Uber is a lesson in KPIs. Uber uses a range of KPIs to measure the impact of its AI systems, from customer satisfaction to operational efficiency. This approach helps Uber understand the true value of its AI systems and make data-driven decisions that drive greater success. It's a powerful reminder of the importance of measuring success and using KPIs to guide your business decisions.

Return on Investment (ROI): The Bottom Line

Return on investment, or ROI, is the bottom line. It helps you understand the financial impact of your AI systems and ensure that they're delivering value to your business. Think of it like this: ROI is like the bottom line of a financial statement, telling you whether your investment in AI is paying off.

The Case of IBM: A Lesson in ROI

The case of IBM is a lesson in ROI. IBM uses ROI to measure the financial impact of its AI systems and ensure that they're delivering value to its business. This approach helps IBM make data-driven decisions that drive greater success and maximize the value of its AI investments. It's a powerful reminder of the importance of measuring ROI and ensuring that your AI systems are delivering value to your business.

Ethical Considerations: The Responsible Approach

The final step in implementing AI in your business is considering the ethical implications. Think of it like this: AI is a powerful tool, but it also comes with significant responsibilities. You gotta make sure you're using it ethically and responsibly to avoid causing harm and maintain the trust of your customers.

Bias and Fairness: The Ethical Dilemma

Bias and fairness are the ethical dilemma. Think of it like this: AI systems can be biased, making decisions that are unfair or discriminatory. It's your responsibility to ensure that your AI systems are fair and unbiased, treating all customers equally and avoiding any form of discrimination.

The Case of Amazon: A Lesson in Bias

The case of Amazon is a lesson in bias. In 2018, it was revealed that Amazongs AI-powered recruiting tool was biased against women. The tool was trained on historical data, which was predominantly male, and as a result, it favored male candidates over female candidates. It was a wake-up call about the dangers of bias in AI and the importance of ensuring fairness and equality in your AI systems.

Privacy and Security: The Ethical Responsibility

Privacy and security are the ethical responsibility. Think of it like this: when you gather data, you gotta make sure you're doing it ethically and responsibly. That means protecting the privacy of your customers, keeping their data secure, and being transparent about how you're using it. It's a crucial aspect of implementing AI in your business and one that cangt be overlooked.

The Case of Facebook: A Lesson in Privacy

The case of Facebook is a lesson in privacy. In 2018, it was revealed that Facebook had allowed the data of millions of its users to be accessed by Cambridge Analytica without their consent. This breach of privacy highlighted the importance of protecting customer data and being transparent about how it's being used. It's a powerful reminder of the ethical responsibilities that come with implementing AI in your business.

The Human Touch: The Role of Leaders and Innovators

But implementing AI in your business aingt just about technology. It's also about people. It's about the leaders and innovators who are pushing the boundaries of what's possible. It's about the visionaries who are dreaming of a future where AI can help us transform the world like never before.

Leaders and innovators are a special breed. They're part strategist, part visionary, part advocate, and part dreamer. They know how to identify opportunities, how to analyze challenges, and how to develop solutions. But more importantly, they know how to communicate their findings in a way that's clear and compelling.

Think of it like this: a leader is like a strategist who can use AI to identify opportunities and develop solutions. An innovator is like a visionary who can use AI to push the boundaries of what's possible and achieve even greater success. Together, they're like a dynamic duo, working hand in hand to unlock the power of ethical AI.

The Future of AI in Business: A World of Possibilities

Chapter 12: AI and the Future of Work: Opportunities and Challenges

But despite the challenges, the future of AI in business is bright. It's a future filled with possibilities, with opportunities to solve problems and improve lives. It's a future where AI can help us transform the world like never before, where it can help us make the world a safer, more efficient, and more prosperous place.

And it's a future that's already here. Every day, we're seeing new breakthroughs, new innovations, new ways of using AI to make the world a better place. It's exciting, it's inspiring, and it's just the beginning.

So, my friends, as we journey through this AI revolution—implementing AI in businesses—let's remember the power and the potential that lies within. Let's remember the pioneers who came before us, the visionaries who dared to dream of a future where AI could help us transform the world like never before. And let's look forward to the exciting journey that lies ahead, as we continue to explore the boundless possibilities of artificial intelligence and the future of business.

PRACTICAL TIPS FOR IMPLEMENTING AI IN BUSINESSES

Chapter 13: Getting Started with AI: A Roadmap for Businesses

Identifying AI Opportunities in Your Business

Introduction: The Gold Rush of AI

Folks, gather 'round and let me spin you a yarn about the gold rush of AI—identifying AI opportunities in your business. Now, I know what you're thinking: "AI opportunities? Sounds like something out of a business strategy book." But fear not, my friends, for I'm here to make it all as clear as a summer's day. So, grab your favorite chair, pour yourself a glass of lemonade, and let's dive right in.

Understanding the Landscape: The Lay of the Land

Before we start digging for gold, we gotta understand the lay of the land. Think of it like this: your business is a vast territory, filled with opportunities just waiting to be discovered. AI is like the gold rush, offering new ways to improve efficiency, enhance customer experiences, and even create new revenue streams.

The Power of Data: The Lifeblood of AI

The power of data is the lifeblood of AI. Think of it like this: data is the fuel that powers AI, making it possible to analyze patterns, identify trends, and make predictions. The more data you have, the more powerful your AI can be. It's like having a super-smart assistant who can see into the future and guide your business to success.

Chapter 13: Getting Started with AI: A Roadmap for Businesses

The Case of Walmart: A Lesson in Data Power

The case of Walmart is a lesson in data power. Walmart uses data to optimize its supply chain, predicting demand and adjusting inventory levels in real-time. This approach helps Walmart reduce costs, improve efficiency, and even increase sales. It's a powerful reminder of the importance of data in driving AI opportunities in your business.

Identifying Pain Points: The Problems to Solve

The first step in identifyng AI opportunities is pinpointing the pain points in your business. Think of it like this: pain points are like the obstacles on your journey to success. They're the problems that need solving, the challenges that need addressing. By identifyng these pain points, you can find the areas where AI can make the biggest impact.

Operational Inefficiencies: The Hidden Costs

Operational inefficiencies are the hidden costs. Think of it like this: inefficiencies in your operations can lead to wasted time, increased costs, and even reduced productivity. AI can help you identify and address these inefficiencies, streamlining your operations and improving your overall performance.

The Case of Amazon: A Lesson in Efficiency

The case of Amazon is a lesson in efficiency. Amazon uses AI to optimize its warehouse operations, from inventory management to order fulfillment. This approach helps Amazon reduce costs, improve efficiency, and even increase customer satisfaction. It's a powerful reminder of the importance of identifyng operational inefficiencies and using AI to address them.

Customer Dissatisfaction: The Silent Killer

Customer dissatisfaction is the silent killer. Think of it like this: unhappy customers can lead to lost sales, damaged reputations, and even reduced loyalty. AI can help you identify the root causes of customer dissatisfaction and develop solutions that improve the customer experience.

The Case of Delta Airlines: A Lesson in Customer Satisfaction

The case of Delta Airlines is a lesson in customer satisfaction. Delta uses AI to analyze customer feedback and identify the root causes of dissatisfaction. This approach helps Delta develop targeted solutions that improve the customer experience and increase loyalty. It's a powerful reminder of the importance of identifyng customer dissatisfaction and using AI to address it.

Analyzing Data: The Treasure Map

The next step in identifyng AI opportunities is analyzing your data. Think of it like this: data is like the treasure map, guiding you to the hidden opportunities in your business. By analyzing your data, you can uncover insights, identify trends, and even make predictions that can drive your business forward.

Descriptive Analytics: The What

Descriptive analytics is the what. Think of it like this: descriptive analytics helps you understand what has happened in your business. It's like looking in the rearview mirror, seeing the past and understanding the present. By analyzing historical data, you can identify trends, patterns, and even anomalies that can guide your business decisions.

The Case of Netflix: A Lesson in Descriptive Analytics

The case of Netflix is a lesson in descriptive analytics. Netflix uses descriptive analytics to understand viewer behavior, identifyng trends and patterns in their watching history. This approach helps Netflix make informed decisions about content creation and distribution, improving the overall viewer experience. It's a powerful reminder of the importance of descriptive analytics in identifyng AI opportunities in your business.

Predictive Analytics: The What If

Predictive analytics is the what if. Think of it like this: predictive analytics helps you understand what might happen in the future. It's like looking into a crystal ball, seeing the future and preparing for what's to come. By analyzing current data, you can make predictions about future trends, customer behavior, and even market conditions.

The Case of Uber: A Lesson in Predictive Analytics

The case of Uber is a lesson in predictive analytics. Uber uses predictive analytics to forecast demand for rides, adjusting prices and optimizing driver schedules in real-time. This approach helps Uber reduce wait times, improve efficiency, and even increase customer satisfaction. It's a powerful reminder of the importance of predictive analytics in identifyng AI opportunities in your business.

Prioritizing Opportunities: The Gold Nuggets

The next step in identifyng AI opportunities is prioritizing the gold nuggets. Think of it like this: not all opportunities are created equal. Some are more valuable, more impactful, and more urgent than others. By prioritizing these opportunities, you can focus your efforts on the areas that will deliver the greatest return on investment.

Impact Analysis: The Big Picture

Impact analysis is the big picture. Think of it like this: impact analysis helps you understand the potential impact of each AI opportunity on your business. It's like looking at the big picture, seeing the forest for the trees, and understanding the broader implications of your decisions. By conducting an impact analysis, you can prioritize the opportunities that will have the greatest impact on your business.

The Case of Google: A Lesson in Impact Analysis

The case of Google is a lesson in impact analysis. Google uses impact analysis to prioritize its AI initiatives, focusing on the areas that will have the greatest impact on its business. This approach helps Google make informed decisions about resource allocation, project prioritization, and even strategic direction. It's a powerful reminder of the importance of impact analysis in identifyng AI opportunities in your business.

Feasibility Analysis: The Reality Check

Feasibility analysis is the reality check. Think of it like this: feasibility analysis helps you understand the practicality of each AI opportunity. It's like looking at the nuts and bolts, seeing the details, and understanding the challenges and limitations of your plans. By conducting a feasibility analysis, you can prioritize the opportunities that are most likely to succeed.

The Case of Tesla: A Lesson in Feasibility Analysis

The case of Tesla is a lesson in feasibility analysis. Tesla uses feasibility analysis to evaluate the practicality of its AI initiatives, from autonomous driving to battery technology. This approach helps Tesla make informed decisions about project feasibility, resource allocation, and even risk management. It's a powerful reminder of the importance of feasibility analysis in identifyng AI opportunities in your business.

Building a Roadmap: The Path to Success

The final step in identifyng AI opportunities is building a roadmap to success. Think of it like this: a roadmap is like the path to success, guiding you through the challenges and opportunities that lie ahead. By building a roadmap, you can plan your journey, set your goals, and even measure your progress along the way.

Defining Objectives: The Destination

Defining objectives is the destination. Think of it like this: objectives are like the destination on your journey to success. They're the goals you want to achieve, the milestones you want to reach, and the outcomes you want to accomplish. By defining clear and measurable objectives, you can focus your efforts and drive your business forward.

The Case of Apple: A Lesson in Objective Setting

The case of Apple is a lesson in objective setting. Apple sets clear and measurable objectives for its AI initiatives, from product innovation to customer experience. This approach helps Apple focus its efforts, drive innovation, and even achieve greater success. It's a powerful reminder of the importance of defining objectives in identifyng AI opportunities in your business.

Developing Strategies: The Plan of Action

Developing strategies is the plan of action. Think of it like this: strategies are like the plan of action, the steps you need to take to achieve your objectives. They're the roadmap that guides your journey, the blueprint that shapes your success. By developing clear and effective strategies, you can turn your AI opportunities into reality.

The Case of Microsoft: A Lesson in Strategy Development

The case of Microsoft is a lesson in strategy development. Microsoft develops clear and effective strategies for its AI initiatives, from cloud computing to enterprise solutions. This approach helps Microsoft turn its AI opportunities into reality, achieving greater success and driving innovation in the tech industry. It's a powerful reminder of the importance of developing strategies in identifyng AI opportunities in your business.

The Human Touch: The Role of Leaders and Innovators

But identifyng AI opportunities in your business aingt just about technology. It's also about people. It's about the leaders and innovators who are pushing the boundaries of what's possible. It's about the visionaries who are dreaming of a future where AI can help us transform the world like never before.

Leaders and innovators are a special breed. They're part strategist, part visionary, part advocate, and part dreamer. They know how to identify opportunities, how to analyze challenges, and how to develop solutions. But more importantly, they know how to communicate their findings in a way that's clear and compelling.

Think of it like this: a leader is like a strategist who can use AI to identify opportunities and develop solutions. An innovator is like a visionary who can use AI to push the boundaries of what's possible and achieve even greater success. Together, they're like a dynamic duo, working hand in hand to unlock the power of ethical AI.

The Future of AI in Business: A World of Possibilities

But despite the challenges, the future of AI in business is bright. It's a future filled with possibilities, with opportunities to solve problems and improve lives. It's a future where AI can help us transform the world like never before, where it can help us make the world a safer, more efficient, and more prosperous place.

And it's a future that's already here. Every day, we're seeing new breakthroughs, new innovations, new ways of using AI to make the world a better place. It's exciting, it's inspiring, and it's just the beginning.

So, my friends, as we journey through this gold rush of AI—identifyng AI opportunities in your business—let's remember the power and the potential that lies within. Let's remember the pioneers who came before us, the visionaries who dared to dream of a future where AI could help us transform the world like never before. And let's look forward to the exciting journey that lies ahead, as we continue to explore the boundless possibilities of artificial intelligence and the future of business.

Building an AI-Ready Team and Infrastructure

Introduction: The New Frontier

Folks, gather 'round and let me spin you a yarn about the new frontier—building an AI-ready team and infrastructure. Now, I know what you're thinking: "AI-ready team and infrastructure? Sounds like something out of a futuristic novel." But fear not, my friends, for I'm here to make it all as clear as a summer's day. So, grab your favorite chair, pour yourself a glass of lemonade, and let's dive right in.

Understanding the Basics: The ABCs of AI

Before we start building our AI-ready team and infrastructure, let's get a handle on the basics. AI, or artificial intelligence, is like having a super-smart assistant who can analyze data, make decisions, and even predict the future. It's a powerful tool that can transform industries and improve lives.

Machine Learning: The Brains Behind AI

Machine learning is the brains behind AI. It's like teaching a computer to think and learn from data. Think of it like this: machine learning is like a super-smart student who can analyze patterns, identify trends, and make predictions based on the data it's given. It's a powerful tool that can help businesses make better decisions, improve efficiency, and even create new opportunities.

Deep Learning: The Next Level

Deep learning is the next level of machine learning. It's like giving your super-smart student a PhD in data analysis. Deep learning uses complex algorithms and neural networks to analyze data at a deeper level, making it possible to solve even more complex problems. It's a powerful tool that can help businesses push the boundaries of what's possible and achieve even greater success.

Building the Team: The Experts You Need

The first step in building an AI-ready team is gathering the right experts. Think of it like this: AI is a complex and ever-changing field, and you need a team of specialists who can help you navigate the challenges and opportunities it presents.

Data Scientists: The Analysts

Data scientists are the analysts. They're the folks who can analyze data, identify patterns, and make predictions based on the insights they uncover. Think of it like this: data scientists are like detectives, sifting through mountains of data to find the clues that can help you make better decisions and achieve greater success.

The Case of Netflix: A Lesson in Data Science

The case of Netflix is a lesson in data science. Netflix uses data scientists to analyze viewer data and make personalized recommendations based on their watching history. This approach helps Netflix build stronger relationships with its viewers and improve their overall experience. It's a powerful reminder of the importance of having a team of data scientists who can help you make the most of your data.

AI Engineers: The Builders

AI engineers are the builders. They're the folks who can design, develop, and implement AI systems that meet your business needs. Think of it like this: AI engineers are like architects, designing and building the systems that can help you achieve your business goals and drive greater success.

The Case of Tesla: A Lesson in AI Engineering

The case of Tesla is a lesson in AI engineering. Tesla uses AI engineers to design and develop the autonomous driving systems that power its vehicles. This approach helps Tesla push the boundaries of what's possible and achieve even greater success in the automotive industry. It's a powerful reminder of the importance of having a team of AI engineers who can help you build the systems you need to succeed.

Data Engineers: The Plumbers

Data engineers are the plumbers. They're the folks who can design, build, and maintain the data infrastructure that supports your AI systems. Think of it like this: data engineers are like the plumbers who keep the water flowing, ensuring that your data is clean, reliable, and accessible when you need it.

The Case of Google: A Lesson in Data Engineering

The case of Google is a lesson in data engineering. Google uses data engineers to design and maintain the data infrastructure that supports its search engine, making it possible to provide accurate and relevant search results to its users. This approach helps Google maintain its position as the world's leading search engine and continue to provide value to its users. It's a powerful reminder of the importance of having a team of data engineers who can help you build and maintain the data infrastructure you need to succeed.

Building the Infrastructure: The Foundation You Need

The next step in building an AI-ready team and infrastructure is laying the foundation. Think of it like this: AI is a powerful tool, but it needs the right infrastructure to support it. Without the right infrastructure, your AI systems wongt be able to function effectively or deliver the results you need.

Cloud Platforms: The Backbone

Cloud platforms are the backbone. They provide the infrastructure and resources you need to build, deploy, and manage your AI systems. Think of it like this: cloud platforms are like the backbone of a body, supporting the entire structure and providing the stability you need to succeed.

The Case of AWS: A Lesson in Cloud Computing

The case of AWS is a lesson in cloud computing. AWS, or Amazon Web Services, provides a range of cloud-based tools and services that can help you build, deploy, and manage your AI systems. This approach helps businesses of all sizes take advantage of the power of AI and achieve even greater success. It's a powerful reminder of the importance of choosing the right cloud platform for your business.

AI Frameworks: The Building Blocks

AI frameworks are the building blocks. They provide the tools and libraries you need to develop and deploy your AI systems. Think of it like this: AI frameworks are like the building blocks of a structure, providing the components you need to create something powerful and effective.

The Case of TensorFlow: A Lesson in AI Frameworks

The case of TensorFlow is a lesson in AI frameworks. TensorFlow is an open-source AI framework developed by Google that provides a range of tools and libraries for developing and deploying AI systems. This approach helps businesses of all sizes take advantage of the power of AI and achieve even greater success. It's a powerful reminder of the importance of choosing the right AI framework for your business.

Data Storage: The Vault

Data storage is the vault. It's where you keep all your valuable data, ensuring that it's safe, secure, and accessible when you need it. Think of it like this: data storage is like the vault in a bank, protecting your most valuable assets and providing the security you need to succeed.

The Case of Dropbox: A Lesson in Data Storage

The case of Dropbox is a lesson in data storage. Dropbox provides a range of data storage solutions that can help you keep your data safe, secure, and accessible when you need it. This approach helps businesses of all sizes protect their most valuable assets and ensure that their data is always available when they need it. It's a powerful reminder of the importance of choosing the right data storage solution for your business.

Training the Team: The Knowledge You Need

The next step in building an AI-ready team and infrastructure is training the team. Think of it like this: AI is a complex and ever-changing field, and your team needs the knowledge and skills to keep up with the latest developments and best practices.

Continuous Learning: The Key to Success

Continuous learning is the key to success. Think of it like this: the world of AI is always changing, and your team needs to be constantly learning and adapting to keep up with the latest developments and best practices. By encouraging continuous learning, you can ensure that your team has the knowledge and skills they need to succeed.

The Case of IBM: A Lesson in Continuous Learning

The case of IBM is a lesson in continuous learning. IBM invests heavily in the continuous learning and development of its employees, offering a wide range of training programs, from online courses to in-person workshops, from technical skills to soft skills. This approach helps IBM stay ahead of the curve, adapt to new technologies, and prepare for the future. It's a powerful reminder of the importance of encouraging continuous learning in your business.

Mentorship Programs: The Guidance You Need

Mentorship programs are the guidance you need. Think of it like this: mentorship programs provide the guidance and support your team needs to develop their skills, gain experience, and achieve their goals. By implementing mentorship programs, you can help your team grow and succeed in the world of AI.

The Case of Microsoft: A Lesson in Mentorship

The case of Microsoft is a lesson in mentorship. Microsoft implements mentorship programs that pair experienced employees with new hires, providing them with the guidance and support they need to develop their skills, gain experience, and achieve their goals. This approach helps Microsoft build a strong and capable team that can drive innovation and achieve greater success. It's a powerful reminder of the importance of implementing mentorship programs in your business.

Measuring Success: The Metrics That Matter

The final step in building an AI-ready team and infrastructure is measuring success. Think of it like this: AI is a powerful tool, but you gotta know how to measure its impact to understand its true value.

Key Performance Indicators (KPIs): The Metrics That Matter

Key performance indicators, or KPIs, are the metrics that matter. They help you measure the impact of your AI systems and understand their true value. Think of it like this: KPIs are like the scorecard of a game, telling you how well you're doing and where you need to improve.

The Case of Uber: A Lesson in KPIs

The case of Uber is a lesson in KPIs. Uber uses a range of KPIs to measure the impact of its AI systems, from customer satisfaction to operational efficiency. This approach helps Uber understand the true value of its AI systems and make data-driven decisions that drive greater success. It's a powerful reminder of the importance of measuring success and using KPIs to guide your business decisions.

Return on Investment (ROI): The Bottom Line

Return on investment, or ROI, is the bottom line. It helps you understand the financial impact of your AI systems and ensure that they're delivering value to your business. Think of it like this: ROI is like the bottom line of a financial statement, telling you whether your investment in AI is paying off.

The Case of IBM: A Lesson in ROI

The case of IBM is a lesson in ROI. IBM uses ROI to measure the financial impact of its AI systems and ensure that they're delivering value to its business. This approach helps IBM make data-driven decisions that drive greater success and maximize the value of its AI investments. It's a powerful reminder of the importance of measuring ROI and ensuring that your AI systems are delivering value to your business.

The Human Touch: The Role of Leaders and Innovators

Chapter 13: Getting Started with AI: A Roadmap for Businesses

But building an AI-ready team and infrastructure aingt just about technology. It's also about people. It's about the leaders and innovators who are pushing the boundaries of what's possible. It's about the visionaries who are dreaming of a future where AI can help us transform the world like never before.

Leaders and innovators are a special breed. They're part strategist, part visionary, part advocate, and part dreamer. They know how to identify opportunities, how to analyze challenges, and how to develop solutions. But more importantly, they know how to communicate their findings in a way that's clear and compelling.

Think of it like this: a leader is like a strategist who can use AI to identify opportunities and develop solutions. An innovator is like a visionary who can use AI to push the boundaries of what's possible and achieve even greater success. Together, they're like a dynamic duo, working hand in hand to unlock the power of ethical AI.

The Future of AI in Business: A World of Possibilities

But despite the challenges, the future of AI in business is bright. It's a future filled with possibilities, with opportunities to solve problems and improve lives. It's a future where AI can help us transform the world like never before, where it can help us make the world a safer, more efficient, and more prosperous place.

And it's a future that's already here. Every day, we're seeing new breakthroughs, new innovations, new ways of using AI to make the world a better place. It's exciting, it's inspiring, and it's just the beginning.

So, my friends, as we journey through this new frontier—building an AI-ready team and infrastructure—let's remember the power and the potential that lies within. Let's remember the pioneers who came before us, the visionaries who dared to dream of a future where AI could help us transform the world like never before. And let's look forward to the exciting journey that lies ahead, as we continue to explore the boundless possibilities of artificial intelligence and the future of business.

Chapter 13: Getting Started with AI: A Roadmap for Businesses

Case Study: How Small Businesses Are Leveraging AI

Introduction: The Little Guys and the Big Ideas

Folks, gather 'round and let me spin you a yarn about the little guys and the big ideas—how small businesses are leveraging AI. Now, I know what you're thinking: "AI in small businesses? Sounds like something out of a futuristic novel." But fear not, my friends, for I'm here to make it all as clear as a summer's day. So, grab your favorite chair, pour yourself a glass of lemonade, and let's dive right in.

The Power of AI: The Great Equalizer

Artificial intelligence is revolutionizing the world as we know it. From healthcare to finance, from transportation to entertainment, AI is transforming industries and improving lives. It's like having a super-smart assistant who can analyze data, make decisions, and even predict the future. But here's the kicker: AI aingt just for the big guys. It's the great equalizer, giving small businesses the power to compete with the giants.

The Case of Square: A Lesson in Leveling the Playing Field

The case of Square is a lesson in leveling the playing field. Square is a small business that provides payment processing solutions to other small businesses. By leveraging AI, Square can offer advanced analytics and insights to its customers, helping them make better decisions and improve their operations. It's a powerful reminder that AI can help small businesses compete with the big guys and achieve greater success.

Customer Service: The Personal Touch

One of the biggest challenges for small businesses is providing excellent customer service. With limited resources and manpower, it can be tough to keep up with customer demands. But AI is changing the game, offering new ways to provide a more personalized and efficient customer experience.

Chatbots: The 24/7 Assistants

Chatbots are the 24/7 assistants. Think of it like this: chatbots are like having a super-smart customer service representative who can answer questions, provide information, and even make recommendations—all without taking a break. By leveraging AI-powered chatbots, small businesses can provide round-the-clock customer support, improving customer satisfaction and loyalty.

The Case of ManyChat: A Lesson in Chatbot Magic

The case of ManyChat is a lesson in chatbot magic. ManyChat is a small business that provides a chatbot platform for other small businesses. By leveraging AI, ManyChat can help its customers create personalized and engaging chatbots that improve customer service and drive sales. It's a powerful reminder that AI can help small businesses provide a more personalized and efficient customer experience.

Personalized Recommendations: The Secret Sauce

Personalized recommendations are the secret sauce. Think of it like this: AI can analyze customer data to identify preferences, behaviors, and even emotions. By leveraging this data, small businesses can provide personalized recommendations that resonate with their customers, improving the overall customer experience and driving sales.

The Case of Stitch Fix: A Lesson in Personalization

The case of Stitch Fix is a lesson in personalization. Stitch Fix is a small business that provides personalized clothing recommendations to its customers. By leveraging AI, Stitch Fix can analyze customer data to identify preferences and behaviors, providing personalized recommendations that resonate with their customers. This approach helps Stitch Fix improve the overall customer experience and drive sales. It's a powerful reminder that AI can help small businesses provide a more personalized and engaging customer experience.

Operational Efficiency: The Streamlined Approach

Another big challenge for small businesses is operational efficiency. With limited resources and manpower, it can be tough to keep up with the demands of running a business. But AI is changing the game, offering new ways to streamline operations and improve efficiency.

Automation: The Time Saver

Automation is the time saver. Think of it like this: AI can automate repetitive and time-consuming tasks, freeing up valuable resources and manpower for more important activities. By leveraging AI-powered automation, small businesses can streamline their operations, improving efficiency and productivity.

The Case of Zapier: A Lesson in Automation

The case of Zapier is a lesson in automation. Zapier is a small business that provides an automation platform for other small businesses. By leveraging AI, Zapier can help its customers automate repetitive tasks, freeing up valuable resources and manpower for more important activities. This approach helps small businesses streamline their operations and improve efficiency and productivity. It's a powerful reminder that AI can help small businesses save time and resources, focusing on what really matters.

Inventory Management: The Balancing Act

Inventory management is the balancing act. Think of it like this: AI can analyze sales data, predict demand, and even optimize inventory levels. By leveraging AI-powered inventory management, small businesses can reduce waste, improve efficiency, and even increase sales.

The Case of Lightspeed: A Lesson in Inventory Management

The case of Lightspeed is a lesson in inventory management. Lightspeed is a small business that provides a point-of-sale and inventory management platform for other small businesses. By leveraging AI, Lightspeed can help its customers analyze sales data, predict demand, and optimize inventory levels. This approach helps small businesses reduce waste, improve efficiency, and even increase sales. It's a powerful reminder that AI can help small businesses manage their inventory more effectively and achieve greater success.

Marketing and Sales: The Growth Engine

Marketing and sales are the growth engine. Think of it like this: AI can analyze customer data, identify trends, and even predict future behaviors. By leveraging this data, small businesses can create more effective marketing campaigns, target the right customers, and even increase sales.

Targeted Marketing: The Bullseye

Targeted marketing is the bullseye. Think of it like this: AI can analyze customer data to identify preferences, behaviors, and even emotions. By leveraging this data, small businesses can create more effective marketing campaigns that resonate with their target audience, improving the overall customer experience and driving sales.

Chapter 13: Getting Started with AI: A Roadmap for Businesses

The Case of Mailchimp: A Lesson in Targeted Marketing

The case of Mailchimp is a lesson in targeted marketing. Mailchimp is a small business that provides a marketing automation platform for other small businesses. By leveraging AI, Mailchimp can help its customers analyze customer data, identify preferences and behaviors, and create more effective marketing campaigns that resonate with their target audience. This approach helps small businesses improve the overall customer experience and drive sales. It's a powerful reminder that AI can help small businesses create more effective and engaging marketing campaigns.

Sales Forecasting: The Crystal Ball

Sales forecasting is the crystal ball. Think of it like this: AI can analyze sales data, identify trends, and even predict future behaviors. By leveraging this data, small businesses can create more accurate sales forecasts, improving their overall business strategy and achieving greater success.

The Case of Salesforce: A Lesson in Sales Forecasting

The case of Salesforce is a lesson in sales forecasting. Salesforce is a small business that provides a customer relationship management (CRM) platform for other small businesses. By leveraging AI, Salesforce can help its customers analyze sales data, identify trends, and create more accurate sales forecasts. This approach helps small businesses improve their overall business strategy and achieve greater success. It's a powerful reminder that AI can help small businesses create more accurate and effective sales forecasts.

The Human Touch: The Role of Leaders and Innovators

But leveraging AI in small businesses aingt just about technology. It's also about people. It's about the leaders and innovators who are pushing the boundaries of what's possible. It's about the visionaries who are dreaming of a future where AI can help us transform the world like never before.

Leaders and innovators are a special breed. They're part strategist, part visionary, part advocate, and part dreamer. They know how to identify opportunities, how to analyze challenges, and how to develop solutions. But more importantly, they know how to communicate their findings in a way that's clear and compelling.

Think of it like this: a leader is like a strategist who can use AI to identify opportunities and develop solutions. An innovator is like a visionary who can use AI to push the boundaries of what's possible and achieve even greater success. Together, they're like a dynamic duo, working hand in hand to unlock the power of ethical AI.

The Future of AI in Small Businesses: A World of Possibilities

But despite the challenges, the future of AI in small businesses is bright. It's a future filled with possibilities, with opportunities to solve problems and improve lives. It's a future where AI can help us transform the world like never before, where it can help us make the world a safer, more efficient, and more prosperous place.

And it's a future that's already here. Every day, we're seeing new breakthroughs, new innovations, new ways of using AI to make the world a better place. It's exciting, it's inspiring, and it's just the beginning.

So, my friends, as we journey through this new frontier—how small businesses are leveraging AI—let's remember the power and the potential that lies within. Let's remember the pioneers who came before us, the visionaries who dared to dream of a future where AI could help us transform the world like never before. And let's look forward to the exciting journey that lies ahead, as we continue to explore the boundless possibilities of artificial intelligence and the future of small businesses.

Chapter 14: Data Strategy: The Fuel for AI Success

Collecting, Storing, and Managing Data Effectively

Introduction: The Gold Rush of Data

Folks, gather 'round and let me spin you a yarn about the gold rush of data—collecting, storing, and managing it effectively. Now, I know what you're thinking: "Data management? Sounds like something out of a tech manual." But fear not, my friends, for I'm here to make it all as clear as a summer's day. So, grab your favorite chair, pour yourself a glass of lemonade, and let's dive right in.

The Power of Data: The Lifeblood of AI

Data is the lifeblood of AI. Think of it like this: data is the fuel that powers AI, making it possible to analyze patterns, identify trends, and make predictions. The more data you have, the more powerful your AI can be. It's like having a super-smart assistant who can see into the future and guide your business to success.

The Case of Google: A Lesson in Data Power

The case of Google is a lesson in data power. Google uses data to power its search engine, making it possible to provide accurate and relevant search results to its users. This approach helps Google maintain its position as the world's leading search engine and continue to provide value to its users. It's a powerful reminder of the importance of data in driving AI opportunities in your business.

Collecting Data: The Treasure Hunt

Chapter 14: Data Strategy: The Fuel for AI Success

The first step in managing data effectively is collecting it. Think of it like this: data collection is like a treasure hunt, where you're searching for valuable information that can help you make better decisions and achieve greater success.

Sources of Data: The Treasure Map

Sources of data are the treasure map. Think of it like this: data can come from a variety of sources, from customer interactions to social media, from sensors to IoT devices. By identifyng the right sources of data, you can gather the information you need to make better decisions and achieve greater success.

The Case of Amazon: A Lesson in Data Collection

The case of Amazon is a lesson in data collection. Amazon collects data from a variety of sources, from customer interactions to product reviews, from browsing history to purchase history. This approach helps Amazon gather the information it needs to make better decisions and improve the overall customer experience. It's a powerful reminder of the importance of identifyng the right sources of data and collecting the information you need to succeed.

Data Quality: The Gold Standard

Data quality is the gold standard. Think of it like this: it's better to have a small amount of high-quality data than a large amount of low-quality data. High-quality data is accurate, complete, and relevant to your business goals. It's the kind of data that can help your AI make accurate predictions and provide valuable insights.

The Case of IBM: A Lesson in Data Quality

The case of IBM is a lesson in data quality. IBM focuses on collecting high-quality data that is accurate, complete, and relevant to its business goals. This approach helps IBM ensure that its AI systems can make accurate predictions and provide valuable insights. It's a powerful reminder of the importance of focusing on data quality and collecting the information you need to succeed.

Storing Data: The Vault

The next step in managing data effectively is storing it. Think of it like this: data storage is like the vault in a bank, protecting your most valuable assets and providing the security you need to succeed.

Data Storage Solutions: The Safe

Data storage solutions are the safe. Think of it like this: data storage solutions provide the infrastructure and resources you need to store your data safely and securely. From cloud storage to on-premises solutions, from databases to data lakes, there are a variety of options available to meet your business needs.

The Case of Dropbox: A Lesson in Data Storage

The case of Dropbox is a lesson in data storage. Dropbox provides a range of data storage solutions that can help you keep your data safe, secure, and accessible when you need it. This approach helps businesses of all sizes protect their most valuable assets and ensure that their data is always available when they need it. It's a powerful reminder of the importance of choosing the right data storage solution for your business.

Data Security: The Lock and Key

Data security is the lock and key. Think of it like this: data security is about protecting your data from unauthorized access, theft, and misuse. It's about ensuring that your data is safe, secure, and only accessible to those who need it.

The Case of Apple: A Lesson in Data Security

The case of Apple is a lesson in data security. Apple focuses on protecting its customers' data from unauthorized access, theft, and misuse. This approach helps Apple build trust with its customers and ensure that their data is safe and secure. It's a powerful reminder of the importance of focusing on data security and protecting your most valuable assets.

Managing Data: The Art of Organization

The final step in managing data effectively is organizing it. Think of it like this: data management is like the art of organization, ensuring that your data is structured, accessible, and easy to use.

Data Governance: The Rules of the Game

Data governance is the rules of the game. Think of it like this: data governance is about establisheng policies, procedures, and standards for managing your data. It's about ensuring that your data is consistent, reliable, and accessible when you need it.

The Case of Microsoft: A Lesson in Data Governance

The case of Microsoft is a lesson in data governance. Microsoft establishes policies, procedures, and standards for managing its data, ensuring that it is consistent, reliable, and accessible when needed. This approach helps Microsoft maintain the integrity of its data and ensure that it is always available when needed. It's a powerful reminder of the importance of data governance and establisheng the rules of the game.

Data Integration: The Puzzle Pieces

Data integration is the puzzle pieces. Think of it like this: data integration is about combining data from different sources and systems to create a unified view of your business. It's about ensuring that your data is connected, accessible, and easy to use.

The Case of Salesforce: A Lesson in Data Integration

The case of Salesforce is a lesson in data integration. Salesforce combines data from different sources and systems to create a unified view of its customers, providing valuable insights and improving the overall customer experience. This approach helps Salesforce make better decisions and achieve greater success. It's a powerful reminder of the importance of data integration and combining the puzzle pieces to create a unified view of your business.

The Human Touch: The Role of Data Managers and Analysts

But collecting, storing, and managing data effectively aingt just about technology. It's also about people. It's about the data managers and analysts who are pushing the boundaries of what's possible. It's about the visionaries who are dreaming of a future where data can help us transform the world like never before.

Data managers and analysts are a special breed. They're part detective, part architect, part advocate, and part dreamer. They know how to identify data sources, how to analyze data quality, and how to develop solutions. But more importantly, they know how to communicate their findings in a way that's clear and compelling.

Think of it like this: a data manager is like a detective who can use data to identify sources and analyze quality. A data analyst is like an architect who can use data to develop solutions and achieve greater success. Together, they're like a dynamic duo, working hand in hand to unlock the power of ethical data management.

The Future of Data Management: A World of Possibilities

But despite the challenges, the future of data management is bright. It's a future filled with possibilities, with opportunities to solve problems and improve lives. It's a future where data can help us transform the world like never before, where it can help us make the world a safer, more efficient, and more prosperous place.

And it's a future that's already here. Every day, we're seeing new breakthroughs, new innovations, new ways of using data to make the world a better place. It's exciting, it's inspiring, and it's just the beginning.

So, my friends, as we journey through this gold rush of data—collecting, storing, and managing it effectively—let's remember the power and the potential that lies within. Let's remember the pioneers who came before us, the visionaries who dared to dream of a future where data could help us transform the world like never before. And let's look forward to the exciting journey that lies ahead, as we continue to explore the boundless possibilities of data management and the future of business.

Data Privacy and Security Best Practices

Introduction: The Guardians of Data

Folks, gather 'round and let me spin you a yarn about the guardians of data—data privacy and security best practices. Now, I know what you're thinking: "Data privacy and security? Sounds like something out of a tech manual." But fear not, my friends, for I'm here to make it all as clear as a summer's day. So, grab your favorite chair, pour yourself a glass of lemonade, and let's dive right in.

The Importance of Data Privacy: The Trust Factor

Data privacy is the trust factor. Think of it like this: when you collect data from your customers, you're entering into a sacred trust. They're sharing their personal information with you, expecting that you'll keep it safe and secure. Breaking that trust can have serious consequences, from loss of business to legal troubles. It's a responsibility that cangt be taken lightly.

The Case of Facebook: A Lesson in Trust

The case of Facebook is a lesson in trust. In 2018, it was revealed that Facebook had allowed the data of millions of its users to be accessed by Cambridge Analytica without their consent. This breach of trust highlighted the importance of protecting customer data and being transparent about how it's being used. It's a powerful reminder of the importance of data privacy and the need to maintain the trust of your customers.

The Importance of Data Security: The Fortress

Data security is the fortress. Think of it like this: data security is about protecting your data from unauthorized access, theft, and misuse. It's about ensuring that your data is safe, secure, and only accessible to those who need it. Without strong data security, your business is vulnerable to attacks, breaches, and even legal consequences.

The Case of Equifax: A Lesson in Vulnerability

The case of Equifax is a lesson in vulnerability. In 2017, Equifax suffered a massive data breach that exposed the personal information of over 147 million people. This breach highlighted the importance of strong data security and the need to protect your data from unauthorized access, theft, and misuse. It's a powerful reminder of the importance of data security and the need to build a fortress around your data.

Best Practices for Data Privacy: The Golden Rules

Now, let's talk about the golden rules—the best practices for data privacy. These are the guidelines that will help you maintain the trust of your customers and protect their personal information.

Transparency: The Open Book

Transparency is the open book. Think of it like this: being transparent about how you collect, use, and store data is crucial for building trust with your customers. They need to know what information you're collecting, why you're collecting it, and how you're using it. By being transparent, you can build a strong and trusting relationship with your customers.

The Case of Apple: A Lesson in Transparency

The case of Apple is a lesson in transparency. Apple is known for its strong commitment to data privacy and transparency. The company provides clear and detailed information about how it collects, uses, and stores customer data. This approach helps Apple build trust with its customers and ensure that their data is safe and secure. It's a powerful reminder of the importance of transparency in data privacy.

Consent: The Agreement

Consent is the agreement. Think of it like this: before you collect any data from your customers, you need to get their explicit consent. This means asking for their permission and explaining exactly what data you're collecting and how you're going to use it. By obtaining consent, you can ensure that your customers are fully aware of and agree to your data collection practices.

The Case of GDPR: A Lesson in Consent

The case of GDPR is a lesson in consent. GDPR, or the General Data Protection Regulation, is a set of rules designed to protect the privacy of EU citizens. One of its key requirements is that companies must obtain explicit consent from their customers before collecting any personal data. This approach helps ensure that customers are fully aware of and agree to the data collection practices. It's a powerful reminder of the importance of obtaining consent in data privacy.

Data Minimization: The Less is More Approach

Data minimization is the less is more approach. Think of it like this: only collect the data you absolutely need. The less data you have, the less risk there is of it being compromised. By minimizing the amount of data you collect, you can reduce the risk of data breaches and ensure that your customers' personal information is protected.

The Case of Google: A Lesson in Data Minimization

The case of Google is a lesson in data minimization. Google focuses on collecting only the data it absolutely needs to provide its services. This approach helps Google reduce the risk of data breaches and ensure that its customers' personal information is protected. It's a powerful reminder of the importance of data minimization in data privacy.

Best Practices for Data Security: The Ironclad Rules

Now, let's talk about the ironclad rules—the best practices for data security. These are the guidelines that will help you protect your data from unauthorized access, theft, and misuse.

Encryption: The Lock and Key

Encryption is the lock and key. Think of it like this: encryption is like putting a lock on your data, making it unreadable to anyone who doesngt have the key. By encrypting your data, you can ensure that it is safe and secure, even if it falls into the wrong hands.

The Case of WhatsApp: A Lesson in Encryption

The case of WhatsApp is a lesson in encryption. WhatsApp uses end-to-end encryption to protect its users' messages, ensuring that only the sender and the recipient can read them. This approach helps WhatsApp protect its users' data from unauthorized access, theft, and misuse. It's a powerful reminder of the importance of encryption in data security.

Access Control: The Gatekeeper

Access control is the gatekeeper. Think of it like this: access control is about limiting who can access your data and what they can do with it. By implementing strong access controls, you can ensure that only authorized individuals have access to your data and that they can only perform the actions they are permitted to.

The Case of Amazon Web Services (AWS): A Lesson in Access Control

The case of Amazon Web Services (AWS) is a lesson in access control. AWS provides robust access control mechanisms that allow businesses to limit who can access their data and what they can do with it. This approach helps businesses protect their data from unauthorized access, theft, and misuse. It's a powerful reminder of the importance of access control in data security.

Regular Updates: The Maintenance Plan

Regular updates are the maintenance plan. Think of it like this: just like you need to maintain your car to keep it running smoothly, you need to regularly update your data security measures to keep them effective. This includes patching vulnerabilities, updating software, and even reviewing your security policies and procedures.

The Case of Microsoft: A Lesson in Regular Updates

The case of Microsoft is a lesson in regular updates. Microsoft regularly releases updates and patches for its software to address vulnerabilities and improve security. This approach helps Microsoft protect its customers' data from unauthorized access, theft, and misuse. It's a powerful reminder of the importance of regular updates in data security.

The Human Touch: The Role of Data Privacy Officers and Security Experts

But data privacy and security best practices aingt just about technology. It's also about people. It's about the data privacy officers and security experts who are pushing the boundaries of what's possible. It's about the visionaries who are dreaming of a future where data can be protected and used ethically to transform the world like never before.

Data privacy officers and security experts are a special breed. They're part guardian, part strategist, part advocate, and part dreamer. They know how to identify risks, how to analyze vulnerabilities, and how to develop solutions. But more importantly, they know how to communicate their findings in a way that's clear and compelling.

Think of it like this: a data privacy officer is like a guardian who can use data to identify risks and develop solutions. A security expert is like a strategist who can use data to analyze vulnerabilities and achieve greater success. Together, they're like a dynamic duo, working hand in hand to unlock the power of ethical data privacy and security.

The Future of Data Privacy and Security: A World of Trust and Protection

But despite the challenges, the future of data privacy and security is bright. It's a future filled with possibilities, with opportunities to build trust and protect lives. It's a future where data can be used ethically and securely to transform the world like never before, where it can help us make the world a safer, more trustworthy, and more prosperous place.

And it's a future that's already here. Every day, we're seeing new breakthroughs, new innovations, new ways of protecting data and building trust. It's exciting, it's inspiring, and it's just the beginning.

So, my friends, as we journey through this guardianship of data—data privacy and security best practices—let's remember the power and the potential that lies within. Let's remember the pioneers who came before us, the visionaries who dared to dream of a future where data could be protected and used ethically to transform the world like never before. And let's look forward to the exciting journey that lies ahead, as we continue to explore the boundless possibilities of data privacy and security and the future of trust and protection.

Chapter 14: Data Strategy: The Fuel for AI Success

Case Study: Data-Driven Success Stories

Introduction: The Power of Data

Folks, gather 'round and let me spin you a yarn about the power of data—data-driven success stories. Now, I know what you're thinking: "Data-driven success stories? Sounds like something out of a tech manual." But fear not, my friends, for I'm here to make it all as clear as a summer's day. So, grab your favorite chair, pour yourself a glass of lemonade, and let's dive right in.

The Rise of Data-Driven Decisions: The New Frontier

Data-driven decisions are the new frontier. Think of it like this: data is the lifeblood of modern businesses, fueling insights, guiding strategies, and driving success. By leveraging data, companies can make better decisions, improve efficiency, and even create new opportunities. It's like having a super-smart assistant who can see into the future and guide your business to success.

The Case of Netflix: A Lesson in Personalization

The case of Netflix is a lesson in personalization. Netflix uses data to analyze viewer behavior, identifyng trends and patterns in their watching history. This approach helps Netflix make personalized recommendations that resonate with their viewers, improving the overall customer experience and driving engagement. It's a powerful reminder of the importance of data in creating a more personalized and engaging customer experience.

Improving Customer Experience: The Personal Touch

One of the biggest benefits of data-driven decisions is improving the customer experience. By analyzing customer data, companies can identify preferences, behaviors, and even emotions. This allows them to create more personalized and engaging experiences that resonate with their customers.

The Case of Amazon: A Lesson in Customer Satisfaction

The case of Amazon is a lesson in customer satisfaction. Amazon uses data to analyze customer behavior, from browsing history to purchase history. This approach helps Amazon make personalized recommendations, optimize product listings, and even improve customer service. By leveraging data, Amazon can create a more personalized and satisfying customer experience, driving loyalty and repeat business. It's a powerful reminder of the importance of data in improving the overall customer experience.

The Case of Spotify: A Lesson in Music Personalization

The case of Spotify is a lesson in music personalization. Spotify uses data to analyze listening behavior, identifyng trends and patterns in their users' music preferences. This approach helps Spotify create personalized playlists, recommend new music, and even curate content that resonates with their users. By leveraging data, Spotify can create a more personalized and engaging music experience, driving user satisfaction and loyalty. It's a powerful reminder of the importance of data in creating a more personalized and engaging customer experience.

Optimizing Operations: The Streamlined Approach

Another big benefit of data-driven decisions is optimizing operations. By analyzing operational data, companies can identify inefficiencies, streamline processes, and improve overall performance. It's like having a super-smart manager who can see the big picture and make the right calls to keep things running smoothly.

The Case of Walmart: A Lesson in Inventory Management

The case of Walmart is a lesson in inventory management. Walmart uses data to analyze sales trends, predict demand, and optimize inventory levels. This approach helps Walmart reduce waste, improve efficiency, and even increase sales. By leveraging data, Walmart can streamline its operations, improving overall performance and achieving greater success. It's a powerful reminder of the importance of data in optimizing operations and improving efficiency.

The Case of UPS: A Lesson in Route Optimization

The case of UPS is a lesson in route optimization. UPS uses data to analyze delivery routes, identifyng the most efficient paths and schedules. This approach helps UPS reduce fuel consumption, minimize delivery times, and even improve customer satisfaction. By leveraging data, UPS can optimize its operations, improving overall performance and achieving greater success. It's a powerful reminder of the importance of data in optimizing operations and improving efficiency.

Driving Innovation: The Creative Spark

Data-driven decisions can also drive innovation. By analyzing data, companies can identify new opportunities, develop new products, and even create new markets. It's like having a super-smart inventor who can see the future and create something truly groundbreaking.

The Case of Tesla: A Lesson in Innovation

The case of Tesla is a lesson in innovation. Tesla uses data to analyze driving behavior, identifyng trends and patterns in their customers' usage. This approach helps Tesla develop new features, improve existing products, and even create new markets. By leveraging data, Tesla can drive innovation, improving overall performance and achieving greater success. It's a powerful reminder of the importance of data in driving innovation and creating new opportunities.

The Case of Airbnb: A Lesson in Market Creation

The case of Airbnb is a lesson in market creation. Airbnb uses data to analyze travel trends, identifyng new opportunities and markets. This approach helps Airbnb expand its offerings, improve its services, and even create new markets. By leveraging data, Airbnb can drive innovation, improving overall performance and achieving greater success. It's a powerful reminder of the importance of data in driving innovation and creating new opportunities.

Enhancing Marketing: The Targeted Approach

Data-driven decisions can also enhance marketing. By analyzing customer data, companies can identify target audiences, develop effective campaigns, and even measure their impact. It's like having a super-smart marketer who can see the big picture and create campaigns that truly resonate with customers.

The Case of Coca-Cola: A Lesson in Targeted Marketing

The case of Coca-Cola is a lesson in targeted marketing. Coca-Cola uses data to analyze customer behavior, identifyng trends and patterns in their consumption habits. This approach helps Coca-Cola develop targeted marketing campaigns that resonate with their customers, improving overall engagement and driving sales. By leveraging data, Coca-Cola can enhance its marketing, improving overall performance and achieving greater success. It's a powerful reminder of the importance of data in enhancing marketing and creating effective campaigns.

The Case of Nike: A Lesson in Personalized Marketing

Chapter 14: Data Strategy: The Fuel for AI Success

The case of Nike is a lesson in personalized marketing. Nike uses data to analyze customer behavior, identifyng trends and patterns in their purchase habits. This approach helps Nike create personalized marketing campaigns that resonate with their customers, improving overall engagement and driving sales. By leveraging data, Nike can enhance its marketing, improving overall performance and achieving greater success. It's a powerful reminder of the importance of data in enhancing marketing and creating effective campaigns.

The Human Touch: The Role of Data Scientists and Analysts

But data-driven success stories aingt just about technology. It's also about people. It's about the data scientists and analysts who are pushing the boundaries of what's possible. It's about the visionaries who are dreaming of a future where data can help us transform the world like never before.

Data scientists and analysts are a special breed. They're part detective, part architect, part advocate, and part dreamer. They know how to identify data sources, how to analyze data quality, and how to develop solutions. But more importantly, they know how to communicate their findings in a way that's clear and compelling.

Think of it like this: a data scientist is like a detective who can use data to identify sources and analyze quality. A data analyst is like an architect who can use data to develop solutions and achieve greater success. Together, they're like a dynamic duo, working hand in hand to unlock the power of ethical data-driven decisions.

The Future of Data-Driven Success: A World of Possibilities

But despite the challenges, the future of data-driven success is bright. It's a future filled with possibilities, with opportunities to solve problems and improve lives. It's a future where data can help us transform the world like never before, where it can help us make the world a safer, more efficient, and more prosperous place.

And it's a future that's already here. Every day, we're seeing new breakthroughs, new innovations, new ways of using data to make the world a better place. It's exciting, it's inspiring, and it's just the beginning.

So, my friends, as we journey through this power of data—data-driven success stories—let's remember the power and the potential that lies within. Let's remember the pioneers who came before us, the visionaries who dared to dream of a future where data could help us transform the world like never before. And let's look forward to the exciting journey that lies ahead, as we continue to explore the boundless possibilities of data-driven decisions and the future of business.

Chapter 15: Implementing AI: From Pilot Projects to Full-Scale Deployment

Designing and Executing AI Pilot Projects

Introduction: The New Frontier of AI

Folks, gather 'round and let me spin you a yarn about the new frontier of AI—designing and executing AI pilot projects. Now, I know what you're thinking: "AI pilot projects? Sounds like something out of a futuristic novel." But fear not, my friends, for I'm here to make it all as clear as a summer's day. So, grab your favorite chair, pour yourself a glass of lemonade, and let's dive right in.

Understanding AI Pilot Projects: The Testing Grounds

AI pilot projects are the testing grounds. Think of it like this: before you roll out a full-scale AI initiative, you need to test the waters, see what works, and what doesngt. Pilot projects allow you to experiment, learn, and refine your AI strategies without the risk of a full-scale implementation. It's like having a practice run before the big game.

The Case of Google: A Lesson in Piloting

The case of Google is a lesson in piloting. Google often starts with small-scale pilot projects to test new AI technologies before rolling them out to the entire company. This approach helps Google identify issues, refine strategies, and ensure that their AI initiatives are successful. It's a powerful reminder of the importance of pilot projects in testing and refining your AI strategies.

Identifying the Right Use Cases: The Target

The first step in designing an AI pilot project is identifyng the right use cases. Think of it like this: you need to find the areas where AI can make the biggest impact, where it can solve real problems and deliver real value. By identifyng the right use cases, you can ensure that your pilot project is focused, relevant, and impactful.

The Case of Amazon: A Lesson in Use Cases

The case of Amazon is a lesson in use cases. Amazon identified the use case of personalized product recommendations as a key area where AI could make a significant impact. By focusing on this use case, Amazon was able to develop and test an AI system that provided personalized recommendations, improving the overall customer experience and driving sales. It's a powerful reminder of the importance of identifyng the right use cases for your AI pilot projects.

Defining Objectives: The Goal

The next step in designing an AI pilot project is defining your objectives. Think of it like this: you need to know what you're aiming for, what you want to achieve, and how you're going to measure success. By defining clear and measurable objectives, you can ensure that your pilot project is focused, aligned with your business goals, and capable of delivering real value.

The Case of IBM: A Lesson in Objectives

The case of IBM is a lesson in objectives. IBM defines clear and measurable objectives for its AI pilot projects, such as improving customer service, optimizing supply chains, or enhancing data analytics. This approach helps IBM ensure that its pilot projects are focused, aligned with its business goals, and capable of delivering real value. It's a powerful reminder of the importance of defining clear and measurable objectives for your AI pilot projects.

Gathering the Right Data: The Fuel

The next step in designing an AI pilot project is gathering the right data. Think of it like this: data is the fuel that powers AI, making it possible to analyze patterns, identify trends, and make predictions. By gathering the right data, you can ensure that your AI pilot project has the information it needs to succeed.

The Case of Netflix: A Lesson in Data Gathering

The case of Netflix is a lesson in data gathering. Netflix collects data on viewer behavior, from watching history to ratings and reviews. This data is used to power its AI systems, providing personalized recommendations and improving the overall viewer experience. It's a powerful reminder of the importance of gathering the right data for your AI pilot projects.

Building the Right Team: The Experts

The next step in designing an AI pilot project is building the right team. Think of it like this: AI is a complex and ever-changing field, and you need a team of experts who can help you navigate the challenges and opportunities it presents. By building the right team, you can ensure that your pilot project has the knowledge, skills, and expertise it needs to succeed.

The Case of Microsoft: A Lesson in Team Building

The case of Microsoft is a lesson in team building. Microsoft assembles teams of data scientists, AI engineers, and domain experts to work on its AI pilot projects. This approach helps Microsoft ensure that its pilot projects have the knowledge, skills, and expertise they need to succeed. It's a powerful reminder of the importance of building the right team for your AI pilot projects.

Selecting the Right Tools: The Technology

The next step in designing an AI pilot project is selecting the right tools. Think of it like this: AI requires the right technology to function effectively, from cloud platforms to AI frameworks, from data storage solutions to analytics tools. By selecting the right tools, you can ensure that your pilot project has the technology it needs to succeed.

The Case of AWS: A Lesson in Tool Selection

The case of AWS (Amazon Web Services) is a lesson in tool selection. AWS provides a range of cloud-based tools and services that can help you build, deploy, and manage your AI pilot projects. This approach helps businesses of all sizes take advantage of the power of AI and achieve even greater success. It's a powerful reminder of the importance of selecting the right tools for your AI pilot projects.

Executing the Pilot Project: The Launch

Once you've designed your AI pilot project, it's time to execute it. Think of it like this: executing the pilot project is like launching a rocket, sending it into the unknown to see what it can achieve. By executing the pilot project, you can test your AI strategies, gather data, and refine your approach.

The Case of Uber: A Lesson in Execution

The case of Uber is a lesson in execution. Uber executed a pilot project to test its AI-powered self-driving cars, gathering data and refining its technology. This approach helped Uber identify issues, refine its strategies, and ensure that its self-driving cars were safe

Chapter 15: Implementing AI: From Pilot Projects to Full-Scale Deployment

and effective. It's a powerful reminder of the importance of executing your AI pilot projects to test and refine your strategies.

Monitoring and Evaluating Performance: The Feedback Loop

The next step in executing an AI pilot project is monitoring and evaluating its performance. Think of it like this: you need to keep a close eye on your pilot project, tracking its progress, identifyng issues, and measuring its impact. By monitoring and evaluating performance, you can gather valuable feedback and make data-driven decisions to improve your AI strategies.

The Case of Tesla: A Lesson in Performance Monitoring

The case of Tesla is a lesson in performance monitoring. Tesla closely monitors the performance of its AI-powered autonomous driving systems, gathering data and identifyng issues. This approach helps Tesla make data-driven decisions to improve its technology and ensure that its autonomous driving systems are safe and effective. It's a powerful reminder of the importance of monitoring and evaluating the performance of your AI pilot projects.

Scaling Up: The Next Step

The final step in executing an AI pilot project is scaling up. Think of it like this: once you've tested and refined your AI strategies, it's time to roll them out on a larger scale, implementing them across your entire business. By scaling up, you can achieve even greater impact and drive significant business value.

The Case of Walmart: A Lesson in Scaling Up

The case of Walmart is a lesson in scaling up. Walmart started with small-scale AI pilot projects to test its inventory management and supply chain optimization strategies. Once these strategies were proven successful, Walmart scaled them up, implementing them across its entire business. This approach helped Walmart achieve even greater impact and drive significant business value. It's a powerful reminder of the importance of scaling up your AI pilot projects to achieve even greater success.

The Human Touch: The Role of Leaders and Innovators

But designing and executing AI pilot projects aingt just about technology. It's also about people. It's about the leaders and innovators who are pushing the boundaries of what's possible. It's about the visionaries who are dreaming of a future where AI can help us transform the world like never before.

Leaders and innovators are a special breed. They're part strategist, part visionary, part advocate, and part dreamer. They know how to identify opportunities, how to analyze challenges, and how to develop solutions. But more importantly, they know how to communicate their findings in a way that's clear and compelling.

Think of it like this: a leader is like a strategist who can use AI to identify opportunities and develop solutions. An innovator is like a visionary who can use AI to push the boundaries of what's possible and achieve even greater success. Together, they're like a dynamic duo, working hand in hand to unlock the power of ethical AI.

The Future of AI Pilot Projects: A World of Possibilities

But despite the challenges, the future of AI pilot projects is bright. It's a future filled with possibilities, with opportunities to solve problems and improve lives. It's a future where AI can help us transform the world like never before, where it can help us make the world a safer, more efficient, and more prosperous place.

And it's a future that's already here. Every day, we're seeing new breakthroughs, new innovations, new ways of using AI to make the world a better place. It's exciting, it's inspiring, and it's just the beginning.

So, my friends, as we journey through this new frontier of AI—designing and executing AI pilot projects—let's remember the power and the potential that lies within. Let's remember the pioneers who came before us, the visionaries who dared to dream of a future where AI could help us transform the world like never before. And let's look forward to the exciting journey that lies ahead, as we continue to explore the boundless possibilities of AI pilot projects and the future of business.

Chapter 15: Implementing AI: From Pilot Projects to Full-Scale Deployment

Scaling AI Solutions Across the Enterprise

Introduction: The New Frontier of AI

Folks, gather 'round and let me spin you a yarn about the new frontier of AI—scaling AI solutions across the enterprise. Now, I know what you're thinking: "Scaling AI solutions? Sounds like something out of a futuristic novel." But fear not, my friends, for I'm here to make it all as clear as a summer's day. So, grab your favorite chair, pour yourself a glass of lemonade, and let's dive right in.

Understanding the Need for Scaling AI

Scaling AI solutions across the enterprise is like spreading a wildfire of innovation. Think of it like this: once you've tested and proven your AI strategies in small-scale pilot projects, it's time to roll them out on a larger scale, implementing them across your entire business. By scaling AI solutions, you can achieve even greater impact and drive significant business value.

The Case of Walmart: A Lesson in Scaling Up

The case of Walmart is a lesson in scaling up. Walmart started with small-scale AI pilot projects to test its inventory management and supply chain optimization strategies. Once these strategies were proven successful, Walmart scaled them up, implementing them across its entire business. This approach helped Walmart achieve even greater impact and drive significant business value. It's a powerful reminder of the importance of scaling AI solutions to achieve even greater success.

Identifying the Right Use Cases: The Target

The first step in scaling AI solutions is identifyng the right use cases. Think of it like this: you need to find the areas where AI can make the biggest impact, where it can solve real problems and deliver real value. By identifyng the right use cases, you can ensure that your AI solutions are focused, relevant, and impactful.

The Case of Amazon: A Lesson in Use Cases

The case of Amazon is a lesson in use cases. Amazon identified the use case of personalized product recommendations as a key area where AI could make a significant impact. By focusing on this use case, Amazon was able to develop and scale an AI system that provided personalized recommendations, improving the overall customer experience and driving sales. It's a powerful reminder of the importance of identifyng the right use cases for your AI solutions.

Defining Objectives: The Goal

The next step in scaling AI solutions is defining your objectives. Think of it like this: you need to know what you're aiming for, what you want to achieve, and how you're going to measure success. By defining clear and measurable objectives, you can ensure that your AI solutions are focused, aligned with your business goals, and capable of delivering real value.

The Case of IBM: A Lesson in Objectives

The case of IBM is a lesson in objectives. IBM defines clear and measurable objectives for its AI solutions, such as improving customer service, optimizing supply chains, or enhancing data analytics. This approach helps IBM ensure that its AI solutions are focused, aligned with its business goals, and capable of delivering real value. It's a powerful reminder of the importance of defining clear and measurable objectives for your AI solutions.

Gathering the Right Data: The Fuel

The next step in scaling AI solutions is gathering the right data. Think of it like this: data is the fuel that powers AI, making it possible to analyze patterns, identify trends, and make predictions. By gathering the right data, you can ensure that your AI solutions have the information they need to succeed.

The Case of Netflix: A Lesson in Data Gathering

The case of Netflix is a lesson in data gathering. Netflix collects data on viewer behavior, from watching history to ratings and reviews. This data is used to power its AI systems, providing personalized recommendations and improving the overall viewer experience. It's a powerful reminder of the importance of gathering the right data for your AI solutions.

Building the Right Team: The Experts

The next step in scaling AI solutions is building the right team. Think of it like this: AI is a complex and ever-changing field, and you need a team of experts who can help you navigate the challenges and opportunities it presents. By building the right team, you can ensure that your AI solutions have the knowledge, skills, and expertise they need to succeed.

The Case of Microsoft: A Lesson in Team Building

The case of Microsoft is a lesson in team building. Microsoft assembles teams of data scientists, AI engineers, and domain experts to work on its AI solutions. This approach helps Microsoft ensure that its AI solutions have the knowledge, skills, and expertise they need to succeed. It's a powerful reminder of the importance of building the right team for your AI solutions.

Selecting the Right Tools: The Technology

Chapter 15: Implementing AI: From Pilot Projects to Full-Scale Deployment

The next step in scaling AI solutions is selecting the right tools. Think of it like this: AI requires the right technology to function effectively, from cloud platforms to AI frameworks, from data storage solutions to analytics tools. By selecting the right tools, you can ensure that your AI solutions have the technology they need to succeed.

The Case of AWS: A Lesson in Tool Selection

The case of AWS (Amazon Web Services) is a lesson in tool selection. AWS provides a range of cloud-based tools and services that can help you build, deploy, and manage your AI solutions. This approach helps businesses of all sizes take advantage of the power of AI and achieve even greater success. It's a powerful reminder of the importance of selecting the right tools for your AI solutions.

Developing a Scaling Strategy: The Roadmap

The next step in scaling AI solutions is developing a scaling strategy. Think of it like this: you need a roadmap, a plan that outlines how you're going to roll out your AI solutions across the enterprise. This roadmap should include timelines, milestones, and key performance indicators (KPIs) to help you track progress and measure success.

The Case of Google: A Lesson in Scaling Strategy

The case of Google is a lesson in scaling strategy. Google develops detailed roadmaps for scaling its AI solutions, including timelines, milestones, and KPIs. This approach helps Google ensure that its AI solutions are rolled out effectively and efficiently, achieving the desired business outcomes. It's a powerful reminder of the importance of developing a scaling strategy for your AI solutions.

Ensuring Data Quality and Security: The Safeguards

As you scale your AI solutions, it's crucial to ensure data quality and security. Think of it like this: data is the lifeblood of your AI solutions, and you need to protect it from unauthorized access, theft, and misuse. By ensuring data quality and security, you can maintain the trust of your customers and protect your business from potential risks.

The Case of Apple: A Lesson in Data Security

The case of Apple is a lesson in data security. Apple focuses on protecting its customers' data from unauthorized access, theft, and misuse. This approach helps Apple build trust with its customers and ensure that their data is safe and secure. It's a powerful reminder of the importance of ensuring data quality and security for your AI solutions.

Monitoring and Evaluating Performance: The Feedback Loop

The next step in scaling AI solutions is monitoring and evaluating their performance. Think of it like this: you need to keep a close eye on your AI solutions, tracking their progress, identifyng issues, and measuring their impact. By monitoring and evaluating performance, you can gather valuable feedback and make data-driven decisions to improve your AI solutions.

The Case of Tesla: A Lesson in Performance Monitoring

The case of Tesla is a lesson in performance monitoring. Tesla closely monitors the performance of its AI-powered autonomous driving systems, gathering data and identifyng issues. This approach helps Tesla make data-driven decisions to improve its technology and ensure that its autonomous driving systems are safe and effective. It's a powerful reminder of the importance of monitoring and evaluating the performance of your AI solutions.

Scaling Across Departments: The Enterprise-Wide Approach

Scaling AI solutions across the enterprise means implementing them across all departments and functions. Think of it like this: AI can benefit every part of your business, from customer service to supply chain management, from marketing to finance. By scaling AI solutions across departments, you can achieve a holistic and integrated approach to AI adoption.

The Case of Uber: A Lesson in Enterprise-Wide Scaling

The case of Uber is a lesson in enterprise-wide scaling. Uber has implemented AI solutions across various departments, from customer service to route optimization, from marketing to fraud detection. This approach helps Uber achieve a holistic and integrated approach to AI adoption, improving overall business performance and achieving greater success. It's a powerful reminder of the importance of scaling AI solutions across departments to achieve a comprehensive and integrated approach.

Training and Supporting Employees: The Knowledge Base

As you scale your AI solutions, it's crucial to train and support your employees. Think of it like this: your employees are the backbone of your business, and they need to understand and embrace AI to make it a success. By providing training and support, you can ensure that your employees have the knowledge and skills they need to effectively use and benefit from AI solutions.

The Case of IBM: A Lesson in Employee Training

The case of IBM is a lesson in employee training. IBM invests heavily in training its employees on AI technologies, providing workshops, online courses, and hands-on experiences. This approach helps IBM ensure that its employees have the knowledge and skills they need to effectively use and benefit from

AI solutions. It's a powerful reminder of the importance of training and supporting your employees as you scale AI solutions across the enterprise.

The Human Touch: The Role of Leaders and Innovators

But scaling AI solutions across the enterprise aingt just about technology. It's also about people. It's about the leaders and innovators who are pushing the boundaries of what's possible. It's about the visionaries who are dreaming of a future where AI can help us transform the world like never before.

Leaders and innovators are a special breed. They're part strategist, part visionary, part advocate, and part dreamer. They know how to identify opportunities, how to analyze challenges, and how to develop solutions. But more importantly, they know how to communicate their findings in a way that's clear and compelling.

Think of it like this: a leader is like a strategist who can use AI to identify opportunities and develop solutions. An innovator is like a visionary who can use AI to push the boundaries of what's possible and achieve even greater success. Together, they're like a dynamic duo, working hand in hand to unlock the power of ethical AI.

The Future of Scaling AI Solutions: A World of Possibilities

But despite the challenges, the future of scaling AI solutions across the enterprise is bright. It's a future filled with possibilities, with opportunities to solve problems and improve lives. It's a future where AI can help us transform the world like never before, where it can help us make the world a safer, more efficient, and more prosperous place.

And it's a future that's already here. Every day, we're seeing new breakthroughs, new innovations, new ways of using AI to make the world a better place. It's exciting, it's inspiring, and it's just the beginning.

So, my friends, as we journey through this new frontier of AI—scaling AI solutions across the enterprise—let's remember the power and the potential that lies within. Let's remember the pioneers who came before us, the visionaries who dared to dream of a future where AI could help us transform the world like never before. And let's look forward to the exciting journey that lies ahead, as we continue to explore the boundless possibilities of scaling AI solutions and the future of business.

Case Study: AI Implementation in Fortune 500 Companies

Introduction: The Giants of Industry

Folks, gather 'round and let me spin you a yarn about the giants of industry—AI implementation in Fortune 500 companies. Now, I know what you're thinking: "AI in Fortune 500 companies? Sounds like something out of a futuristic novel." But fear not, my friends, for I'm here to make it all as clear as a summer's day. So, grab your favorite chair, pour yourself a glass of lemonade, and let's dive right in.

The Power of AI: The Game Changer

Artificial intelligence is revolutionizing the world as we know it. From healthcare to finance, from transportation to entertainment, AI is transforming industries and improving lives. It's like having a super-smart assistant who can analyze data, make decisions, and even predict the future. But here's the kicker: AI aingt just for the little guys. It's the game changer for the giants of industry, the Fortune 500 companies.

The Case of Amazon: A Lesson in Innovation

The case of Amazon is a lesson in innovation. Amazon uses AI to optimize its supply chain, predict demand, and even personalize customer experiences. This approach helps Amazon reduce costs, improve efficiency, and even increase customer satisfaction. It's a powerful reminder of the importance of AI in transforming industries and improving lives.

Customer Experience: The Personal Touch

One of the biggest benefits of AI implementation in Fortune 500 companies is improving the customer experience. By analyzing customer data, companies can identify preferences, behaviors, and even emotions. This allows them to create more personalized and engaging experiences that resonate with their customers.

The Case of Netflix: A Lesson in Personalization

The case of Netflix is a lesson in personalization. Netflix uses AI to analyze viewer behavior, identifyng trends and patterns in their watching history. This approach helps Netflix make personalized recommendations that resonate with their viewers, improving the overall customer experience and driving engagement. It's a powerful reminder of the importance of AI in creating a more personalized and engaging customer experience.

The Case of Starbucks: A Lesson in Customer Satisfaction

The case of Starbucks is a lesson in customer satisfaction. Starbucks uses AI to analyze customer data, identifyng trends and patterns in their purchase history. This approach helps Starbucks make personalized recommendations, optimize store layouts, and even improve customer service. By leveraging AI, Starbucks can create a more satisfying customer experience, driving loyalty and repeat business. It's a powerful reminder of the importance of AI in improving the overall customer experience.

Operational Efficiency: The Streamlined Approach

Another big benefit of AI implementation in Fortune 500 companies is operational efficiency. By analyzing operational data, companies can identify inefficiencies, streamline processes, and improve overall performance. It's like having a super-smart manager who can see the big picture and make the right calls to keep things running smoothly.

The Case of Walmart: A Lesson in Inventory Management

The case of Walmart is a lesson in inventory management. Walmart uses AI to analyze sales trends, predict demand, and optimize inventory levels. This approach helps Walmart reduce waste, improve efficiency, and even increase sales. By leveraging AI, Walmart can streamline its operations, improving overall performance and achieving greater success. It's a powerful reminder of the importance of AI in optimizing operations and improving efficiency.

The Case of UPS: A Lesson in Route Optimization

The case of UPS is a lesson in route optimization. UPS uses AI to analyze delivery routes, identifyng the most efficient paths and schedules. This approach helps UPS reduce fuel consumption, minimize delivery times, and even improve customer satisfaction. By leveraging AI, UPS can optimize its operations, improving overall performance and achieving greater success. It's a powerful reminder of the importance of AI in optimizing operations and improving efficiency.

Innovation and Product Development: The Creative Spark

AI implementation in Fortune 500 companies can also drive innovation and product development. By analyzing data, companies can identify new opportunities, develop new products, and even create new markets. It's like having a super-smart inventor who can see the future and create something truly groundbreaking.

The Case of Tesla: A Lesson in Innovation

The case of Tesla is a lesson in innovation. Tesla uses AI to analyze driving behavior, identifyng trends and patterns in their customers' usage. This approach helps Tesla develop new features, improve existing products, and even create new markets. By leveraging AI, Tesla can drive innovation, improving overall performance and achieving greater success. It's a powerful reminder of the importance of AI in driving innovation and creating new opportunities.

The Case of Apple: A Lesson in Product Development

The case of Apple is a lesson in product development. Apple uses AI to analyze customer data, identifyng trends and patterns in their usage. This approach helps Apple develop new products, improve existing features, and even create new markets. By leveraging AI, Apple can drive innovation, improving overall performance and achieving greater success. It's a powerful reminder of the importance of AI in driving innovation and creating new opportunities.

Marketing and Sales: The Targeted Approach

AI implementation in Fortune 500 companies can also enhance marketing and sales. By analyzing customer data, companies can identify target audiences, develop effective campaigns, and even measure their impact. It's like having a super-smart marketer who can see the big picture and create campaigns that truly resonate with customers.

The Case of Coca-Cola: A Lesson in Targeted Marketing

The case of Coca-Cola is a lesson in targeted marketing. Coca-Cola uses AI to analyze customer behavior, identifyng trends and patterns in their consumption habits. This approach helps Coca-Cola develop targeted marketing campaigns that resonate with their customers, improving overall engagement and driving sales. By leveraging AI, Coca-Cola can enhance its marketing, improving overall performance and achieving greater success. It's a powerful reminder of the importance of AI in enhancing marketing and creating effective campaigns.

The Case of Nike: A Lesson in Personalized Marketing

The case of Nike is a lesson in personalized marketing. Nike uses AI to analyze customer behavior, identifyng trends and patterns in their purchase habits. This approach helps Nike create personalized marketing campaigns that resonate with their customers, improving overall engagement and driving sales. By leveraging AI, Nike can enhance its marketing, improving overall performance and achieving greater success. It's a powerful reminder of the importance of AI in enhancing marketing and creating effective campaigns.

The Human Touch: The Role of Leaders and Innovators

But AI implementation in Fortune 500 companies aingt just about technology. It's also about people. It's about the leaders and innovators who are pushing the boundaries of what's possible. It's about the visionaries who are dreaming of a future where AI can help us transform the world like never before.

Leaders and innovators are a special breed. They're part strategist, part visionary, part advocate, and part dreamer. They know how to identify opportunities, how to analyze challenges, and how to develop solutions. But more importantly, they know how to communicate their findings in a way that's clear and compelling.

Think of it like this: a leader is like a strategist who can use AI to identify opportunities and develop solutions. An innovator is like a visionary who can use AI to push the boundaries of what's possible and achieve even greater success. Together, they're like a dynamic duo, working hand in hand to unlock the power of ethical AI.

The Future of AI in Fortune 500 Companies: A World of Possibilities

But despite the challenges, the future of AI in Fortune 500 companies is bright. It's a future filled with possibilities, with opportunities to solve problems and improve lives. It's a future where AI can help us transform the world like never before, where it can help us make the world a safer, more efficient, and more prosperous place.

And it's a future that's already here. Every day, we're seeing new breakthroughs, new innovations, new ways of using AI to make the world a better place. It's exciting, it's inspiring, and it's just the beginning.

So, my friends, as we journey through this world of giants—AI implementation in Fortune 500 companies—let's remember the power and the potential that lies within. Let's remember the pioneers who came before us, the visionaries who dared to dream of a future where AI could help us transform the world like never before. And let's look forward to the exciting journey that lies ahead, as we continue to explore the boundless possibilities of AI implementation and the future of business.

Chapter 16: Measuring Success: Metrics and KPIs for AI Projects

Defining Success Metrics for AI Initiatives

Introduction: The Measure of Success

Folks, gather 'round and let me spin you a yarn about the measure of success—defining success metrics for AI initiatives. Now, I know what you're thinking: "Success metrics for AI? Sounds like something out of a business textbook." But fear not, my friends, for I'm here to make it all as clear as a summer's day. So, grab your favorite chair, pour yourself a glass of lemonade, and let's dive right in.

The Importance of Success Metrics: The Compass

Success metrics are the compass. Think of it like this: without clear and measurable success metrics, you're navigating without a map, wandering aimlessly in the wilderness of AI initiatives. Success metrics help you understand what you're aiming for, what you want to achieve, and how you're going to measure success. By defining clear and measurable success metrics, you can ensure that your AI initiatives are focused, aligned with your business goals, and capable of delivering real value.

The Case of Google: A Lesson in Metrics

The case of Google is a lesson in metrics. Google defines clear and measurable success metrics for its AI initiatives, such as improving search accuracy, optimizing ad performance, or enhancing user experience. This approach helps Google ensure that its AI initiatives are focused, aligned with its business goals, and capable of delivering real value. It's a powerful reminder of the importance of defining clear and measurable success metrics for your AI initiatives.

Key Performance Indicators (KPIs): The Metrics That Matter

Key Performance Indicators, or KPIs, are the metrics that matter. Think of it like this: KPIs are like the scorecard of a game, telling you how well you're doing and where you need to improve. By defining the right KPIs, you can measure the impact of your AI initiatives and understand their true value.

The Case of Amazon: A Lesson in KPIs

The case of Amazon is a lesson in KPIs. Amazon uses a range of KPIs to measure the impact of its AI initiatives, from customer satisfaction to operational efficiency. This approach helps Amazon understand the true value of its AI initiatives and make data-driven decisions to improve its business performance. It's a powerful reminder of the importance of defining the right KPIs for your AI initiatives.

Customer-Centric Metrics: The Voice of the People

Customer-centric metrics are the voice of the people. Think of it like this: your customers are the heart of your business, and their satisfaction is crucial to your success. By defining customer-centric metrics, you can measure the impact of your AI initiatives on customer experience, satisfaction, and loyalty.

Customer Satisfaction (CSAT): The Smile Factor

Customer Satisfaction, or CSAT, is the smile factor. Think of it like this: CSAT measures how happy your customers are with your products or services. By tracking CSAT, you can understand the impact of your AI initiatives on customer satisfaction and make improvements where needed.

The Case of Netflix: A Lesson in CSAT

The case of Netflix is a lesson in CSAT. Netflix tracks CSAT to measure the impact of its AI-powered personalized recommendations on customer satisfaction. This approach helps Netflix understand how its AI initiatives are affecting customer satisfaction and make improvements where needed. It's a powerful reminder of the importance of defining customer-centric metrics for your AI initiatives.

Net Promoter Score (NPS): The Loyalty Factor

Net Promoter Score, or NPS, is the loyalty factor. Think of it like this: NPS measures how likely your customers are to recommend your products or services to others. By tracking NPS, you can understand the impact of your AI initiatives on customer loyalty and make improvements where needed.

The Case of Apple: A Lesson in NPS

The case of Apple is a lesson in NPS. Apple tracks NPS to measure the impact of its AI-powered customer service on customer loyalty. This approach helps Apple understand how its AI initiatives are affecting customer loyalty and make improvements where needed. It's a powerful reminder of the importance of defining customer-centric metrics for your AI initiatives.

Operational Metrics: The Efficiency Factor

Operational metrics are the efficiency factor. Think of it like this: operational efficiency is crucial to the success of your business, and AI can play a significant role in improving it. By defining operational metrics, you can measure the impact of your AI initiatives on operational efficiency, productivity, and cost savings.

Operational Efficiency: The Streamlined Approach

Operational efficiency is the streamlined approach. Think of it like this: operational efficiency measures how well your business processes are running. By tracking operational efficiency, you can understand the impact of your AI initiatives on streamlining processes, improving productivity, and reducing costs.

The Case of Walmart: A Lesson in Operational Efficiency

The case of Walmart is a lesson in operational efficiency. Walmart tracks operational efficiency to measure the impact of its AI-powered inventory management and supply chain optimization on streamlining processes, improving productivity, and reducing costs. This approach helps Walmart understand how its AI initiatives are affecting operational efficiency and make improvements where needed. It's a powerful reminder of the importance of defining operational metrics for your AI initiatives.

Cost Savings: The Bottom Line

Cost savings are the bottom line. Think of it like this: cost savings measure how much money your AI initiatives are saving your business. By tracking cost savings, you can understand the financial impact of your AI initiatives and ensure that they are delivering' value to your business.

The Case of UPS: A Lesson in Cost Savings

The case of UPS is a lesson in cost savings. UPS tracks cost savings to measure the impact of its AI-powered route optimization on reducing' fuel consumption, minimizing delivery times, and improving customer satisfaction. This approach helps UPS understand the financial impact of its AI initiatives and ensure that they are delivering value to its business. It's a powerful reminder of the importance of defining operational metrics for your AI initiatives.

Financial Metrics: The Dollar Sign

Financial metrics are the dollar sign. Think of it like this: financial performance is the ultimate measure of success for your business, and AI can play a significant role in improving it. By defining financial metrics, you can measure the impact of your AI initiatives on revenue growth, profitability, and return on investment (ROI).

Revenue Growth: The Top Line

Revenue growth is the top line. Think of it like this: revenue growth measures how much money your AI initiatives are generating for your business. By tracking revenue growth, you can understand the financial impact of your AI initiatives and ensure that they are contributing to the success of your business.

The Case of Tesla: A Lesson in Revenue Growth

The case of Tesla is a lesson in revenue growth. Tesla tracks revenue growth to measure the impact of its AI-powered autonomous driving systems on generating revenue for its business. This approach helps Tesla understand the financial impact of its AI initiatives and ensure that they are contributing to the success of its business. It's a powerful reminder of the importance of defining financial metrics for your AI initiatives.

Return on Investment (ROI): The Bottom Line

Return on Investment, or ROI, is the bottom line. Think of it like this: ROI measures how much value your AI initiatives are generating for your business compared to the investment you made in them. By tracking ROI, you can understand the financial impact of your AI initiatives and ensure that they are delivering value to your business.

The Case of IBM: A Lesson in ROI

Chapter 15: Implementing AI: From Pilot Projects to Full-Scale Deployment

The case of IBM is a lesson in ROI. IBM tracks ROI to measure the financial impact of its AI initiatives on generating value for its business. This approach helps IBM understand the financial impact of its AI initiatives and ensure that they are delivering value to its business. It's a powerful reminder of the importance of defining financial metrics for your AI initiatives.

Innovation Metrics: The Creative Spark

Innovation metrics are the creative spark. Think of it like this: innovation is the lifeblood of your business, and AI can play a significant role in driving it. By defining innovation metrics, you can measure the impact of your AI initiatives on creating new opportunities, developing new products, and even entering new markets.

New Product Development: The Invention Factor

New product development is the invention factor. Think of it like this: new product development measures how many new products your AI initiatives are helping to create. By tracking new product development, you can understand the impact of your AI initiatives on driving innovation and creating new opportunities for your business.

The Case of Apple: A Lesson in New Product Development

The case of Apple is a lesson in new product development. Apple tracks new product development to measure the impact of its AI initiatives on creating new products, such as the iPhone, iPad, and Apple Watch. This approach helps Apple understand the impact of its AI initiatives on driving innovation and creating new opportunities for its business. It's a powerful reminder of the importance of defining innovation metrics for your AI initiatives.

Market Expansion: The Growth Factor

Market expansion is the growth factor. Think of it like this: market expansion measures how many new markets your AI initiatives are helping you to enter. By tracking market expansion, you can understand the impact of your AI initiatives on growing your business and entering new markets.

The Case of Amazon: A Lesson in Market Expansion

The case of Amazon is a lesson in market expansion. Amazon tracks market expansion to measure the impact of its AI initiatives on entering new markets, such as cloud computing, digital content, and even physical stores. This approach helps Amazon understand the impact of its AI initiatives on growing its business and entering new markets. It's a powerful reminder of the importance of defining innovation metrics for your AI initiatives.

The Human Touch: The Role of Leaders and Innovators

But defining success metrics for AI initiatives aingt just about technology. It's also about people. It's about the leaders and innovators who are pushing the boundaries of what's possible. It's about the visionaries who are dreaming of a future where AI can help us transform the world like never before.

Leaders and innovators are a special breed. They're part strategist, part visionary, part advocate, and part dreamer. They know how to identify opportunities, how to analyze challenges, and how to develop solutions. But more importantly, they know how to communicate their findings in a way that's clear and compelling.

Think of it like this: a leader is like a strategist who can use AI to identify opportunities and develop solutions. An innovator is like a visionary who can use AI to push the boundaries of what's possible and achieve even greater success. Together, they're like a dynamic duo, working hand in hand to unlock the power of ethical AI.

The Future of AI Initiatives: A World of Possibilities

But despite the challenges, the future of AI initiatives is bright. It's a future filled with possibilities, with opportunities to solve problems and improve lives. It's a future where AI can help us transform the world like never before, where it can help us make the world a safer, more efficient, and more prosperous place.

And it's a future that's already here. Every day, we're seeing new breakthroughs, new innovations, new ways of using AI to make the world a better place. It's exciting, it's inspiring, and it's just the beginning.

So, my friends, as we journey through this measure of success—defining success metrics for AI initiatives—let's remember the power and the potential that lies within. Let's remember the pioneers who came before us, the visionaries who dared to dream of a future where AI could help us transform the world like never before. And let's look forward to the exciting journey that lies ahead, as we continue to explore the boundless possibilities of AI initiatives and the future of business.

Continuous Improvement and Optimization

Introduction: The Journey of Progress

Folks, gather 'round and let me spin you a yarn about the journey of progress—continuous improvement and optimization. Now, I know what you're thinking: "Continuous improvement? Sounds like something out of a management textbook." But fear not, my friends, for I'm here to make it all as clear as a summer's day. So, grab your favorite chair, pour yourself a glass of lemonade, and let's dive right in.

The Importance of Continuous Improvement: The Path to Excellence

Continuous improvement is the path to excellence. Think of it like this: in today's fast-paced world, standing still is like moving backward. You gotta keep improving, keep innovating, keep pushing the boundaries of what's possible. By embracing continuous improvement, you can ensure that your business stays ahead of the curve, adapting to new challenges and opportunities.

The Case of Toyota: A Lesson in Continuous Improvement

The case of Toyota is a lesson in continuous improvement. Toyota's famous "Kaizen" philosophy is all about continuous improvement, encouraging employees to constantly seek ways to improve processes, reduce waste, and enhance quality. This approach has helped Toyota become one of the most successful and respected automakers in the world. It's a powerful reminder of the importance of embracing continuous improvement in your business.

The Role of Data and Analytics: The Compass

Data and analytics are the compass. Think of it like this: to improve, you need to know where you stand, where you're going, and how you're getting there. Data and analytics provide the insights and direction you need to make informed decisions and drive continuous improvement.

The Case of Google: A Lesson in Data-Driven Improvement

The case of Google is a lesson in data-driven improvement. Google uses data and analytics to constantly monitor and improve its search algorithms, advertising platforms, and user experiences. This approach helps Google stay at the forefront of innovation, delivering the best possible experiences to its users. It's a powerful reminder of the importance of leveraging data and analytics for continuous improvement.

Feedback Loops: The Circle of Progress

Feedback loops are the circle of progress. Think of it like this: continuous improvement is a cycle, a never-ending loop of gathering feedback, analyzing data, and making improvements. By establishing effective feedback loops, you can ensure that your business is always learning, always improving, and always moving forward.

The Case of Amazon: A Lesson in Feedback Loops

The case of Amazon is a lesson in feedback loops. Amazon uses customer feedback, sales data, and operational metrics to continuously improve its products, services, and processes. This approach helps Amazon stay ahead of the competition, delivering exceptional customer experiences and achieving remarkable business success. It's a powerful reminder of the importance of establishing effective feedback loops for continuous improvement.

Agile Methodologies: The Flexible Approach

Agile methodologies are the flexible approach. Think of it like this: in a world that's always changing, you need to be agile, able to adapt and respond quickly to new challenges and opportunities. Agile methodologies provide a framework for continuous improvement, encouraging iteration, collaboration, and rapid adaptation.

The Case of Spotify: A Lesson in Agile Methodologies

The case of Spotify is a lesson in agile methodologies. Spotify uses agile methodologies to continuously improve its music streaming service, iterating quickly and responding to user feedback and market trends. This approach helps Spotify stay at the forefront of the music industry, delivering innovative and engaging experiences to its users. It's a powerful reminder of the importance of adopting agile methodologies for continuous improvement.

Lean Principles: The Efficiency Mindset

Lean principles are the efficiency mindset. Think of it like this: continuous improvement is about more than just making things better; it's about making things more efficient, more streamlined, and more effective. Lean principles focus on eliminating waste, optimizing processes, and maximizing value for customers.

The Case of Tesla: A Lesson in Lean Principles

The case of Tesla is a lesson in lean principles. Tesla applies lean principles to its manufacturing processes, continuously improving efficiency, reducing waste, and maximizing value for its customers. This approach helps Tesla stay competitive, delivering high-quality products at a lower cost. It's a powerful reminder of the importance of adopting lean principles for continuous improvement.

Innovation and Creativity: The Spark of Progress

Innovation and creativity are the spark of progress. Think of it like this: continuous improvement isngt just about making small tweaks and adjustments; it's about thinking big, dreaming big, and innovating big. By encouraging innovation and creativity, you can drive transformative change and achieve remarkable success.

The Case of Apple: A Lesson in Innovation and Creativity

The case of Apple is a lesson in innovation and creativity. Apple continuously innovates, introducing groundbreaking products like the iPhone, iPad, and Apple Watch. This approach helps Apple stay at the forefront of the tech industry, delivering exceptional user experiences and achieving unprecedented business success. It's a powerful reminder of the importance of encouraging innovation and creativity for continuous improvement.

Employee Engagement: The Heart of Improvement

Employee engagement is the heart of improvement. Think of it like this: your employees are the lifeblood of your business, and their engagement and involvement are crucial to continuous improvement. By encouraging employee engagement, you can tap into their knowledge, skills, and creativity, driving meaningful and lasting change.

The Case of Southwest Airlines: A Lesson in Employee Engagement

The case of Southwest Airlines is a lesson in employee engagement. Southwest Airlines fosters a culture of employee engagement, encouraging employees to share their ideas, collaborate, and drive continuous improvement. This approach helps Southwest Airlines deliver exceptional customer service and achieve remarkable business success. It's a powerful reminder of the importance of encouraging employee engagement for continuous improvement.

Technology and Tools: The Enablers

Technology and tools are the enablers. Think of it like this: continuous improvement requires the right tools and technologies to gather data, analyze insights, and drive change. By leveraging the right technology and tools, you can accelerate continuous improvement and achieve greater success.

The Case of Microsoft: A Lesson in Technology and Tools

The case of Microsoft is a lesson in technology and tools. Microsoft provides a range of tools and technologies, from Azure to Power BI, that help businesses gather data, analyze insights, and drive continuous improvement. This approach helps businesses stay ahead of the curve, adapting to new challenges and opportunities. It's a powerful reminder of the importance of leveraging the right technology and tools for continuous improvement.

The Human Touch: The Role of Leaders and Innovators

But continuous improvement and optimization aingt just about technology. It's also about people. It's about the leaders and innovators who are pushing the boundaries of what's possible. It's about the visionaries who are dreaming of a future where continuous improvement can help us transform the world like never before.

Leaders and innovators are a special breed. They're part strategist, part visionary, part advocate, and part dreamer. They know how to identify opportunities, how to analyze challenges, and how to develop solutions. But more importantly, they know how to communicate their findings in a way that's clear and compelling.

Think of it like this: a leader is like a strategist who can use continuous improvement to identify opportunities and develop solutions. An innovator is like a visionary who can use continuous improvement to push the boundaries of what's possible and achieve even greater success. Together, they're like a dynamic duo, working hand in hand to unlock the power of ethical continuous improvement.

The Future of Continuous Improvement: A World of Progress

But despite the challenges, the future of continuous improvement is bright. It's a future filled with possibilities, with opportunities to solve problems and improve lives. It's a future where continuous improvement can help us transform the world like never before, where it can help us make the world a safer, more efficient, and more prosperous place.

And it's a future that's already here. Every day, we're seeing new breakthroughs, new innovations, new ways of using continuous improvement to make the world a better place. It's exciting, it's inspiring, and it's just the beginning.

So, my friends, as we journey through this path of progress—continuous improvement and optimization—let's remember the power and the potential that lies within. Let's remember the pioneers who came before us, the visionaries who dared to dream of a future where continuous improvement could help us transform the world like never before. And let's look forward to the exciting journey that lies ahead, as we continue to explore the boundless possibilities of continuous improvement and the future of business.

Case Study: Measuring the Impact of AI in Customer Service

Introduction: The New Frontier of Customer Service

Folks, gather 'round and let me spin you a yarn about the new frontier of customer service—measuring the impact of AI. Now, I know what you're thinking: "AI in customer service? Sounds like something out of a futuristic novel." But fear not, my friends, for I'm here to make it all as clear as a summer's day. So, grab your favorite chair, pour yourself a glass of lemonade, and let's dive right in.

The Power of AI in Customer Service: The Game Changer

Artificial intelligence is revolutionizing the world of customer service. Think of it like this: AI can analyze data, understand customer needs, and even make decisions in real-time, improving the overall customer experience and driving business success. It's like having a super-smart assistant who can see into the future and guide your business to success.

The Case of Amazon: A Lesson in Personalization

The case of Amazon is a lesson in personalization. Amazon uses AI to analyze customer behavior, identifyng trends and patterns in their purchase history. This approach helps Amazon make personalized recommendations, optimize product listings, and even improve customer service. By leveraging AI, Amazon can create a more personalized and satisfying customer experience, driving loyalty and repeat business. It's a powerful reminder of the importance of AI in transforming customer service and improving lives.

Measuring the Impact: The Metrics That Matter

Measuring the impact of AI in customer service is crucial. Think of it like this: without clear and measurable metrics, you're navigating without a map, wandering aimlessly in the wilderness of AI initiatives. By defining the right metrics, you can understand the true value of your AI investments and make data-driven decisions to improve your customer service.

Customer Satisfaction (CSAT): The Smile Factor

Customer Satisfaction, or CSAT, is the smile factor. Think of it like this: CSAT measures how happy your customers are with your products or services. By tracking CSAT, you can understand the impact of your AI initiatives on customer satisfaction and make improvements where needed.

The Case of Netflix: A Lesson in CSAT

The case of Netflix is a lesson in CSAT. Netflix tracks CSAT to measure the impact of its AI-powered personalized recommendations on customer satisfaction. This approach helps Netflix understand how its AI initiatives are affecting customer satisfaction and make improvements where needed. It's a powerful reminder of the importance of defining customer-centric metrics for your AI initiatives.

Net Promoter Score (NPS): The Loyalty Factor

Net Promoter Score, or NPS, is the loyalty factor. Think of it like this: NPS measures how likely your customers are to recommend your products or services to others. By tracking NPS, you can understand the impact of your AI initiatives on customer loyalty and make improvements where needed.

The Case of Apple: A Lesson in NPS

The case of Apple is a lesson in NPS. Apple tracks NPS to measure the impact of its AI-powered customer service on customer loyalty. This approach helps Apple understand how its AI initiatives are affecting customer loyalty and make improvements where needed. It's a powerful reminder of the importance of defining customer-centric metrics for your AI initiatives.

Operational Efficiency: The Streamlined Approach

AI in customer service can also drive operational efficiency. Think of it like this: AI can automate repetitive tasks, reduce response times, and even optimize resource allocation. By measuring operational efficiency, you can understand the impact of your AI initiatives on streamlining processes, improving productivity, and reducing costs.

Response Time: The Speed Factor

Response time is the speed factor. Think of it like this: response time measures how quickly your customer service team can address customer inquiries. By tracking response time, you can understand the impact of your AI initiatives on improving the speed and efficiency of your customer service.

The Case of Uber: A Lesson in Response Time

The case of Uber is a lesson in response time. Uber uses AI to automate customer inquiries, reducing response times and improving the overall customer experience. This approach helps Uber understand the impact of its AI initiatives on improving the speed and efficiency of its customer service. It's a powerful reminder of the importance of measuring operational efficiency for your AI initiatives.

Cost Savings: The Bottom Line

Cost savings are the bottom line. Think of it like this: cost savings measure how much money your AI initiatives are saving your business. By tracking cost savings, you can understand the financial impact of your AI initiatives and ensure that they are delivering value to your business.

The Case of Walmart: A Lesson in Cost Savings

The case of Walmart is a lesson in cost savings. Walmart uses AI to optimize its customer service processes, reducing costs and improving efficiency. This approach helps Walmart understand the financial impact of its AI initiatives and ensure that they are delivering value to its business. It's a powerful reminder of the importance of measuring operational efficiency for your AI initiatives.

Customer Engagement: The Connection Factor

AI in customer service can also enhance customer engagement. Think of it like this: AI can provide personalized and interactive experiences, engaging customers and building stronger relationships. By measuring customer engagement, you can understand the impact of your AI initiatives on connecting with your customers and building loyalty.

Engagement Rate: The Interaction Factor

Engagement rate is the interaction factor. Think of it like this: engagement rate measures how often your customers interact with your AI-powered customer service tools. By tracking engagement rate, you can understand the impact of your AI initiatives on engaging customers and building stronger relationships.

The Case of Starbucks: A Lesson in Engagement Rate

The case of Starbucks is a lesson in engagement rate. Starbucks uses AI to provide personalized and interactive customer experiences, engaging customers and building stronger relationships. This approach helps Starbucks understand the impact of its AI initiatives on engaging customers and building loyalty. It's a powerful reminder of the importance of measuring customer engagement for your AI initiatives.

Customer Retention: The Loyalty Factor

Customer retention is the loyalty factor. Think of it like this: customer retention measures how many of your customers continue to do business with you over time. By tracking customer retention, you can understand the impact of your AI initiatives on building loyalty and maintaining long-term customer relationships.

The Case of Amazon: A Lesson in Customer Retention

The case of Amazon is a lesson in customer retention. Amazon uses AI to provide personalized and engaging customer experiences, building loyalty and maintaining long-term customer relationships. This approach helps Amazon understand the impact of its AI initiatives on building loyalty and maintaining long-term customer relationships. It's a powerful reminder of the importance of measuring customer engagement for your AI initiatives.

The Human Touch: The Role of Leaders and Innovators

But measuring the impact of AI in customer service aingt just about technology. It's also about people. It's about the leaders and innovators who are pushing the boundaries of what's possible. It's about the visionaries who are dreaming of a future where AI can help us transform the world like never before.

Leaders and innovators are a special breed. They're part strategist, part visionary, part advocate, and part dreamer. They know how to identify opportunities, how to analyze challenges, and how to develop solutions. But more importantly, they know how to communicate their findings in a way that's clear and compelling.

Think of it like this: a leader is like a strategist who can use AI to identify opportunities and develop solutions. An innovator is like a visionary who can use AI to push the boundaries of what's possible and achieve even greater success. Together, they're like a dynamic duo, working hand in hand to unlock the power of ethical AI.

The Future of AI in Customer Service: A World of Possibilities

But despite the challenges, the future of AI in customer service is bright. It's a future filled with possibilities, with opportunities to solve problems and improve lives. It's a future where AI can help us transform the world like never before, where it can help us make the world a safer, more efficient, and more prosperous place.

And it's a future that's already here. Every day, we're seeing new breakthroughs, new innovations, new ways of using AI to make the world a better place. It's exciting, it's inspiring, and it's just the beginning.

So, my friends, as we journey through this new frontier of customer service—measuring the impact of AI—let's remember the power and the potential that lies within. Let's remember the pioneers who came before us, the visionaries who dared to dream of a future where AI could help us transform the world like never before. And let's look forward to the exciting journey that lies ahead, as we continue to explore the boundless possibilities of AI in customer service and the future of business.

Conclusion: The AI Revolution: Where We Go from Here

Introduction: The Dawn of a New Era

Folks, gather 'round and let me spin you a yarn about the dawn of a new era—the AI revolution. Now, I know what you're thinking: "AI revolution? Sounds like something out of a futuristic novel." But fear not, my friends, for I'm here to make it all as clear as a summer's day. So, grab your favorite chair, pour yourself a glass of lemonade, and let's dive right in.

The Journey So Far: A Look Back

We've come a long way in our journey through the world of AI. From the early days of simple algorithms to the complex neural networks of today, AI has transformed industries, improved lives, and opened up new possibilities. We've seen AI revolutionize healthcare, finance, transportation, and entertainment. We've witnessed the power of AI in customer service, marketing, and operations. And we've explored the importance of data privacy, security, and ethical considerations.

The Case of DeepMind: A Lesson in AI Evolution

The case of DeepMind is a lesson in AI evolution. DeepMind, a subsidiary of Alphabet Inc., has developed groundbreaking AI technologies, from AlphaGo, which defeated the world champion in the game of Go, to AlphaFold, which predicts the structure of proteins with unprecedented accuracy. This journey highlights the incredible progress AI has made and the potential it holds for the future.

The Power of AI: The Game Changer

Chapter 15: Implementing AI: From Pilot Projects to Full-Scale Deployment

Artificial intelligence is a game changer. Think of it like this: AI can analyze data, understand patterns, make decisions, and even predict the future. It's like having a super-smart assistant who can see into the future and guide your business to success. But the power of AI goes beyond just business; it has the potential to transform the world, making it a safer, more efficient, and more prosperous place.

The Case of AI in Healthcare: A Lesson in Life-Saving Technology

The case of AI in healthcare is a lesson in life-saving technology. AI is being used to diagnose diseases, develop new treatments, and even predict outbreaks. For example, AI algorithms can analyze medical images to detect cancer with greater accuracy than human doctors. This approach helps save lives, improving healthcare outcomes and making the world a healthier place.

The Challenges Ahead: The Roadblocks

But the AI revolution is not without its challenges. Think of it like this: as we venture into this new frontier, we'll encounter roadblocks, obstacles that we need to overcome. These challenges include data privacy and security, ethical considerations, and the need for continuous improvement and optimization.

The Case of Facial Recognition: A Lesson in Ethical Considerations

The case of facial recognition is a lesson in ethical considerations. While facial recognition technology has the potential to enhance security and convenience, it also raises concerns about privacy, bias, and misuse. This highlights the importance of addressing ethical considerations as we develop and deploy AI technologies.

The Role of Leaders and Innovators: The Visionaries

But the AI revolution aingt just about technology. It's also about people. It's about the leaders and innovators who are pushing the boundaries of what's possible. It's about the visionaries who are dreaming of a future where AI can help us transform the world like never before.

Leaders and innovators are a special breed. They're part strategist, part visionary, part advocate, and part dreamer. They know how to identify opportunities, how to analyze challenges, and how to develop solutions. But more importantly, they know how to communicate their findings in a way that's clear and compelling.

Think of it like this: a leader is like a strategist who can use AI to identify opportunities and develop solutions. An innovator is like a visionary who can use AI to push the boundaries of what's possible and achieve even greater success. Together, they're like a dynamic duo, working hand in hand to unlock the power of ethical AI.

The Future of AI: A World of Possibilities

But despite the challenges, the future of AI is bright. It's a future filled with possibilities, with opportunities to solve problems and improve lives. It's a future where AI can help us transform the world like never before, where it can help us make the world a safer, more efficient, and more prosperous place.

And it's a future that's already here. Every day, we're seeing new breakthroughs, new innovations, new ways of using AI to make the world a better place. It's exciting, it's inspiring, and it's just the beginning.

The Case of AI in Education: A Lesson in Transformative Potential

The case of AI in education is a lesson in transformative potential. AI is being used to personalize learning, enhance teaching, and even predict student outcomes. For example, AI tutors can provide personalized learning experiences, adapting to each student's unique needs and helping them achieve their full potential. This approach helps transform education, improving outcomes and making the world a more educated place.

Where We Go from Here: The Path Forward

So, my friends, as we stand on the brink of this new era—the AI revolution—let's remember the power and the potential that lies within. Let's remember the pioneers who came before us, the visionaries who dared to dream of a future where AI could help us transform the world like never before. And let's look forward to the exciting journey that lies ahead, as we continue to explore the boundless possibilities of AI and the future of humanity.

Embracing Continuous Learning: The Key to Success

Embracing continuous learning is the key to success. Think of it like this: the world of AI is always changing, always evolving, and we need to keep learning, keep adapting, and keep improving. By embracing continuous learning, we can stay ahead of the curve, adapting to new challenges and opportunities.

The Case of Coursera: A Lesson in Continuous Learning

The case of Coursera is a lesson in continuous learning. Coursera offers online courses and specializations in AI, helping individuals and organizations stay up-to-date with the latest developments in the field. This approach helps foster a culture of continuous learning, ensuring that we are always prepared for the future.

Fostering Collaboration: The Power of Partnerships

Fostering collaboration is the power of partnerships. Think of it like this: the AI revolution is too big, too complex for any one person or organization to tackle alone. We need to work together, collaborating, sharing knowledge, and building partnerships. By fostering collaboration, we can accelerate innovation, overcome challenges, and achieve even greater success.

The Case of AI Partnerships: A Lesson in Collaboration

The case of AI partnerships is a lesson in collaboration. Companies like IBM, Google, and Microsoft are forming partnerships with universities, research institutions, and other organizations to advance the field of AI. This approach helps foster collaboration, accelerating innovation and achieving even greater success.

Promoting Ethical AI: The Responsibility

Promoting ethical AI is the responsibility. Think of it like this: as we develop and deploy AI technologies, we have a responsibility to ensure that they are used ethically, respecting privacy, promoting fairness, and avoiding harm. By promoting ethical AI, we can build trust, foster acceptance, and create a better future for all.

The Case of Ethical AI Guidelines: A Lesson in Responsibility

The case of ethical AI guidelines is a lesson in responsibility. Organizations like the European Commission and the IEEE are developing guidelines and frameworks for ethical AI, ensuring that AI technologies are used responsibly and ethically. This approach helps promote ethical AI, building trust and fostering acceptance.

The Call to Action: The Journey Ahead

So, my friends, as we embark on this exciting journey—the AI revolution—let's remember the power and the potential that lies within. Let's remember the pioneers who came before us, the visionaries who dared to dream of a future where AI could help us transform the world like never before. And let's look forward to the exciting journey that lies ahead, as we continue to explore the boundless possibilities of AI and the future of humanity.

Let's embrace continuous learning, foster collaboration, and promote ethical AI. Let's work together, sharing knowledge, building partnerships, and creating a better future for all. Let's seize the opportunities, overcome the challenges, and achieve even greater success.

The AI revolution is here, and it's up to us—the leaders, the innovators, the visionaries—to shape its future. So, let's roll up our sleeves, put on our thinking caps, and get to work. The world is waiting, and the future is ours to create.

CONCLUSION: THE AI REVOLUTION: WHERE WE GO FROM HERE

Chapter 17: The Future of AI: Predictions and Possibilities

Emerging Trends and Technologies in AI

Introduction: The Frontier of Tomorrow

Folks, gather 'round and let me spin you a yarn about the frontier of tomorrow—emerging trends and technologies in AI. Now, I know what you're thinking: "Emerging trends in AI? Sounds like something out of a futuristic novel." But fear not, my friends, for I'm here to make it all as clear as a summer's day. So, grab your favorite chair, pour yourself a glass of lemonade, and let's dive right in.

The Power of AI: The Game Changer

Artificial intelligence is revolutionizing the world as we know it. From healthcare to finance, from transportation to entertainment, AI is transforming industries and improving lives. It's like having a super-smart assistant who can analyze data, make decisions, and even predict the future. But the power of AI goes beyond just business; it has the potential to transform the world, making it a safer, more efficient, and more prosperous place.

The Case of DeepMind: A Lesson in AI Evolution

The case of DeepMind is a lesson in AI evolution. DeepMind, a subsidiary of Alphabet Inc., has developed groundbreaking AI technologies, from AlphaGo, which defeated the world champion

Chapter 17: The Future of AI: Predictions and Possibilities

in the game of Go, to AlphaFold, which predicts the structure of proteins with unprecedented accuracy. This journey highlights the incredible progress AI has made and the potential it holds for the future.

Emerging Trends: The Wave of the Future

Emerging trends in AI are the wave of the future. Think of it like this: as AI continues to evolve, new trends and technologies are emerging, opening up new possibilities and transforming the way we live and work. By staying ahead of these trends, you can ensure that your business is at the forefront of innovation, adapting to new challenges and opportunities.

AI in Healthcare: The Life-Saving Technology

AI in healthcare is a life-saving technology. Think of it like this: AI can analyze medical data, diagnose diseases, and even predict outbreaks. For example, AI algorithms can analyze medical images to detect cancer with greater accuracy than human doctors. This approach helps save lives, improving healthcare outcomes and making the world a healthier place.

The Case of AI in Diagnostics: A Lesson in Accuracy

The case of AI in diagnostics is a lesson in accuracy. AI algorithms can analyze medical images, such as X-rays and MRIs, to detect diseases with greater accuracy than human doctors. This approach helps improve healthcare outcomes, saving lives and making the world a healthier place. It's a powerful reminder of the importance of AI in transforming healthcare and improving lives.

AI in Finance: The Smart Money

AI in finance is the smart money. Think of it like this: AI can analyze financial data, predict market trends, and even make investment decisions. For example, AI algorithms can analyze stock market data to predict price movements and make profitable trades. This approach helps improve financial outcomes, making the world a more prosperous place.

The Case of AI in Trading: A Lesson in Profitability

The case of AI in trading is a lesson in profitability. AI algorithms can analyze stock market data to predict price movements and make profitable trades. This approach helps improve financial outcomes, making the world a more prosperous place. It's a powerful reminder of the importance of AI in transforming finance and improving lives.

AI in Transportation: The Road to Efficiency

AI in transportation is the road to efficiency. Think of it like this: AI can optimize routes, reduce traffic congestion, and even improve safety. For example, AI algorithms can analyze traffic data to predict congestion and suggest alternative routes. This approach helps improve transportation efficiency, making the world a more connected place.

The Case of AI in Logistics: A Lesson in Optimization

The case of AI in logistics is a lesson in optimization. AI algorithms can analyze traffic data to predict congestion and suggest alternative routes. This approach helps improve transportation efficiency, making the world a more connected place. It's a powerful reminder of the importance of AI in transforming transportation and improving lives.

Emerging Technologies: The Tools of Tomorrow

Emerging technologies in AI are the tools of tomorrow. Think of it like this: as AI continues to evolve, new technologies are emerging, providing the tools and resources needed to drive innovation and transformation. By leveraging these technologies, you can stay ahead of the curve, adapting to new challenges and opportunities.

Natural Language Processing (NLP): The Language of AI

Natural Language Processing, or NLP, is the language of AI. Think of it like this: NLP enables AI to understand, interpret, and generate human language. For example, AI chatbots can use NLP to engage in conversations with customers, providing personalized and interactive experiences. This approach helps improve customer service, making the world a more connected place.

The Case of AI Chatbots: A Lesson in Interaction

The case of AI chatbots is a lesson in interaction. AI chatbots can use NLP to engage in conversations with customers, providing personalized and interactive experiences. This approach helps improve customer service, making the world a more connected place. It's a powerful reminder of the importance of NLP in transforming customer service and improving lives.

Computer Vision: The Eyes of AI

Computer Vision is the eyes of AI. Think of it like this: computer vision enables AI to see and understand the world around it. For example, AI algorithms can analyze images and videos to detect objects, recognize faces, and even interpret scenes. This approach helps improve security, enhance user experiences, and even enable autonomous vehicles.

The Case of AI in Security: A Lesson in Safety

The case of AI in security is a lesson in safety. AI algorithms can analyze images and videos to detect objects, recognize faces, and even interpret scenes. This approach helps improve security, making the world a safer place. It's a powerful reminder of the importance of computer vision in transforming security and improving lives.

Reinforcement Learning: The Game of AI

Reinforcement Learning is the game of AI. Think of it like this: reinforcement learning enables AI to learn from experience, making decisions and improving over time. For example, AI algorithms can play games, such as chess or Go, learning from their mistakes and improving their strategies. This approach helps improve AI performance, making the world a more intelligent place.

The Case of AlphaGo: A Lesson in Strategy

The case of AlphaGo is a lesson in strategy. AlphaGo, developed by DeepMind, is an AI algorithm that plays the game of Go. By learning from experience, AlphaGo has become one of the best Go players in the world, defeating human champions and improving its strategies over time. It's a powerful reminder of the importance of reinforcement learning in transforming AI and improving lives.

Generative AI: The Creativity of AI

Generative AI is the creativity of AI. Think of it like this: generative AI enables AI to create new content, from images and music to text and videos. For example, AI algorithms can generate realistic images, compose music, and even write stories. This approach helps unlock new creative possibilities, making the world a more imaginative place.

The Case of AI in Art: A Lesson in Creativity

The case of AI in art is a lesson in creativity. AI algorithms can generate realistic images, compose music, and even write stories. This approach helps unlock new creative possibilities, making the world a more imaginative place. It's a powerful reminder of the importance of generative AI in transforming creativity and improving lives.

The Human Touch: The Role of Leaders and Innovators

But emerging trends and technologies in AI aingt just about technology. It's also about people. It's about the leaders and innovators who are pushing the boundaries of what's possible. It's about the visionaries who are dreaming of a future where AI can help us transform the world like never before.

Leaders and innovators are a special breed. They're part strategist, part visionary, part advocate, and part dreamer. They know how to identify opportunities, how to analyze challenges, and how to develop solutions. But more importantly, they know how to communicate their findings in a way that's clear and compelling.

Think of it like this: a leader is like a strategist who can use AI to identify opportunities and develop solutions. An innovator is like a visionary who can use AI to push the boundaries of what's possible and achieve even greater success. Together, they're like a dynamic duo, working hand in hand to unlock the power of ethical AI.

The Future of AI: A World of Possibilities

But despite the challenges, the future of AI is bright. It's a future filled with possibilities, with opportunities to solve problems and improve lives. It's a future where AI can help us transform the world like never before, where it can help us make the world a safer, more efficient, and more prosperous place.

And it's a future that's already here. Every day, we're seeing new breakthroughs, new innovations, new ways of using AI to make the world a better place. It's exciting, it's inspiring, and it's just the beginning.

So, my friends, as we journey through this frontier of tomorrow—emerging trends and technologies in AI—let's remember the power and the potential that lies within. Let's remember the pioneers who came before us, the visionaries who dared to dream of a future where AI could help us transform the world like never before. And let's look forward to the exciting journey that lies ahead, as we continue to explore the boundless possibilities of AI and the future of humanity.

Chapter 17: The Future of AI: Predictions and Possibilities

The Role of AI in Solving Global Challenges

Introduction: The Dawn of a New Era

Folks, gather 'round and let me spin you a yarn about the dawn of a new era—the role of AI in solving global challenges. Now, I know what you're thinking: "AI solving global challenges? Sounds like something out of a futuristic novel." But fear not, my friends, for I'm here to make it all as clear as a summer's day. So, grab your favorite chair, pour yourself a glass of lemonade, and let's dive right in.

The Power of AI: The Game Changer

Artificial intelligence is revolutionizing the world as we know it. From healthcare to finance, from transportation to entertainment, AI is transforming industries and improving lives. It's like having a super-smart assistant who can analyze data, make decisions, and even predict the future. But the power of AI goes beyond just business; it has the potential to transform the world, making it a safer, more efficient, and more prosperous place.

The Case of DeepMind: A Lesson in AI Evolution

The case of DeepMind is a lesson in AI evolution. DeepMind, a subsidiary of Alphabet Inc., has developed groundbreaking AI technologies, from AlphaGo, which defeated the world champion in the game of Go, to AlphaFold, which predicts the structure of proteins with unprecedented accuracy. This journey highlights the incredible progress AI has made and the potential it holds for the future.

Global Challenges: The Problems of Our Time

Global challenges are the problems of our time. Think of it like this: we're facing some of the biggest and most complex issues the world has ever seen, from climate change to poverty, from disease to inequality. These challenges require innovative solutions, and AI has the potential to provide them.

Climate Change: The Environmental Crisis

Climate change is the environmental crisis. Think of it like this: our planet is facing a crisis, with rising temperatures, melting ice caps, and extreme weather events. AI can help us tackle this crisis by analyzing environmental data, predicting climate patterns, and even developing sustainable solutions.

The Case of AI in Climate Modeling: A Lesson in Prediction

The case of AI in climate modeling is a lesson in prediction. AI algorithms can analyze environmental data to predict climate patterns, helping us understand the impacts of climate change and develop sustainable solutions. This approach helps us tackle the environmental crisis, making the world a more sustainable place. It's a powerful reminder of the importance of AI in solving global challenges and improving lives.

Poverty: The Economic Divide

Poverty is the economic divide. Think of it like this: millions of people around the world are living in poverty, facing hunger, lack of education, and limited access to healthcare. AI can help us tackle this divide by analyzing economic data, identifyng areas of need, and even developing targeted interventions.

The Case of AI in Microfinance: A Lesson in Empowerment

The case of AI in microfinance is a lesson in empowerment. AI algorithms can analyze economic data to identify areas of need and develop targeted interventions, such as microloans and financial education. This approach helps empower individuals and communities, reducing poverty and making the world a more equitable place. It's a powerful reminder of the importance of AI in solving global challenges and improving lives.

Disease: The Health Crisis

Disease is the health crisis. Think of it like this: diseases like cancer, HIV, and malaria are causing suffering and death around the world. AI can help us tackle this crisis by analyzing medical data, diagnosing diseases, and even developing new treatments.

The Case of AI in Disease Diagnostics: A Lesson in Accuracy

The case of AI in disease diagnostics is a lesson in accuracy. AI algorithms can analyze medical data to diagnose diseases with greater accuracy than human doctors. This approach helps improve healthcare outcomes, saving lives and making the world a healthier place. It's a powerful reminder of the importance of AI in solving global challenges and improving lives.

Inequality: The Social Divide

Inequality is the social divide. Think of it like this: inequality in education, healthcare, and economic opportunities is creating a divide between the rich and the poor, the privileged and the marginalized. AI can help us tackle this divide by analyzing social data, identifyng areas of inequality, and even developing targeted interventions.

The Case of AI in Education: A Lesson in Accessibility

The case of AI in education is a lesson in accessibility. AI algorithms can analyze social data to identify areas of inequality and develop targeted interventions, such as personalized learning experiences and educational resources. This approach helps improve access to education, reducing inequality and making the world a more equitable place. It's a powerful reminder of the importance of AI in solving global challenges and improving lives.

The Role of AI: The Solution

AI has the potential to be the solution to these global challenges. Think of it like this: AI can analyze data, identify patterns, make predictions, and even develop solutions. By leveraging the power of AI, we can tackle these challenges head-on, improving lives and making the world a better place.

Data Analysis: The Key to Insight

Data analysis is the key to insight. Think of it like this: AI can analyze vast amounts of data, identifyng patterns and trends that would be impossible for humans to detect. By analyzing data, AI can provide valuable insights that help us understand and address global challenges.

The Case of AI in Data Analysis: A Lesson in Insight

The case of AI in data analysis is a lesson in insight. AI algorithms can analyze vast amounts of data, identifyng patterns and trends that help us understand and address global challenges. This approach provides valuable insights, helping us tackle these challenges head-on and improving lives. It's a powerful reminder of the importance of data analysis in solving global challenges and improving lives.

Predictive Analytics: The Power of Foresight

Predictive analytics is the power of foresight. Think of it like this: AI can use historical data to make predictions about the future, helping us anticipate and prepare for global challenges. By leveraging predictive analytics, we can develop proactive solutions that address these challenges before they become crises.

The Case of AI in Predictive Analytics: A Lesson in Foresight

The case of AI in predictive analytics is a lesson in foresight. AI algorithms can use historical data to make predictions about the future, helping us anticipate and prepare for global challenges. This approach helps us develop proactive solutions, addressing these challenges before they become crises and improving lives. It's a powerful reminder of the importance of predictive analytics in solving global challenges and improving lives.

Solution Development: The Path to Progress

Solution development is the path to progress. Think of it like this: AI can help us develop innovative solutions to global challenges, from new technologies to policy interventions. By leveraging AI, we can create solutions that are effective, efficient, and sustainable.

The Case of AI in Solution Development: A Lesson in Innovation

The case of AI in solution development is a lesson in innovation. AI can help us develop innovative solutions to global challenges, from new technologies to policy interventions. This approach helps us create solutions that are effective, efficient, and sustainable, improving lives and making the world a better place. It's a powerful reminder of the importance of solution development in solving global challenges and improving lives.

The Human Touch: The Role of Leaders and Innovators

But the role of AI in solving global challenges aingt just about technology. It's also about people. It's about the leaders and innovators who are pushing the boundaries of what's possible. It's about the visionaries who are dreaming of a future where AI can help us transform the world like never before.

Leaders and innovators are a special breed. They're part strategist, part visionary, part advocate, and part dreamer. They know how to identify opportunities, how to analyze challenges, and how to develop solutions. But more importantly, they know how to communicate their findings in a way that's clear and compelling.

Think of it like this: a leader is like a strategist who can use AI to identify opportunities and develop solutions. An innovator is like a visionary who can use AI to push the boundaries of what's possible and achieve even greater success. Together, they're like a dynamic duo, working hand in hand to unlock the power of ethical AI.

The Future of AI: A World of Possibilities

But despite the challenges, the future of AI is bright. It's a future filled with possibilities, with opportunities to solve problems and improve lives. It's a future where AI can help us transform the world like never before, where it can help us make the world a safer, more efficient, and more prosperous place.

And it's a future that's already here. Every day, we're seeing new breakthroughs, new innovations, new ways of using AI to make the world a better place. It's exciting, it's inspiring, and it's just the beginning.

So, my friends, as we journey through this dawn of a new era—the role of AI in solving global challenges—let's remember the power and the potential that lies within. Let's remember the pioneers who came before us, the visionaries who dared to dream of a future where AI could help us transform the world like never before. And let's look forward to the exciting journey that lies ahead, as we continue to explore the boundless possibilities of AI and the future of humanity.

Chapter 17: The Future of AI: Predictions and Possibilities

A Vision for a Responsible and Inclusive AI Future

Introduction: The Dawn of a New Era

Folks, gather 'round and let me spin you a yarn about the dawn of a new era—a vision for a responsible and inclusive AI future. Now, I know what you're thinking: "Responsible and inclusive AI? Sounds like something out of a futuristic novel." But fear not, my friends, for I'm here to make it all as clear as a summer's day. So, grab your favorite chair, pour yourself a glass of lemonade, and let's dive right in.

The Power of AI: The Game Changer

Artificial intelligence is revolutionizing the world as we know it. From healthcare to finance, from transportation to entertainment, AI is transforming industries and improving lives. It's like having a super-smart assistant who can analyze data, make decisions, and even predict the future. But the power of AI goes beyond just business; it has the potential to transform the world, making it a safer, more efficient, and more prosperous place.

The Case of DeepMind: A Lesson in AI Evolution

The case of DeepMind is a lesson in AI evolution. DeepMind, a subsidiary of Alphabet Inc., has developed groundbreaking AI technologies, from AlphaGo, which defeated the world champion in the game of Go, to AlphaFold, which predicts the structure of proteins with unprecedented accuracy. This journey highlights the incredible progress AI has made and the potential it holds for the future.

The Need for Responsibility: The Ethical Imperative

But with great power comes great responsibility. Think of it like this: as AI continues to evolve and become more integrated into our lives, we need to ensure that it is used ethically, respecting privacy, promoting fairness, and avoiding harm. A responsible AI future is one where AI is used for the benefit of all, improving lives and making the world a better place.

The Case of Facial Recognition: A Lesson in Ethical Considerations

The case of facial recognition is a lesson in ethical considerations. While facial recognition technology has the potential to enhance security and convenience, it also raises concerns about privacy, bias, and misuse. This highlights the importance of addressing ethical considerations as we develop and deploy AI technologies.

The Importance of Inclusivity: The Equitable Approach

Inclusivity is the equitable approach. Think of it like this: AI has the potential to benefit everyone, but only if it is designed and implemented in a way that is inclusive and accessible to all. An inclusive AI future is one where everyone has the opportunity to participate in and benefit from the AI revolution, regardless of their background, abilities, or circumstances.

The Case of AI in Education: A Lesson in Accessibility

The case of AI in education is a lesson in accessibility. AI algorithms can analyze social data to identify areas of inequality and develop targeted interventions, such as personalized learning experiences and educational resources. This approach helps improve access to education, reducing inequality and making the world a more equitable place. It's a powerful reminder of the importance of inclusivity in the AI revolution.

The Role of Leaders and Innovators: The Visionaries

But a responsible and inclusive AI future aingt just about technology. It's also about people. It's about the leaders and innovators who are pushing the boundaries of what's possible. It's about the visionaries who are dreaming of a future where AI can help us transform the world like never before.

Leaders and innovators are a special breed. They're part strategist, part visionary, part advocate, and part dreamer. They know how to identify opportunities, how to analyze challenges, and how to develop solutions. But more importantly, they know how to communicate their findings in a way that's clear and compelling.

Think of it like this: a leader is like a strategist who can use AI to identify opportunities and develop solutions. An innovator is like a visionary who can use AI to push the boundaries of what's possible and achieve even greater success. Together, they're like a dynamic duo, working hand in hand to unlock the power of ethical AI.

The Principles of Responsible AI: The Guiding Light

To achieve a responsible and inclusive AI future, we need to follow a set of guiding principles. Think of it like this: these principles are the guiding light, the compass that will help us navigate the complex and ever-changing world of AI. By adhering to these principles, we can ensure that AI is used ethically, responsibly, and for the benefit of all.

Transparency: The Key to Trust

Transparency is the key to trust. Think of it like this: for AI to be trusted, it must be transparent. People need to understand how AI systems work, what data they use, and how they make decisions. By promoting transparency, we can build trust in AI and ensure that it is used responsibly.

The Case of Explainable AI: A Lesson in Transparency

The case of explainable AI is a lesson in transparency. Explainable AI systems are designed to be understandable to humans, providing insights into how they make decisions. This approach helps build trust in AI, ensuring that it is used responsibly and ethically. It's a powerful reminder of the importance of transparency in the AI revolution.

Accountability: The Responsibility Factor

Accountability is the responsibility factor. Think of it like this: for AI to be used responsibly, there must be accountability. Organizations and individuals who develop and deploy AI systems must be held accountable for their actions, ensuring that AI is used ethically and for the benefit of all.

The Case of AI Regulation: A Lesson in Accountability

The case of AI regulation is a lesson in accountability. Governments and regulatory bodies are developing frameworks and guidelines to ensure that AI is used responsibly and ethically. This approach helps promote accountability, ensuring that AI is used for the benefit of all. It's a powerful reminder of the importance of accountability in the AI revolution.

Fairness: The Equity Principle

Fairness is the equity principle. Think of it like this: for AI to be inclusive, it must be fair. AI systems must be designed and implemented in a way that is free from bias and discrimination, ensuring that everyone has the opportunity to participate in and benefit from the AI revolution.

Chapter 17: The Future of AI: Predictions and Possibilities

The Case of Bias in AI: A Lesson in Fairness

The case of bias in AI is a lesson in fairness. AI systems can inadvertently perpetuate or even amplify existing biases if they are not designed and implemented carefully. This highlights the importance of addressing bias in AI, ensuring that it is used fairly and equitably. It's a powerful reminder of the importance of fairness in the AI revolution.

Privacy: The Protection Factor

Privacy is the protection factor. Think of it like this: for AI to be trusted, it must respect privacy. AI systems must be designed and implemented in a way that protects personal data, ensuring that it is used responsibly and ethically.

The Case of Data Privacy: A Lesson in Protection

The case of data privacy is a lesson in protection. AI systems must be designed and implemented in a way that protects personal data, ensuring that it is used responsibly and ethically. This approach helps build trust in AI, ensuring that it is used for the benefit of all. It's a powerful reminder of the importance of privacy in the AI revolution.

The Path to a Responsible and Inclusive AI Future: The Journey Ahead

So, my friends, as we journey through this dawn of a new era—a vision for a responsible and inclusive AI future—let's remember the power and the potential that lies within. Let's remember the pioneers who came before us, the visionaries who dared to dream of a future where AI could help us transform the world like never before. And let's look forward to the exciting journey that lies ahead, as we continue to explore the boundless possibilities of AI and the future of humanity.

Chapter 17: The Future of AI: Predictions and Possibilities

Embracing Continuous Learning: The Key to Success

Embracing continuous learning is the key to success. Think of it like this: the world of AI is always changing, always evolving, and we need to keep learning, keep adapting, and keep improving. By embracing continuous learning, we can stay ahead of the curve, adapting to new challenges and opportunities.

The Case of Coursera: A Lesson in Continuous Learning

The case of Coursera is a lesson in continuous learning. Coursera offers online courses and specializations in AI, helping individuals and organizations stay up-to-date with the latest developments in the field. This approach helps foster a culture of continuous learning, ensuring that we are always prepared for the future.

Fostering Collaboration: The Power of Partnerships

Fostering collaboration is the power of partnerships. Think of it like this: the AI revolution is too big, too complex for any one person or organization to tackle alone. We need to work together, collaborating, sharing knowledge, and building partnerships. By fostering collaboration, we can accelerate innovation, overcome challenges, and achieve even greater success.

The Case of AI Partnerships: A Lesson in Collaboration

The case of AI partnerships is a lesson in collaboration. Companies like IBM, Google, and Microsoft are forming partnerships with universities, research institutions, and other organizations to advance the field of AI. This approach helps foster collaboration, accelerating innovation and achieving even greater success.

Promoting Ethical AI: The Responsibility

Promoting ethical AI is the responsibility. Think of it like this: as we develop and deploy AI technologies, we have a responsibility to ensure that they are used ethically, respecting privacy, promoting fairness, and avoiding harm. By promoting ethical AI, we can build trust, foster acceptance, and create a better future for all.

The Case of Ethical AI Guidelines: A Lesson in Responsibility

The case of ethical AI guidelines is a lesson in responsibility. Organizations like the European Commission and the IEEE are developing guidelines and frameworks for ethical AI, ensuring that AI technologies are used responsibly and ethically. This approach helps promote ethical AI, building trust and fostering acceptance.

The Future of AI: A World of Possibilities

But despite the challenges, the future of AI is bright. It's a future filled with possibilities, with opportunities to solve problems and improve lives. It's a future where AI can help us transform the world like never before, where it can help us make the world a safer, more efficient, and more prosperous place.

And it's a future that's already here. Every day, we're seeing new breakthroughs, new innovations, new ways of using AI to make the world a better place. It's exciting, it's inspiring, and it's just the beginning.

So, my friends, as we journey through this dawn of a new era—a vision for a responsible and inclusive AI future—let's remember the power and the potential that lies within. Let's remember the pioneers who came before us, the visionaries who dared to dream of a future where AI could help us transform the world like never before. And let's look forward to the exciting journey that lies ahead, as we continue to explore the boundless possibilities of AI and the future of humanity.

www.ingramcontent.com/pod-product-compliance
Lightning Source LLC
Chambersburg PA
CBHW031608210526
45464CB00004B/1475